S0-BYW-899

ENGAGING
INDIA

ALSO BY STROBE TALBOTT

The Russia Hand

At the Highest Levels
(with Michael Beschloss)

The Master of the Game

Reagan and Gorbachev
(with Michael Mandelbaum)

Deadly Gambits

Reagan and the Russians

Endgame

The Age of Terror:
America and the World after September 11
(edited with Nayan Chanda)

EDITED AND TRANSLATED

Khrushchev Remembers: The Last Testament

Khrushchev Remembers

ENGAGING INDIA

DIPLOMACY, DEMOCRACY, AND THE BOMB

REVISED EDITION

STROBE TALBOTT

To Paul —
with thanks for your
knowledge & ...

BROOKINGS INSTITUTION PRESS
Washington, D.C.

06/09/02

Copyright © 2004
Paperback edition copyright © 2006
THE BROOKINGS INSTITUTION
1775 Massachusetts Avenue, N.W., Washington, D.C. 20036
www.brookings.edu

All rights reserved

The Library of Congress has cataloged the hardcover edition as follows:
Talbott, Strobe.
  Engaging India : diplomacy, democracy, and the bomb / Strobe Talbott.
    p.   cm.
  Includes bibliographical references and index.
  ISBN 0-8157-8300-0 (cloth : alk. paper)
  1. United States—Foreign relations—India. 2. India—Foreign relations—United
States. 3. United States—Foreign relations—Pakistan. 4. Pakistan—Foreign
relations—United States. 5. Atomic bomb—India. 6. Atomic bomb—Pakistan.
7. India—Military policy. 8. Pakistan—Military policy. 9. Talbott, Strobe. I. Title.
  E183.8.I4T35   2004
  327.73054'09'049—dc   222004012803
              ISBN-13: 978-0-8157-8301-5 (pbk. : alk. paper)
                     ISBN-10: 0-8157-8301-9

2 4 6 8 9 7 5 3 1

The paper used in this publication meets minimum requirements of the
American National Standard for Information Sciences—Permanence of Paper
for Printed Library Materials: ANSI Z39.48-1992.

Typeset in Adobe Caslon

Composition by Cynthia Stock
Silver Spring, Maryland

Printed by R. R. Donnelley
Harrisonburg, Virginia

FOR ONE FAMILY AND
THREE GENERATIONS OF FRIENDS

Amarjit and Bhagwant Singh

Nayan Chanda and Geetanjali Singh

Amit and Ateesh Chanda

CONTENTS

Strobe Talbott and Jaswant Singh
Hyderabad House, New Delhi, January 29, 1999

(Photograph courtesy of *The Hindu*)

ONE

THE LOST HALF CENTURY

WHEN I ARRIVED for work that damp, overcast morning of Monday, May 11, 1998, I was expecting a relatively normal week, at least by State Department standards. There was plenty to do at the office and plenty to worry about in the world, but nothing that quite qualified as a crisis.

Shortly after 8:00 a.m., I chaired the daily meeting of the department's senior staff. As deputy secretary, I was supposed to keep tabs on what was going on in the building and around the globe. Assembled at a mahogany table in the windowless conference room across from my office on the seventh floor were about twenty assistant secretaries. Their bureaus either covered various geographical regions or sought to advance such global objectives as the promotion of democracy and human rights, the protection of the environment, the struggle against terrorism, and the effort to stop the proliferation of lethal armaments, materials, designs and technologies.

Each official reported briefly on what had happened over the weekend and reviewed what lay ahead. The British government and Sinn Fein, the political wing of the Irish Republican Army, were looking for help in bringing peace to Northern Ireland. A team of American diplomats was in the Balkans trying to avert war over Kosovo. Iraq's deputy prime minister, Tariq Aziz, was barnstorming through Europe, lobbying for an end to the U.S.-led campaign to isolate the Baghdad regime. The annual summit of the Group of Seven major industrial democracies, or G-7, was coming up later in the week in Birmingham, England. Boris Yeltsin, the president of Russia, would be attending for the first time as a full member of the group, making it the G-8. As the administration's point man on Russia, I planned to spend most of the coming days preparing for the private session that President Bill Clinton would have with Yeltsin in Birmingham.

When the senior staff meeting ended, I returned to my office and settled behind the desk to read the *New York Times*. I skimmed articles on the front page about the latest Arab-Israeli tensions and drug trafficking in the Caribbean but skipped a feature article about India. That country could hardly have been further from my mind. In government, it is often said, the urgent drives out the merely important. India—the world's second most populous country, its largest democracy, and the most powerful country in a region that is home to nearly a quarter of humanity—seemed permanently stuck in the latter category.

At that moment, Phyllis Oakley, the foreign service officer in charge of the department's bureau of intelligence and research, was returning to her own office from the senior staff meeting when her deputy intercepted her in the corridor with the news that India had set off a nuclear device several hours earlier. Phyllis was stunned. How had we learned? she asked. From CNN, she was told. She winced, then rushed back to my office to make sure I had gotten the word. I hadn't. After sitting motionless for a moment with my eyes closed, I swiveled around in my chair and picked up the handset of the "red switch" phone behind my desk. The buttons on this clunky device, each labeled with bureaucratic initials, connected me by encrypted lines with my counterparts in other departments and agencies of the government. I punched the button that put me through to John Gordon, a four-star Air Force general who was deputy director of central intelligence at the CIA's headquarters in Langley, Virginia, nine miles up the Potomac River. I assumed John would be able to give me some details on what had happened overnight in India. We had been friends for about ten years, since the first Bush administration, when he had served on the staff of the National Security Council and I had been a *Time* magazine reporter covering foreign policy. John had just arrived at work, so instead of learning anything from him, I succeeded only in ruining his week just as it started. After hearing what I had to say, he, like me a few moments before, needed at first to absorb the magnitude of the news in silence. He then remarked that the only thing worse than being scooped by CNN was being scooped by the State Department.

Phyllis took some consolation from this exchange, since her bureau was microscopic compared with the CIA. "It looks like we're all having a bad government day," she said over her shoulder as she hurried back to her office for more information. I got on the phone again, this time to the secretary of state, Madeleine Albright, who was at the White House in the office of Sandy Berger, the president's national security adviser. They had just heard what happened, also courtesy of CNN.

"When it rains, it pours," said Madeleine. She and Sandy had their hands full dealing with the latest setback in the Middle East peace process. The Israeli government had just rebuffed a U.S. proposal for a compromise with the Palestinians.

Also in the meeting was Bruce Riedel, a career intelligence officer on assignment to the National Security Council staff. He was in charge of the NSC office that covered South Asia as well as the Middle East and the Persian Gulf, which meant riding herd on U.S. diplomacy with the Arabs and Israelis and on U.S. military operations in Iraq. On learning of the Indian test, Bruce commented that he suddenly felt overemployed.

Phyllis Oakley soon returned to my office with a sheaf of printouts of classified cables and faxes that were by now pouring in from some extremely embarrassed offices around the U.S. government, especially in Langley. She had brought a map to show me where the explosion had occurred—in the northwestern Indian state of Rajasthan. Phyllis knew the political geography of South Asia, having lived and worked in Pakistan in the late 1980s and early 1990s when her husband, Bob, served as U.S. ambassador there. The test site, she noted, was just over ninety miles from the Pakistani border, so the subterranean explosion must have set off seismographs in Pakistan.

"Let's just hope that's all it sets off," she added.

The week was no longer normal, and India was no longer merely important.

WHAT FOLLOWS IS the story of the negotiation—or, as we agreed to call it, the dialogue—that the Indian statesman Jaswant Singh and I conducted over the next two and a half years. We met fourteen times at ten locations in seven countries on three continents. Those encounters added up to the most intense and prolonged set of exchanges ever between American and Indian officials at a level higher than ambassadors.

I held a parallel series of meetings with various Pakistani officials. That exercise, too, was called a dialogue, but it barely qualified as such. Why that was the case is also a subject of this book.

In a successful dialogue, the two parties do more than just talk to each other. Each makes an effort to understand what the other has said and to incorporate that understanding into a reply. A dialogue does not, however, necessarily mean that the participants change each other's minds. Hence the other term that figured prominently in the way Jaswant Singh and I defined our task: engagement. That word can connote eye-to-eye contact, a firm handshake, a pledge, or a long-term commitment. But engagement can also refer to the crossing of swords, a clash of armies or warships or wills. Both elements, conciliation and contest, were present in what went on between Jaswant Singh and me.

India's decision to conduct nuclear tests was a manifestation of long-festering differences over the rules governing the international system and our countries' self-assigned positions in that system. Jaswant Singh and I began the dialogue hoping that before it ended—or, better yet, once it became permanent and institutionalized—the United States and India would be able to reach agreement on some of those fundamental questions and, where we could not resolve our disagreements, we would be better able to manage them. To that extent, he and I were dealing with each other on behalf of two governments that shared a desire to fix something that had been broken for a long time: the U.S.-Indian relationship.

But first we had to grapple with the issue at hand, which was India's acquisition of the bomb. That thoroughly unwelcome development had occurred not just in the face of American objections but also against the backdrop of the United States, Britain, China, France, and Russia having acquired bombs of their own many years before.

From the American perspective, what was at stake was the stability of the global nuclear order. If India felt it had to have a bomb, other counties would conclude that they must have one too, and the world would become a much more dangerous place.

For their part, the Indians saw the matter in terms of sovereignty, security, and equity: if those other five powers had an internationally recognized right to be nuclear armed, why did India not have the same prerogative?

My government attempted to finesse that question with what was essentially a compromise: the United States would limit the extent to which the Indian bomb was an obstacle to better relations if India would, by explicit agreement, limit the development and deployment of its nuclear arsenal.

But the Indian government was, from the outset, disinclined to compromise. Its short-term goal was to resist precisely the sort of abnegation the United States proposed. Its strategy was to play for the day when the United States would get over its huffing and puffing and, with a sigh of exhaustion or a shrug of resignation, accept a nuclear-armed India as a fully responsible and fully entitled member of the international community.

The Indians conducted their test knowing that it would provoke American castigation but also hoping it might have another consequence: perhaps it would force the United States to pay them serious, sustained, and respectful attention of a kind the Indians felt they had never received before. Engagement gave the Indians a chance to resist the Americans' pressure face-to-face. In that sense, the dialogue could be its own reward, as both a means and an end. By weathering the storm of U.S. disapproval—by outlasting and outtalking the Americans in the marathon of diplomacy spurred by the test, in short, by *not* compromising—the Indians would prove their resolve and their resilience, thereby giving a boost to their national self-esteem and self-confidence.

As one of the architects of the Indian strategy, Jaswant Singh came closer to achieving his objective in the dialogue than I did to achieving mine. Insofar as what follows is that story, it stands as an exception to Dean Acheson's maxim that the author of a memorandum of conversation never comes out second best.

However, there is more to the tale told here than that. This book can be read as a parable about a benign version of the law of unintended consequences. The annals of diplomacy are replete with examples of accords that backfired, apparent breakthroughs that led to disastrous breakdowns, signatures on peace treaties that lit fuses to war. But the opposite can also occur. Sometimes a negotiation that fails to resolve a specific dispute can have general and lasting benefits, especially if it is a dialogue in fact as well as name. Diplomacy that meets that standard can improve and even transform the overall quality of relations between states. It can make it possible for governments to cooperate in areas that had previously been out of bounds and, at moments of crisis, enable their leaders to avert catastrophe.

That, too, is a theme of this book: it is the story of the turning point in U.S.-Indian relations.

The bad news from Rajasthan that Monday morning in May of 1998 marked a new low between two countries that had seen very few highs. Jaswant Singh and I sat down across from each other for the first time a month later. Yet a little more than a year after that, his prime minister trusted my president enough to let him play a decisive role in defusing a conflict between India and Pakistan that could have escalated to nuclear war. Then, in March 2000, President Clinton's triumphal visit to India established that these two countries were finally engaged in the unambiguously positive sense of that word. They remain so today.

That is all to the good. The great shame is that it took so long to happen.

THE OPPOSITE OF engagement is estrangement. By 1993, when the Clinton administration came into office, that word, which has no positive connotation, had become standard in describing the United States's dealings with India.[1]

Relations between states often take on the attributes, in the minds and language of their citizens and political leaders, of relations between individuals. Countries are described as friends or enemies, partners or rivals; they feel good will toward each other, or they regard each other with irritation and disappointment.

The U.S.-Indian relationship has had this personalized aspect for half a century, especially on the Indian side, where the political and intellectual elite has felt neglected, patronized, or bullied by the U.S. government. Why, it is often asked, did two countries with so many political values in common, not get off to a better start?

Part of the answer is to be found in a difference between their historical experiences. In the seventeenth and eighteenth centuries, America was, like India, a British colony—but with a major difference: it was made up largely of people transplanted from Britain itself, while Indians were of a different race and culture. They were bearers of a great and ancient civilization who had been treated, in Rudyard Kipling's famous phrase, as a burden to be borne by the white man. A lingering sense of being objects of racism and condescension made many Indians all the more wary when, just as their own country was breaking free of the Raj in the late 1940s, America seemed to be inheriting from Britain the mantle of global empire.

On the U.S. side, too, the relationship was jinxed. For most of the next forty years, India was a target of American ideological and geopolitical antagonism. The affinity that might have otherwise existed was a victim of incompatible obsessions—India's with Pakistan and America's with the Soviet Union. One reason that the United States and India were so at odds for so long was that each was on such good terms with the other's principal enemy. The dissolution of the Soviet Union created an opening for the Clinton administration to free the United States's relations with South Asia from the strictures and distortions of the cold war.

But Pakistan was still on the map, and for many Indians, its very existence rankled. They resented what they saw as America's continuing patronage of their misbegotten neighbor.

MOHANDAS GANDHI AND Jawaharlal Nehru had conceived of India as an inclusive state in which the Hindu majority would coexist with Muslims, Sikhs, Jains, Buddhists, Christians, Jews, and others. Muhammad Ali Jinnah and most other influential Muslim leaders, however, insisted that Hindus and Muslims were two nations and that Muslims should have a state of their own. That was, they believed, the only way to safeguard their community's interests and way of life. They did not fear religious persecution so much as political and social discrimination. When the people of British India won their freedom in 1947, the proponents of Pakistan insisted that independence be accompanied by partition, which brought with it massive transfers of populations, carnage on a horrendous scale, and an enduring legacy of mutual mistrust.

The prevailing inclination of many Indians was, for many years, not to accept the logic or the legitimacy of the two-nation theory. They regarded the idea of Pakistan not just as a mistake but as an insult to the idea of India.

Pakistanis not only reciprocated this hostility—they felt intimidated by India, which had more than three times the territory and four times the population, vast numbers of whom were Muslims.

The vision of India as a secular, pluralistic democracy was controversial within India itself. The Rashtriya Swayamsevak Sangh (National Volunteers Association), or RSS, had been founded in 1925 on the principle that India could achieve national unity only on the basis of Hindu supremacy. That position put the RSS in opposition to Gandhi, the founding father and guiding spirit of modern India—whom most Indians and much of the world had come to refer to as the Mahatma, or Great Soul. When Gandhi died five months after independence at the hands of a militant affiliated with a Hindu extremist organization, officials of the Congress Party, which was then the dominant force in Indian politics and would remain so for a long time, accused the RSS of complicity in the assassination, and the Congress-led government banned the organization. The RSS formed a political wing that subsequently became the Bharatiya Janata Party, or BJP. After decades in opposition, the BJP eventually surpassed the Congress Party in electoral support and led the government of India through most of the period covered in this book.

PAKISTAN, WHILE POLITICALLY united around the idea of a separate state for Muslims, was geographically split between noncontiguous eastern and western portions, since those were the principal areas of British India that had Muslim majorities. The disparities and tensions between the dominant, relatively prosperous Pakistanis of the west, especially the Punjabis with their martial tradition, and the poorer but equally proud and more numerous Bengalis of the east constituted a further source of weakness, insecurity, instability, and division for Pakistan.

Another anomaly of partition created a sense among Pakistanis of having been deprived of territory and population rightfully their own. The princely state of Jammu and Kashmir, a mountainous region in the northern part of the subcontinent, had a Muslim majority but a Hindu maharaja who at first wanted independence for his realm but quickly gave in to pressure from New Delhi to join India after Pakistani irregulars mounted an invasion. The ensuing war left India in control of two-thirds of Kashmir, including the verdant Srinagar Valley.

With the end of hostilities in 1949, the two governments established a cease-fire line between the Pakistani and Indian portions of Kashmir. It was an interim arrangement intended to buy time for a permanent settlement.

The United Nations had passed a resolution the year before calling for the complete withdrawal of Pakistani forces from Kashmir, a reduction (though not the withdrawal) of the Indian forces, and a plebiscite whereby the Kashmiri people could determine their future status. At the time, India had a good chance of winning the plebiscite, since Kashmir's nationalist hero, Sheikh Abdullah, even though he was a Muslim, was an ally of Prime Minister Nehru. Later, however, when Abdullah began flirting with the idea of independence, Nehru had him jailed and local opinion began to turn against India. The Indians backed away from holding the plebiscite because they did not want to give the Kashmiris a chance to vote themselves out of the union.

Since Kashmir was the only Muslim-majority state in a Hindu-majority union, Indians saw its retention as an affirmation of their success in building a society that welcomed Muslims along with everyone else.

From the Pakistanis' viewpoint, Indian rule over Kashmir was the theft of their birthright, a foreign occupation of what should have been part of Pakistan, and an abomination against Pakistan's definition of itself as a homeland for the subcontinent's Muslims.[2]

I HAVE ALWAYS associated this intractable conflict with a recollection from childhood. Sometime in the 1950s, my parents attended a speech by Norman Cousins, the liberal internationalist editor of the *Saturday Review of Literature*. What stuck in their minds, and mine when they told me about it, was Cousins's warning that World War III would begin in the Vale of Kashmir. That prediction made an impression on me in part because the name of the place made it sound so exotic and beautiful, but also because those were the days when the possibility of global thermonuclear war was a nightmare for all Americans, including children who practiced duck-and-cover drills in their schoolrooms.

The global rivalry between the United States and the Soviet Union was a crucial factor in determining American relations with both India and Pakistan. Those two countries came into being at a time when the United States was enlisting allies around the periphery of the Soviet empire and when the principal objective of Pakistani foreign policy was to protect itself against India. Pakistan signed up for two U.S. regional anti-Soviet alliances in the 1950s—the Central Treaty Organization, known early on as the Baghdad Pact, and the Southeast Asian Treaty Organization, or Manila Pact. It was from an airfield near Peshawar in Pakistan that Francis Gary Powers took off in his U-2 spy plane on his doomed flight over the Soviet Union in 1960.

Looking for a protector in Asia, Pakistan developed close ties with China, which was embroiled in a border dispute with India that flared into war in 1962. That conflict ended in a humiliating defeat for India.

By then, there were already signs of a Sino-Soviet schism, which meant that Pakistan had now allied itself with the USSR's two principal foes—the United States and China. That gave India yet another reason to cultivate the best possible relations with the Soviet Union as an offset to both the Chinese threat and the American alliance with Pakistan.

Nehru was a founding member of the so-called Non-Aligned Movement, made up of developing (or third world) nations that vowed to steer clear of the two superpowers. But for many of the movement's members, nonalignment had a distinct pro-Moscow slant, which irritated Washington no end. India was a prime example, since it accepted symbolically potent Soviet aid for steel mills and public works projects, equipped its air force with MiGs, and often voted with Moscow against Washington in the United Nations.

THERE WERE A few brief periods when relations between the United States and India showed some promise of improvement. Dwight Eisenhower had a genuine, though publicly muted, rapport with Nehru, whom he entertained in 1956 at his farm in Gettysburg. In 1959 he became the first American president to visit India. President Kennedy's ambassador to New Delhi, John Kenneth Galbraith, developed a close friendship with Nehru, and the Kennedy administration responded favorably to Indian pleas for military help during the 1962 Sino-Indian war in the Himalayas.

Jacqueline Kennedy's visit to India in March of that year was a tour de force of goodwill diplomacy. She took in the Taj Mahal by moonlight, put on an expert display of equestrian skills, and charmed Indian politicians on numerous occasions, listening to them talk, as she later recalled, "about what they were reading, about people, and about some of the insanities of foreign policy." She called the experience "the most magical two weeks in my life." For his part, Nehru was so charmed that he insisted she move from the Galbraiths' guest house into the prime ministerial residence.[3]

Galbraith's successor as ambassador in New Delhi, Chester Bowles, was a champion of the idea that India should be seen not as a quasi-ally of the USSR but as a vast developing country that, in contrast to China, had chosen democracy over communism.*

But advocates of that view were relatively scarce, primarily because of India's close relations with the USSR, and moments of warmth in the U.S.-Indian relationship were exceptions to the general chill.

IN 1964, THE YEAR that Nehru died, China conducted its first test of a nuclear weapon. India sought security guarantees from the United States, the United Kingdom, and the Soviet Union. That idea went nowhere. Washington regarded India as a country that was, if not playing for the Soviet side, then at least rooting for Moscow from the sidelines. In any event, the United States was not about to commit itself to going to war with China if there was another Sino-Indian conflict.

Now that their giant, intimidating, and recently hostile neighbor possessed the bomb, the Indians had a classic strategic rationale for developing one of their own. They also had world-class talent in physics, most notably Homi Bhabha, a Cambridge-educated scientist, the founder and prime mover of India's nuclear energy program.

THE FOLLOWING YEAR, 1965, the dispute over Kashmir further poisoned Indo-Pakistani relations and roiled the internal politics of Pakistan itself. A short but bloody war between India and Pakistan solidified an autocratic military regime in Pakistan dominated by officers from the western part of the country, a state of affairs that exacerbated tensions with the eastern part. In 1971 civil war broke out between the west and east. Seizing the opportunity to weaken its enemy, India helped bring about the breakup of Pakistan. The newly independent eastern part of the country took the name Bangladesh. The number of Muslim citizens

*Bowles had served a previous tour as U.S. envoy to India during the Eisenhower administration. After succeeding Galbraith in 1963, he stayed on in his post into the Johnson administration.

of India now exceeded the entire population of Pakistan, making India the second largest Muslim country in the world, after Indonesia.

Throughout this turmoil, the United States remained protective of its Pakistani ally, dispatching the aircraft carrier *Enterprise* to the Bay of Bengal—a show of force that India saw as all too reminiscent of British gunboat diplomacy.

Around the same time, Richard Nixon and his national security adviser, Henry Kissinger, used Pakistan as a channel for the American rapprochement with India's other adversary, China. This was further evidence, as seen from New Delhi, that the United States was on its way to becoming not only the enemy of India's Soviet friend but the friend of India's Pakistani *and* Chinese enemies.

A new word entered the lexicon of U.S.-South Asian relations: both in Washington and New Delhi there was perceived to be an American "tilt" toward Pakistan.[4]

In 1972, at a summit in Simla, the prime ministers of India and Pakistan—Nehru's daughter, Indira Gandhi, and Zulfikar Ali Bhutto—pledged that each country's forces would stay on their own side of the 1949 cease-fire line, which was renamed the Line of Control, until future negotiations could yield a solution to the problem.[*]

While the Simla Accord helped maintain a precarious peace in South Asia, it represented the regional demarcation of the global standoff between countries like Pakistan that clung to their ties to Washington and those like India that leaned more toward Moscow.

IT WAS AGAINST this setting of multilayered cold war enmities that India took a big step in the direction of breaking, once and for all, with the Nuclear Non-Proliferation Treaty, or NPT.

The NPT grew out of a global grand bargain that Dwight Eisenhower proposed in what became known as the Atoms for Peace Speech to the United Nations General Assembly in 1953: countries that did not possess nuclear weapons would receive international assistance in gaining access to the benefits of peaceful applications of nuclear energy. In the aftermath of the first Chinese nuclear test in 1964, India proclaimed itself

---

[*]Indira Gandhi had taken the name of her late husband, who was no relation to Mohandas Gandhi.

in favor of a treaty that would have required China and the other four states that had tested—Britain, France, the Soviet Union, and the United States—to give up their weapons. When the NPT was finally completed, in 1968, it obliged its signatories "to pursue negotiations in good faith on effective measures relating to cessation of the nuclear arms race at an early date and to nuclear disarmament, and on a treaty on general and complete disarmament under strict and effective international control." This provision was never taken seriously by the five nuclear "haves"—it was a sop to the "have-nots." In effect, the treaty grandfathered those that had established themselves as nuclear weapons states and required everyone else to forgo the option forever. The overwhelming majority of countries went along with this arrangement, however lopsided it might be, on the theory that the only way to avert a free-for-all among them was to accept the ban. In keeping with Eisenhower's original idea, the treaty made the non-nuclear weapons states eligible to receive financial and technical assistance in peaceful uses of nuclear energy for medicine, agriculture, water management, and the generation of electric power.

India was one of the few holdouts, refusing to sign the NPT on the grounds that it was the charter for an inherently discriminatory club. As a result, India was excluded from receiving atoms-for-peace help.

The willingness of the rest of the world to let China join the NPT as a nuclear weapons state was especially infuriating to the Indians. Why, they asked, should the world's largest tyranny be permitted to have the bomb, while the world's largest democracy—projected to be the world's most populous country by the middle of the twenty-first century—was not? The answer, which India found neither logical nor fair, was that since the testing of the Chinese bomb predated the signing of the NPT, its status as a nuclear weapons state was a reality that the rest of the world had to accept.

Indira Gandhi decided to confront the world with a new reality.

AFTER THE 1971 war with Pakistan, the Indian government had established a fifty-mile-long firing range in Rajasthan near the town of Pokhran, named after a fourteenth-century red sandstone fortress at the junction of three roads that were part of the ancient Silk Route. Within the walls of the old city was an open market locally known for an annual cattle fair and ringed by cafes where truck drivers stopped for lunch on their way to and from Jodhpur, ninety miles away. The people of Pokhran and the adjacent areas often complained of warplanes screeching overhead as they conducted target runs in the nearby Thar, or Great Indian Desert.

On May 18, 1974, the Thar shook, breaking windows and cracking mud-brick walls in villages on the edge of the Pokhran range. Officials supervising the underground nuclear test sent a flash message to Prime Minister Gandhi reporting that "the Buddha has smiled," as though to mock the notion that India, as the birthplace of a pacific religion and of an earlier Gandhi who preached nonviolence, was somehow culturally and ethically obliged to deprive itself of the most potent weaponry.

A normally reserved Indian diplomat I knew in Washington at the time could not contain his glee. He reminded me of what the father of the American atomic bomb, J. Robert Oppenheimer, had thought when he witnessed the world's first successful test of an atomic bomb near Alamogordo, New Mexico, in 1945. Watching that spectacle, Oppenheimer recalled a line from a Hindu holy text, the Bhagavad-Gita, in which the warrior Arjuna has a vision of Krishna as a charioteer guiding him into battle:

If the radiance of a thousand suns
Were to burst at once into the sky
That would be like the splendor of the Mighty one . . .
I am become Death,
The shatterer of Worlds.

"You Americans may have expropriated our deity when your scientists broke open this great secret," said my acquaintance, "but that did not give you a permanent monopoly on morality or on technology."

Publicly, the Indian government was restrained to the point of subterfuge about what had happened at Pokhran. The event itself was "a peaceful nuclear explosion," a concept first propounded by U.S. and Soviet scientists who, in the 1950s and 1960s, believed that nuclear explosions could be used for mining and excavation. Although that concept never proved feasible or cost-effective, it provided a handy cover story for the Indians. It was also consistent with the position taken by Indira Gandhi's father, Nehru, that India would use its nuclear expertise exclusively for peaceful purposes. "There is a difference," said Mrs. Gandhi, "between a nuclear country and a nuclear *weapons* country; we are *not* a nuclear weapons country; we don't have any bombs." She later added that India would "keep its options open," but she and her five successors as prime minister resisted pressure from many in the nation's political, scientific, and military elite who believed that India could never attain either full security or the full respect of the world unless it had a truly modern defense capability, and that meant a nuclear weapons program.

LATER IN 1974 I made my first trip to India. There was some irony in the way the opportunity came about. I had been working for three years as a foreign affairs reporter for *Time* but had yet to travel with Kissinger, who was by then President Gerald Ford's secretary of state. In October Kissinger was making a journey that would begin with several days of talks in Moscow. My specialty at *Time* was coverage of the Soviet Union, so the chief diplomatic correspondent, Jerrold Schecter, gave up his seat on Kissinger's Air Force 707 and let me go in his stead.

The Soviet authorities, however, had other ideas. Several months earlier they had labeled me "an unacceptable person" and a "young sprout of the CIA" because I had been the translator and editor of two volumes of memoirs that Nikita Khrushchev dictated into a tape recorder in the last years of his life when he was under virtual house arrest. The Kremlin and KGB, which were furious at the publication of the books in the West, refused me permission to enter the country, even as part of the Kissinger entourage. At the urging of my companions in the airborne press corps, Kissinger appealed the decision while we were en route from Washington to Moscow. When the Russians refused to yield, Kissinger came to the back of the plane and told me that I would have to get off during a refueling stop in Copenhagen. I cut a mournful figure as I hustled down the rear stairs, hastily collected my bags from the hold, and dragged them across the tarmac to the commercial terminal.

From Copenhagen I leapfrogged ahead of Kissinger to what would be his next stop, New Delhi, so that I could join him for the remaining six stops on his itinerary.* I hooked up with Jacques Leslie, a Yale classmate

*Recalled from the vantage point of many years later, the trip has a macabre aspect. Of the foreign leaders Kissinger met, only Leonid Brezhnev died in his own bed and in his own country. All Kissinger's other hosts—Indira Gandhi of India, Sheikh Mujibur Rahman of Bangladesh, Zulfikar Ali Bhutto of Pakistan, Mohammed Daud of Afghanistan, the Shah of Iran, and Anwar Sadat of Egypt—were assassinated, executed or, in the case of the Shah, destined to die in exile.

who was the South Asia correspondent for the *Los Angeles Times*, and tagged along on a reporting swing he made through several cities and villages. In Agra we toured the Taj Mahal with Elizabeth Moynihan, an expert in Mogul gardens and the wife of the U.S. ambassador, Daniel Patrick Moynihan.

Back in New Delhi, I called on Moynihan himself, who was as intellectually passionate a public figure as I have ever known. He was enthralled by what he saw as the defining strength of Indian civilization: its ability to "absorb synergistically" the culture of outsiders, such as the Moguls, thereby "conquering its conquerors."

In Delhi I also met Bhagwant and Amarjit Singh and their daughter Geetanjali, the "Indian family" of my wife, Brooke Shearer, who had lived with them in 1968 when traveling in India under the auspices of the Experiment in International Living.*

By the time I rejoined the Kissinger road show, I felt as though I had just taken a crash course in a country that I had not known—and it was all thanks to the Soviets for keeping me out of the country that I had devoted years to studying.

KISSINGER CAME TO New Delhi primarily to consult with Indira Gandhi. Like many American officials during her long tenure as prime minister, he found her hard to take. He complained in his memoirs about "her assumption of almost hereditary moral superiority" and "a disdain for capitalism quite fashionable in developing countries."[5]

But Kissinger also found in Mrs. Gandhi a steeliness of character and a hardheadedness about the ways of the world with which he could relate. He was a master of *realpolitik* who had attained prominence in the 1950s with a book that explained how the possession of nuclear weaponry could be an effective instrument of a nation's foreign and security policy and how the balance of terror was a corollary to the balance of power. Briefings that Kissinger gave to reporters who traveled with him to New Delhi suggested that he accepted, and even grudgingly admired, the way Mrs. Gandhi put that theory into practice with the Buddha's smile test. He said as much to her privately in New Delhi, although with a heavy dose

*Singh (which means lion) is one of the most common Indian names, especially among Sikhs, like Amarjit, Bhagwant, and Geetanjali, but it is also found among Hindus from northern provinces such as Rajasthan, like Jaswant Singh.

of his trademark sarcasm: "Congratulations. You did it, you showed you could build nuclear weapons. You have the bomb. Now what do we do to keep from blowing up the world?"[6]

Implicit in the rhetorical question and the pronoun "we" was the premise that India had joined the United States as one of those countries responsible for keeping the nuclear peace. Kissinger assumed that India would conduct more tests and asked only that they be postponed until after the NPT came up for its periodic review and renewal the following year.

During Kissinger's visit to New Delhi, I attended a speech he gave to the Indian Council of World Affairs. He engaged in none of the finger-wagging his audience expected. Instead, he called for a more "mature" relationship, based on America's recognition of India's preeminence in the region.[7] Later Kissinger directed that the United States adopt a "basic policy of not pressuring the [Indians] on their nuclear weapons program."[8]

The Indians appreciated Kissinger's reaction to the Buddha's smile test. Twenty-four years later, they wished they had like-minded Americans to deal with when they made the Thar shake again. But even in 1974, Kissinger was in a small minority in Washington who saw a nuclear-capable India as something the United States would just have to get used to. Over his objections, the U.S. Congress insisted on barring international help to India for developing nuclear energy unless the government in New Delhi agreed to place all its nuclear facilities under international inspections.* India refused to do so. Prime Minister Gandhi did indeed consider follow-up tests but decided to let Buddha's smile speak for itself.[9]

THE PAKISTANIS, MEANWHILE, were not waiting passively to see what happened next. Prime Minister Bhutto, a charismatic populist, proclaimed that his people were prepared to "eat grass" if that was what it took to get the bomb. The key figure in the Pakistani program was Abdul Qadeer Khan. Born in the central Indian city of Bhopal, he had been eleven at the time of partition and experienced the full horror of his family's flight to Pakistan. A metallurgist by profession, he was instrumental

---

*The Nuclear Non-Proliferation Act of 1978 precludes U.S. nuclear cooperation or commerce with countries that have not accepted International Atomic Energy Agency safeguards. This feature of American law was later adopted by the multilateral Nuclear Suppliers Group as a precondition for a country's eligibility for nuclear commerce.

in the purchase and theft of European designs for devices to produce weapons-grade uranium at a plant in Kahuta, about thirty miles east of the capital, Islamabad. China, seeing Pakistan as a regional counterbalance to Indian power, provided some help.[10]

In putting the Pakistani program into high gear, Bhutto hoped not only to give his country a way of trumping India militarily but also to give himself, as a civilian leader, a way of trumping the political power of the Pakistani army. Instead, the program fell under the control of the military, which was, consequently, emboldened both against India and against Bhutto. He was overthrown in a coup in 1977, then hanged by General Muhammad Zia ul-Haq, the chief of the army staff who made himself president.[11]

PAKISTAN'S NUCLEAR PROGRAM complicated and in many ways soured its relationship with the United States. Members of the U.S. Congress, fearing nuclear proliferation in general and an "Islamic bomb" in particular, imposed sanctions on Pakistan. The executive branch, under Republican and Democratic administrations, still saw Pakistan as a bulwark against Soviet expansionism in the region. When the USSR invaded Pakistan's neighbor Afghanistan in December 1979, the administration of Jimmy Carter waived the sanctions and made Pakistan the U.S. base of operations for support of the Islamic guerrillas who were fighting the Soviets.

The U.S.-backed resistance of the Soviet occupation in Afghanistan was the last battle of the cold war and, as it turned out, the terminal debacle of the USSR. While that proxy war was under way, it confirmed Pakistan's value to the United States. Ronald Reagan offered Pakistan a multibillion-dollar package of economic and military assistance, including F-16 fighters. Congress reluctantly went along.

In 1985 the State Department, in an effort to protect U.S. relations with Pakistan, persuaded Senator Larry Pressler, a Republican from South Dakota, to sponsor legislation allowing foreign assistance to go forward as long as the president could certify annually that Pakistan did not possess a nuclear explosive device. Pressler turned out to be less pliable than the administration hoped, and the amendment that bore his name became a means for nonproliferation advocates in Congress to put pressure on both the State Department and Pakistan. Officials of the Reagan and first Bush administrations had to engage in increasingly elaborate casuistry to exempt Pakistan from sanctions. American intelligence analysts, who were convinced that Pakistan had everything it took to make the bomb, felt under pressure from their political masters to give the Pakistanis the benefit of an almost nonexistent doubt. Holding their noses, they stopped short of concluding that Pakistan had completed the fabrication and assembly of a nuclear device.

The Pakistanis, however, made it increasingly hard for the United States to practice denial on their behalf. In 1987, at a time of increased military tensions between India and Pakistan, with 370,000 troops squared off against each other along the border, President Zia told *Time*, "Pakistan has the capability of building the bomb. You can write today that Pakistan can build a bomb whenever it wishes. Once you have acquired the technology, which Pakistan has, you can do whatever you like."[12]

The following year, American monitoring of the program Zia was boasting about compelled President Reagan to issue a public warning that future U.S. military sales to Pakistan would become "difficult or impossible." He was yielding not just to the facts but to the waning of the geopolitical justification for the tilt toward Pakistan, since the Soviet Union was in the early phases of withdrawing from Afghanistan and, as it turned out, from the stage of history.

THAT SAME YEAR, 1987, India took another step away from playing coy about its own nuclear capability. Rajiv Gandhi was prime minister, having succeeded his mother after she was gunned down by her Sikh bodyguards in 1984 in reprisal for her use of force to end a siege by Sikh militants in Amritsar. Rajiv Gandhi conducted a personal campaign on behalf of global nuclear disarmament, most dramatically in an address to the United Nations in June 1988. He attached a deadline to India's original position on the NPT: if the nuclear weapons powers would promise to eliminate their arsenals by 2010, India would give up the option of becoming a nuclear weapons state that his mother had left open. The unstated but unmistakable implication was that if the United States and the other nuclear weapons states did not move toward real disarmament, India might conclude it had not just the right but the need to join their ranks.

To make sure that that option was available to his successors, Rajiv
Gandhi secretly ordered a series of steps that would enable India to manufacture the components for a bomb that could be tested at Pokhran.

His premiership was plagued by financial scandals, and he was voted
out of office in 1989, although he remained head of the Congress Party.
In 1991 he was assassinated by a suicide bomber connected with a Sri
Lankan Tamil separatist movement—the third Indian political leader
(and the third named Gandhi) to fall victim to the dark side of the region's kaleidoscopic diversity.*

IN 1989 AND 1990, after almost two decades of relative calm, Kashmir
suffered renewed unrest, partly because many in the local population still
seethed with resentment against New Delhi after Indira Gandhi's government had flagrantly manipulated state elections. Homegrown secessionists took inspiration from the disintegration of the USSR. Islamist
freedom fighters who had succeeded in driving the Soviets out of
Afghanistan turned their attention to the liberation of Kashmir. They did
so with the support of the Pakistani intelligence services. Benazir Bhutto,
the prime minister of Pakistan at the time (and the daughter of Zulfikar
Ali Bhutto), vowed a "thousand-year war" in support of Kashmiri Muslims bent on driving out the Indian "occupiers."

During this upsurge in trouble, the United States saw an alarming
buildup of conventional forces and training exercises on both sides of the
Line of Control. There was evidence that the Pakistani military might
have assembled one or more nuclear weapons and might even be preparing them for use.[13]

President Bush dispatched his deputy national security adviser, Robert
Gates, and Richard Haass of the NSC staff to the region. They secured a
Pakistani promise to shut down training camps for insurgents who had
been infiltrating Kashmir and carrying out acts of terrorism, and India
agreed to "confidence-building measures" that were intended to reduce
the danger of a border incident getting out of control.

This discreet and successful intervention did not earn much gratitude
from New Delhi at the time. The Indians had little doubt that the

---

*The Tamils, while Hindu, are a distinct ethnic and language group that makes up a
majority in the southern Indian state of Tamil Nadu and significant minorities in Sri Lanka
as well as the Indian states of Kerala, Karnataka, and Andhra Pradesh.

Pakistanis would soon resume infiltration—which in fact happened. The Indians also wanted to squelch any suggestion that the Kashmir dispute had been "internationalized" (that is, mediated), lest other would-be peace brokers might someday think they could step in and insist on allowing Kashmir's Muslim majority to join Pakistan or gain independence. Years later, however, the Gates-Haass mission of May 1990 came to be recognized in India as an example of the right kind of quiet American diplomatic assistance and therefore a potential precedent for how the United States might help in future crises.[14]

BY OCTOBER 1990 the Pakistanis' covert nuclear program had advanced to the point that Bush could no longer certify to Congress that they did not possess an explosive device. He also had less reason to try, now that the Soviets had given up in Afghanistan, and Eastern Europe was breaking free of Moscow's control. The Pressler amendment required the United States to cancel further economic and military assistance to Pakistan and stop the remaining shipment of twenty-eight of the F-16s for which the Pakistanis had already partially paid. Feeling cheated and abandoned by the United States, and also concerned about the efficacy of their deterrent, the Pakistanis stepped up their efforts to find another means of signaling their determination to stand up to India.

The arms race on the subcontinent moved into yet another lane: a competition over the acquisition of ballistic missiles.

India already had a rocketry program, masterminded by the aeronautical engineer A. P. J. Abdul Kalam. As head of the Indian Defense Research and Development Organization, he was heavily involved in the development of nuclear weaponry as well. By the end of the first Bush administration, India had two missiles in the testing stage. One, the medium-range Agni, was named for the Hindu god of fire, while the other was a short-range missile called Prithvi, which means earth. As "delivery vehicles" for nuclear weapons, these rockets would be able to reach targets in Pakistan much more quickly than India's French Mirage and Soviet Sukhoi-30 fighter-bombers—and without the risk of being intercepted or shot down en route by Pakistani antiaircraft defenses.

The Pakistanis did not have an indigenous missile program, but in the early 1990s they acquired the short-range M-11 from China. Then, in 1998, they got the medium-range No Dong from North Korea and renamed it the Ghauri, after a twelfth-century Muslim leader who had stormed the Hindu lands to the south and defeated a ruler of Delhi named Prithviraj Chauhan. Pakistan's other two missiles, the Abdali and Shaheen, were also named after Muslim warriors who had invaded India.

Thus, even the nomenclature of the weaponry accumulating in South Asia kept alive, on both sides, vengeful and largely mythologized memories from nine centuries earlier.

TWO

THE DESERT RISES

BILL CLINTON HAS had a fascination with India since I first knew him when we were students together at Oxford in the late 1960s. He has always been a voracious reader of history and biography—especially, in those years and in that setting, books about Britain in the heyday of its empire. I remember him toting around Robert Blake's biography of Disraeli for several weeks in the fall of 1969 and talking about it in pubs and in the kitchen of the house we shared. That same year he read E. M. Forster's *Passage to India* for the first time.

We stayed in touch over the next twenty-five years. Since my reporting career at *Time* was devoted almost entirely to international affairs, Clinton gravitated in that direction when we talked on the phone, corresponded, and got together. My focus was largely on the communist world, and—with the cold war still the dominant factor in American foreign policy—that subject tended to come up more than others. After five years of being banned from visiting the USSR because of my part in the publication of the Khrushchev memoirs, I was allowed to travel there again in 1980 and did so frequently.

When I visited Bill and Hillary Clinton at the governor's mansion in Little Rock in 1987, they asked me, as usual, about what was going on in the Soviet Union now that Mikhail Gorbachev was in charge. But somewhat to my surprise, they were more eager to talk about South Asia. That region was on their minds because it seemed to be a laboratory for experiments in grass-roots democratization and social entrepreneurship, such as the microcredit banks and women's self-help organizations that were taking hold in Bangladesh and northern India. Since her freshman year at Wellesley, Hillary had been interested in India and had considered spending a year teaching or studying there before she decided to go to law school instead.

When Clinton was elected president, he asked me to help him and Secretary of State Warren Christopher deal with Russia and the former Soviet Union. In brainstorming sessions at the White House during the first year of the administration, I noticed that the subject of India came up more often than one might have expected, given the paucity of headline news coming from that part of the world. Policymakers (like journalists) tend to focus on bad news, and there was plenty of that. Yet Clinton was always looking for a bigger and brighter picture of what was going on in the world, and he would often cite India—with its resilient democracy, its vibrant high-tech sector, its liberal reforms that had begun to revitalize a statist and sclerotic economy, and its huge consumer market—as a natural beneficiary of globalization and therefore potentially a much more important partner for the United States than was then the case.

At his request, Hillary toured the subcontinent in March 1995 to demonstrate the administration's interest in the region and Clinton's desire to make a trip of his own. On her return, she gave a speech in the State Department auditorium accentuating the positive of what she had seen. By then I was deputy secretary of state and, in that capacity, her host because Secretary Christopher was traveling. As we were waiting at the podium for the overflow crowd to settle, she told me that she was all the more convinced that the administration should make "a new opening" to India a hallmark of its foreign policy.[1]

One of my colleagues in the department, Tom Pickering, provided an additional argument for increased presidential attention to India. A legendarily energetic and broad-gauge foreign service officer, Tom had been ambassador to New Delhi when Clinton assumed the presidency in 1993. Before taking up his next post, in Moscow, Tom sent Clinton a cable stressing the opportunity that the United States had to revitalize relations with India now that the fifty-year rivalry with the Soviet Union was over.

This argument resonated with Clinton. He believed he would have lost to George H. W. Bush in 1992 had it not been for the end of the cold war. He was looking for every possible way to seize the opportunities that came with being the first post-cold-war president. Those included building partnerships with Russia and the other former Soviet states, but also repairing relations with major developing—and nonaligned—countries that had previously kept their distance from the United States. The foremost example was India.

Yet the Clinton administration paid less attention to that country during its first six years in office than the president wanted. New initiatives stand the best chance of success at the beginning of an administration, but they require full presidential endorsement and engagement. The urgencies that competed for Clinton's attention between 1993 and 1995 were civil wars in the Balkans and Somalia, a political crisis in Russia (Boris Yeltsin was squared off against a Communist-dominated parliament), a humanitarian catastrophe just off American shores (thousands of Haitian refugees were fleeing a brutal military dictatorship in rickety boats, many drowning in the attempt), and the demands and frustrations of the Middle East peace process.

INDIA'S REFUSAL TO join the Nuclear Non-Proliferation Treaty also made it hard for the Clinton administration to develop traction with India. Like his predecessor Bush, Clinton believed in a new global order that would be based on international laws, treaties, and institutions. That meant making the most of a United Nations that was no longer riven by the U.S.-Soviet standoff, transforming NATO from an anti-Soviet alliance into a comprehensive and inclusive security structure for Eurasia, and consolidating regional groupings in Latin America, Africa, the Far East, and Southeast Asia. It also meant strengthening the international arms control and nonproliferation regime, especially the NPT.

In the American view, the NPT had proved its value many times over in the more than two decades it had been in force, disproving John F. Kennedy's famous prediction in 1963 that within ten years there might be more than twenty states armed with atomic and hydrogen bombs.[2] Germany and Japan, which had forsworn nuclear weapons after World War II, looked to the NPT as insurance against other countries acquiring them. Many other advanced industrial states—such as Australia,

Canada, Italy, Spain, and Sweden—could easily have gone nuclear but decided that their interests were best served by not doing so. A number of nations that had set out to develop nuclear weapons in the 1970s and 1980s—Argentina, Brazil, South Africa, South Korea, and Taiwan—agreed to cancel their programs (or in South Africa's case, destroy the nuclear capability it had developed) and join the NPT as non-nuclear-weapons states.

As the Soviet Union began to unravel at the beginning of the 1990s, the world faced the possibility that four newly independent nuclear weapons states might soon occupy the territory of the old USSR: Russia, Ukraine, Belarus, and Kazakhstan. The international community, led by the United States, prevailed upon the three smaller countries to let Russia be the sole successor state to the Soviet Union as a nuclear power. The legitimacy that came with membership in the NPT was a powerful inducement for getting Ukraine, Belarus, and Kazakhstan to relinquish their Soviet-era nuclear weapons.

Even Iran, Iraq, Libya, and North Korea joined the NPT, although they used their membership as a cover under which they pursued their ambitions to develop the bomb.

Israel, which refused to sign the NPT, was alleged to have nuclear weapons, although neither its own government nor that of the United States has ever confirmed the fact. The Kennedy and Johnson administrations reportedly tried to persuade Israel not to go nuclear.[3] From the time of the 1973 Middle East war, during the Nixon administration, the United States avoided making an issue of the matter, in effect treating Israel as a special case, since it was surrounded by Arab enemies who wanted to wipe it off the map. During the Clinton administration, the United States publicly and privately urged Israel to accede to the NPT. Nonetheless, Washington's perceived willingness to give Israel a pass on the NPT made it harder for American diplomats to argue for the sanctity and universal applicability of the treaty.

For many Indian politicians, government officials, defense experts, and commentators, the NPT embodied "the three D's" of U.S. nuclear policy—dominance, discrimination, and double standards.

THE WIDESPREAD ANTIPATHY toward the NPT in India had a champion in the Bharatiya Janata Party, which by the early 1990s had become a potent force in Indian politics. The BJP portrayed the Congress Party, which had governed the country for most of the past forty-plus years, as complacent, lumbering, weak-willed, corrupt—and so eager to demonstrate its secularism that it had turned Hindus into second-class citizens.

Many adherents and advocates of the BJP objected when Indian and foreign political observers described the party's program as Hindu nationalist. What it offered, they said, was an alternative vision of a Hindu national identity—a concept known as Hindutva—that was cultural rather than religious. The term, they believed, should be understood to embrace Muslims and followers of other faiths.

But the fact remained that the BJP included—and not just on its fringes—sectarian zealots who were implicated in incidents of communal violence. The party had evolved from the political wing of the RSS, the organization that rejected root-and-branch Mohandas Gandhi's concept of nationhood based on diversity as a virtue of Indian society and inclusiveness as a necessity of Indian politics.

By 1986 the president of the BJP was Lal Krishna Advani, a journalist-turned-politician who had joined the RSS as a teenager nearly fifty years earlier. In 1990, riding in a Toyota festooned to look like a chariot out of a Hindu epic, surrounded by militants on motorcycles in full combat gear, Advani led a steadily swelling procession of BJP activists from Gujarat to Uttar Pradesh for demonstrations at an unused sixteenth-century mosque in Ayodhya. By legend, Babur, the founder of the Mogul dynasty, had built the mosque on the spot thought to be the birthplace of Ram, the mythical Hindu king, and a Hindu shrine had once stood there. Fiery rhetoric against the perceived sacrilege whipped the crowds into a frenzy. Two years later, a similar protest turned into a riot. Mobs armed with knives, swords, and pickaxes tore down the mosque and slaughtered thirteen Muslims who were too slow to flee the scene. Thousands more died in the mayhem that spread during the days and weeks that followed. Ayodhya has remained ever since a focus of Hindu-versus-Muslim tension and a flashpoint for occasional outbreaks of bloodletting.

Because of incidents like this and the ideology that incited their perpetrators, most non-Hindu Indians saw the BJP as fundamentally hostile toward their communities. Many Hindus saw it as anathema to the founding principles of Indian statehood, and many BJP members disavowed the fanaticism for which Ayodhya became an enduring symbol, as did others who voted for the BJP out of disillusionment with the Congress Party.

However, no matter what the differences within the BJP on other issues, there was near-unanimity within its ranks and among its supporters in other parties on the importance of nuclear weaponry as a guarantee of India's safety and strength and an enhancement of its international prestige. Indeed, on this issue, the BJP struck a chord across the political spectrum. Most Indians, regardless of political stripe, rejected as unfair and insulting the insistence of the United States and others that the NPT, to which India was not a signatory, nonetheless imposed obligations and limitations on India. Even those who believed in forgoing the bomb tended to do so not out of deference to the United States but for some combination of economic reasons and moral ones derived from an international version of Gandhi's belief in dealing peacefully with enemies.

The principal figures in the BJP, as the party's idea of Hindutva would suggest, did not share the reverence of many Indians for Gandhi. In their debates with those preaching nuclear abstinence, BJP spokesmen portrayed themselves as realists who saw nuclear weapons as a necessary means of ensuring India's security in a world where half a dozen countries, including the two most threatening to India—China and Pakistan—already had such weapons and several more were bent on acquiring them. Even moderates in the party believed in India's entitlement to nuclear weaponry as a basic right that came with sovereignty. Forces in Indian politics who held this view—and who were by no means limited to the BJP—were gaining momentum about the time that Bill Clinton won the presidency in the United States.

THE CLINTON ADMINISTRATION set about designing a policy toward South Asia that would allow it to pursue three objectives that were in some tension with one another: keeping the lid on the proliferation of nuclear and ballistic missile technology, nudging U.S.-Indian relations forward, and maintaining support for Pakistan as a quasi-democratic, relatively pro-Western Islamic state.

Within the executive branch, the difficulty of striking this three-way balance sometimes produced friction between two groups: the *functionalists*, whose job was to advance global goals like nonproliferation (and human rights and sensible environmental policies); and the *regionalists*, who were charged with maintaining decent relations with countries that often had poor records on one or more of those issues. The functionalists would argue that the United States needed to crack down on prolifera- tors (and human-rights abusers and nature despoilers), while the region- alists would reply that lines of communication should remain open in order to bring American influence to bear on the offending governments. In principle, an integrated and coherent policy would emerge from the resulting dialectic. In practice, there were wrangles that resulted in win- ners and losers, with the losers coming back to fight another day—or in compromises that left no one entirely satisfied.

Nonetheless, the system worked reasonably well in the case of U.S. policy toward South Asia during the 1990s. That was largely because each group made an effort to understand—and, as much as possible, accommodate—the other's views.

The most experienced, imaginative, and diplomatically skillful of the State Department's nonproliferationists was Robert Einhorn, a civil ser- vant who had worked on disarmament and arms control since the 1970s. I had known Bob for more than a dozen years, first as a specialist on U.S.-Soviet arms control, the subject of several books I wrote, then as a close personal friend, and, once I came into government in 1993, as a key colleague.

I spent the first year of the administration identified as a regionalist because I headed a newly created bureau responsible for relations with the countries of the former Soviet Union. As it happened, however, one of my principal concerns was nonproliferation, so in that sense I had a foot in the functionalist camp as well. In addition to many months devoted to "denuclearizing" the non-Russian former Soviet republics, I spent considerable time in 1993 helping President Clinton and Secretary Christopher dissuade the Russians from supplying rocket engines and related technology to India for use in its missile program.[4]

When Christopher made me his deputy in early 1994, one of my assignments was to help the nonproliferationists and the regionalists rec- oncile their differences and develop a comprehensive policy. That was one purpose of the morning senior staff meetings that brought all the assis- tant secretaries together in my conference room.

IN APRIL 1994, two weeks after I was sworn in as deputy secretary, Clinton and Christopher sent me to South Asia to sound out the Indians and Pakistanis on some ideas that might, if adopted, slow down and regulate the arms race between them.

The Pakistanis were telling us privately they had stopped producing highly enriched uranium for their weapons program. If that was true, we might be able to get them to announce they were freezing production of so-called fissile material—the stuff of which the explosive part of a bomb is made—and open their enrichment facility at Kahuta to international inspection. In exchange, the United States would give them what we called "Pressler relief"—that is, relaxation of the sanctions required by the amendment Senator Pressler had sponsored in 1985. One result would have been delivery of the F-16s that the Pakistanis had bought but that were sitting at an Air Force base in Arizona. A promise to press Congress for sanctions relief was just about the only carrot I had to take with me to Pakistan.

I STOPPED FIRST in New Delhi to try to persuade the Indians that halting Pakistani production of fissile material was sufficiently in India's interest to justify letting the Pakistanis have the F-16s. Any hope of success was dashed even before I landed. News of our proposal was already splashed all over the Indian media, prompting indignation that the United States was even thinking about letting the Pakistanis have the F-16s ("all the better to bomb us with!"). If we released the planes, Indian officials hinted, they would deploy their missiles within striking distance of Pakistan's major cities.

The Indians were even more upset at the prospect of the United States easing old sanctions against Pakistan while keeping on the books another American law that would impose new sanctions against any state that conducted a nuclear test in defiance of the NPT. That legislation had been sponsored by Senator John Glenn in order to strengthen laws that had been in effect since the Indians' "peaceful test" in 1974 and that were intended to hold a sword of Damocles over the Indians' head in case they set off another device. Glenn, an Ohio Democrat and America's first astronaut to orbit the earth, was a figure of immense authority in the realm of rocketry, space, and national security. He was the leader of Congress's antiproliferation hawks who wanted the administration to be tough on any country that refused to accept the NPT, regardless of other strategic considerations. Once I arrived in New Delhi, several Indians whom I knew to be in the pro-nuclear camp fulminated against American nonproliferation laws. They regarded the Glenn amendment in particular as typical of the American penchant for intimidation and arrogance, and they hoped their government would not let itself be cowed.

My visit would have been a total bust were it not for a long private conversation with Prime Minister Narasimha Rao at his office in South Block (so-called because of its location in the vast complex of administrative buildings built in the early twentieth century under the Raj). A quiet, erudite, cautious former foreign minister, Rao would have had me believe he was predisposed to maintain Indira Gandhi's policy of nuclear ambiguity. He told me that he and his cabinet—especially his highly regarded finance minister, Manmohan Singh, the architect of the nation's economic reforms—understood that security depended on prosperity. Prosperity, in turn, depended on integration into world markets and close relations with the United States. That objective, he seemed to recognize, would be in jeopardy if India overplayed its nuclear card.

I brought with me a formal invitation for Rao to make a visit to Washington in May. Rao readily agreed, but he confided that the trip would entail some political risk, especially if it created the impression that he was going to the White House to be badgered on nonproliferation. He did not elaborate, but he did not need to: the Congress Party's opponents, and particularly those in the BJP, were showing increased strength in regional elections and in the parliament.

IN ISLAMABAD I quickly discovered that Prime Minister Benazir Bhutto was feeling even more heat from her domestic political enemies than Rao was from his. Benazir was a smart, tough Radcliffe graduate who came across as thoroughly Americanized and sure of herself when dealing with visitors from Washington. But the substance of her positions was unbendingly nationalistic, and her assertive, self-confident style did not disguise how vulnerable she was politically. She told me that the inspections that would be required under the U.S. proposal would be seen as an infringement of Pakistani sovereignty and that she would pay a big price for any concession on that front. She warned that Muhammad Nawaz Sharif, the son of a wealthy Lahore industrialist and the leader of the parliamentary opposition, would exploit any concessions she made as part of his campaign to drive her out of office.

But it was the military that concerned her most. All Pakistani prime ministers have had to keep a wary eye in the direction of the garrison town of Rawalpindi, southwest of Islamabad, but Benazir had particular cause for wariness, given her father's death on the gallows at the order of Zia ul-Haq.

That episode in Pakistani political history was on my mind when I called on General Abdul Wahid Kakar, one of Zia's successors as chief of the army staff. General Wahid's rejection of the American proposal made Benazir Bhutto's look mild. His country, he said, was not going to accept a moratorium when everyone knew India was hell-bent to produce as much fissile material as quickly as possible for its own bomb program. As for our offer of relief on the Pressler amendment, he said, naturally Pakistan wanted delivery of the planes it had bought "and paid good money for—but not on your terms." Mimicking the look of a man being hanged (an image that was already fixed in my mind), he added, "We will *choke* on your carrots!"

The U.S. government's task was not made easier when, back in Washington, Senator Pressler himself, encouraged by the Indian embassy, publicly vowed to keep sanctions in place even if the Pakistanis agreed to the U.S. plan.

During several public appearances I made during the brief visit, I saw, for the only time in my career, signs reading, "Talbott Go Home!"

It seemed like just the thing to do.

As RAO's VISIT to Washington drew closer, he came under heightened pressure from those who were advocating a nuclear test to prove that India was not going to be pushed around by the United States. One shot across the prime minister's bow came from A. P. J. Abdul Kalam, the head of the Indian rocketry program, who gave an interview trumpeting successful missile tests as a refutation of the "racial prejudice" that led other nations to believe that they had a monopoly on sophisticated technology.[5] More on the political defensive than ever, Rao publicly vowed to a group of army officers that he would not let anyone dictate to India limitations on its nuclear program.[6]

That spring, the United States and India resorted to a standard means of maintaining the appearance of momentum when in fact diplomacy is going nowhere: talks about talks. It was agreed that experts of the two governments would conduct quiet discussions on the terms for a series of meetings that would include nine countries—India as well as Pakistan, along with the five NPT-recognized nuclear weapons states, plus Germany and Japan (as the economically most powerful of the non-nuclear weapons states). The stated goal of the meetings would be to identify measures to promote arms control and disarmament on a global basis but with special emphasis on South Asia.

The hope in Washington was that the proposed conference might lead eventually to India's and Pakistan's acceptance of UN-supervised regulation of the arms race between them. The administration hoped that since Rao was letting his experts talk with U.S. experts about the possibility of such a conference, he was slightly relaxing his government's long-standing refusal to consider international constraints on its military programs.

The United States was making a concession of its own: by proposing the discussions, our government was tacitly signaling a willingness to live with India's and Pakistan's undeclared, untested, but undisputed nuclear capabilities rather than insisting on their formal accession to the NPT.

When the experts' talks took place at the end of April, it was with an advance understanding, at Indian insistence, that there would be no publicity and that the meeting would occur on the neutral and unofficial ground of a London hotel. The Indian specialists insisted on adding three more countries—Iran, Libya, and North Korea—to the list of nine that Washington was proposing for the conference. As the Indians put it, these three states were "of relevance to the nuclear issues." So they were. Even though Iran, Libya, and North Korea were signatories to the NPT, they were making a mockery of its intent by seeking to acquire nuclear weapons. The Indians' proposal was at best a way of putting meaningful diplomacy on hold and, at worst, a guarantee that there would no progress.

The meeting looked all the more like a setup when someone on the Indian side leaked word of the "secret" talks to the press. In the ensuing uproar, Rao was lambasted by his political opponents, especially in the BJP, on the grounds that by even agreeing to let the meeting take place he had knuckled under to U.S. pressure.

WHEN THE PRIME MINISTER arrived at the White House on May 19, Clinton suggested they meet alone in the Oval Office. While Rao's advisors fidgeted nervously nearby in the Cabinet Room, Clinton played for nearly an hour on Rao's desire for a "qualitatively new and better relationship than anything we could ever have during all those decades when we seemed always to be mad at each other about one thing or another." Instead of broaching the question of testing directly, he said, "Let's not let anything upset the apple cart and keep us from accomplishing what we can do together if we really look to the future and all its possibilities."

When the private meeting concluded, Clinton and Rao emerged arm-in-arm and beaming, to the obvious apprehension of Rao's aides. Clinton took me aside as the two delegations made their way to a lunch in the residence. "I think I may have softened him up," he said. "Now you go give him the hard message."

That afternoon I went to see Rao at his suite in the Willard Hotel and, invoking the president's name, asked to see him one-on-one. He excused his assistants, who were now looking unhappier than ever. I stressed that I was under the president's instructions to fill in the blanks of what Rao had heard in the Oval Office. I said I realized there were pressures on him and alluded to reports that some in the Indian strategic community might be preparing for a change of policy and a round of highly provocative tests of missiles and perhaps of nuclear devices as well. President Clinton, I said, hoped Rao would resist what we recognized was a powerful temptation.

Rao replied that he had been heartened by what he had heard from Clinton about the possibilities for the U.S.-Indian relationship and understood the connection between that prospect and what I was saying, but he gave no concrete assurances.

Shortly after Rao's return to New Delhi from Washington, the BJP leader, Lal Krishna Advani, told cheering supporters, "India should go ahead with its nuclear weapons program to prevent our neighbors and superpowers from intimidating us."[7]

LATE 1994 AND early 1995 saw shifts in American and Indian domestic politics that spelled new and lasting trouble for arms control and nonproliferation.

The American mid-term elections in 1994 swept the Republicans into control of both houses of Congress. Powerful, ultraconservative senators like Jesse Helms of North Carolina and members of the House of Representatives like Newt Gingrich of Georgia campaigned against what they denounced as the Democrats' ill-conceived arms control initiatives that would "denuclearize" American defenses. High on the Republican target list was the Comprehensive Test Ban Treaty (CTBT).

THE QUEST FOR a global prohibition on all nuclear testing had its origins in the 1950s, during the Eisenhower administration. A Limited Test Ban Treaty—which outlawed tests above ground, in the atmosphere and in outer space but permitted them to continue underground—went into effect, and the Indians signed it, during the Kennedy administration.

Some U.S. military officers, weapons scientists, and conservative politicians opposed a comprehensive test ban on the grounds that continued subterranean testing was necessary to check the reliability of the American nuclear stockpile and to perfect new, specialized bombs. Furthermore, some intelligence experts feared that if the United States agreed to stop underground testing, it would be at a disadvantage in its competition with the Soviet Union, which would cheat on the ban by setting off relatively low-yield devices deep in the earth or in outer space. Largely because of this opposition, the idea of a CTBT languished through the Reagan administration.

Then, under pressure from a Democratic-controlled Congress, the first President Bush reluctantly signed into law a bill calling for a CTBT within four years. Clinton, who saw the test ban as vital to strengthening the global nonproliferation regime, came into office determined to meet that deadline.

One of the earliest advocates of a comprehensive test ban had been Nehru, but over time, the Indians came to oppose it for the same reason they were against the NPT: they saw it as part of a U.S.-led effort to keep them from developing nuclear weapons of their own and to make permanent a nuclear monopoly that excluded India.

That suspicion was confirmed in 1995. Just as negotiators were putting the finishing touches on the text of the CTBT, the United States pulled out all the stops to secure an indefinite extension of the NPT. The administration succeeded in getting 174 member states of the United Nations to agree. That number would rise to 186 over the next three years. From New Delhi's standpoint, the permanent extension of the NPT was dismaying because it drastically reduced the chance that the treaty might someday be amended to allow India to join as a nuclear weapons state. The Indians feared that the Clinton administration would next push for "universalizing" the CTBT—that is, making the test ban applicable to all countries, whether they joined the treaty or not—thereby foreclosing India's option of further testing and consigning India forever to a kind of purgatory in the eyes of the rest of the world for its refusal to sign the NPT and CTBT.

The Indians' first line of defense was to try to block the CTBT as negotiations on a final text of the treaty moved into the endgame. Even if that last-ditch effort failed, they could still hope that the Republicans in the U.S. Senate would prevent the treaty from ever being ratified.

In their opposition to the CTBT, the Indian government looked for support to the increasingly influential Indian-American community. During the 1970s Indian educational institutions had produced large numbers of scientists, engineers, doctors, and other professionals who had trouble finding work in their own stagnating economy. In the 1980s and 1990s the number of Indian Americans more than tripled, from fewer than 400,000 to more than 1.2 million (ten times the number of Pakistani Americans).

Many of the Indians who settled in the United States had formed professional associations and political organizations that soon exercised impressive clout. During the 1990s they doubled their contributions to political candidates. A bipartisan Congressional Caucus on India and Indian Americans burgeoned from 8 members to 115, more than a quarter of the entire House of Representatives. Whatever the issue, Indian Americans pushed an increasingly responsive Congress for more leniency toward New Delhi on virtually all issues. Their influence added to congressional opposition to the CTBT.[8]

Meanwhile, in India, the ruling Congress Party lost a number of crucial elections, including in Prime Minister Rao's home state of Andhra Pradesh and in Karnataka in the south, both of which had long been considered bastions of Congress strength. Then, in March 1995, the BJP scored further gains in two other large states—Gujarat, where Gandhi was born, and Maharashtra, the capital of which is Mumbai, formerly known as Bombay, the financial and entertainment center of the country.

As 1995 drew to a close, the Clinton administration was gearing up for a major fight with the Republicans over ratification of the CTBT just as pressure was mounting on the politically vulnerable Rao to give in to the nuclear lobby.

IN EARLY DECEMBER, Frank Wisner, the U.S. ambassador to India, was back in Washington for consultations. Like Tom Pickering, whom he had replaced in New Delhi after Tom was transferred to Moscow, Frank held the rank of career ambassador, which marked him as one of the most experienced and respected foreign service officers of his generation. Before returning to his post, Frank paid a courtesy call on Secretary Christopher. Chris (as he was called) only half-jokingly remarked that given his own preoccupations with the Middle East, the Balkans, Russia, and China, he hoped Frank would keep the subcontinent under control—and definitely not get him involved in Kashmir, which was regarded as the ultimate diplomatic tar baby.

Within minutes after leaving the secretary's office, Frank learned that American satellites passing over the Pokhran test site had photographed evidence of suspicious activity. Cables were now running through L-shaped tunnels, presumably to transmit data from an underground blast. Frank went to the CIA to get a full briefing and arrange for copies of the pictures to be sent to the U.S. embassy in New Delhi.

While Frank was en route to India, the *New York Times* carried an article under the headline "U.S. Suspects India Prepares to Conduct Nuclear Test," with attribution to American intelligence experts. The United States, said the story, was "working to discourage [the test], fearing a political chain reaction."[9]

As soon as Frank arrived in New Delhi, he arranged a private meeting with A. N. Varma, Prime Minister Rao's principal secretary (in effect, his chief of staff). Frank showed Varma a single sample of the satellite imagery, put it back in his pocket, then warned that a test would backfire against India, incurring a full dose of sanctions under the terms of the Glenn amendment. When Clinton called Rao to reinforce Frank's message, Rao replied only that India would not act irresponsibly.

While that statement was far from reassuring, Rao did, as Clinton hoped he would, pull the plug on the test, largely because he did not want to provoke American sanctions that would do harm to the Indian economy.[10]

For proponents of testing, the lesson was clear: next time India would have to maintain the same sort of secrecy, and attain the same degree of surprise, that Indira Gandhi had achieved with Buddha's smile in 1974.

THE BJP ISSUED a statement calling the *Times* story a "ploy" by Washington to "coerce" India into signing the CTBT. The BJP's deputy parliamentary leader was quoted in one of the press reports that came across my desk as saying, "India is not a colony to be bent or threatened into submission"; American bullying was just one more reason to "strengthen India's nuclear policies."[11]

I believe this was the first time I focused on the name of Jaswant Singh. If so, it was largely because of his rhetorical flair. The quotation that caught my eye captured in just a few words a combination of characteristics that I would later come to associate with him: personal forcefulness, national pride, political resolve, and a long memory for historical grievances. From then on, I scanned press and government reports for more rumblings from this outspoken representative for what was clearly a rising force in Indian politics and also for more background on the man himself.

Jaswant Singh was a Rajput (Hindi for son of a king), a member of the warrior community that had produced rulers and nobility in a vast area in northern India that had managed, over the centuries, to preserve a degree of self-rule under Moguls and British alike. He was born in 1938 in the desert village of Jasol in Rajasthan, about sixty miles southwest of Pokhran. He joined the army as a young man, served in a cavalry unit, rose to the rank of major, and resigned his commission to go into politics in 1966. He did not become a member of the BJP until the 1980s, yet he rose quickly within its ranks to become a spokesman on matters of technology, national security, and military affairs. He was elected to the lower house of parliament in 1989 and served as chairman of a variety of legislative committees. He publicly—and with a bluntness that showed real political courage—deplored the RSS-backed and often RSS-instigated practice of tearing down mosques and burning churches. Identifying himself as a liberal democrat, he said, "I believe that this country cannot be constructed through demolitions."[12]

Partly because of his outspokenness as an internationalist who believed that globalization could work to India's advantage and as a moderate on domestic policy, Jaswant Singh was regarded with some suspicion by the RSS. But that did not stop him from becoming a close friend and trusted lieutenant of Atal Bihari Vajpayee, who had served as India's foreign minister in a coalition government twenty years before and who had taken over as leader of the BJP in 1996 after Advani resigned his parliamentary seat when he was implicated in a wide-reaching bribery scandal.*

IN EARLY 1996 the Congress Party, which had been in power for most of the forty-eight years of India's independence, lost in national elections. The defeat occurred for a host of reasons—slippage of support in key states, the rise of regional parties, disaffection with a hung parliament, and an anti-incumbent mood in the electorate. The BJP formed a tenuous minority government, with Vajpayee as prime minister and Jaswant Singh as finance minister. Vajpayee quickly ordered the resumption of preparations for an underground test at Pokhran, and U.S. satellites spotted increased activity at Pokhran.[13]

That test was suspended when, after only two weeks in power, the BJP-led government fell after losing a vote of confidence in the parliament. The coalition that formed a new government had Congress as its linchpin member but was led by two compromise figures from the Janata Dal ("the People's Movement"), Deve Gowda as prime minister and Inder Gujral as foreign minister. In public they adopted a more conciliatory stance toward India's neighbors and sent signals to Washington suggesting that they would not go ahead with the test that Vajpayee had authorized.

ON SEPTEMBER 24, 1996, Clinton was the first of 146 world leaders to sign the Comprehensive Test Ban Treaty, which had finally emerged after two and a half years of negotiation and logrolling. Using the pen with

---

*A legal inquiry cleared Advani of the charges in April 1997, and he returned actively to politics in early 1998.

which Kennedy had signed the Limited Test Ban thirty-three years before, Clinton proclaimed the CTBT "the longest-sought, hardest-fought prize in the history of arms control" and vowed to push the Senate to ratify it during his second term.

However, while the Republicans might not be able to keep Clinton from being reelected that November, the polls showed they stood a good chance of maintaining control of Congress, so Senate ratification of the CTBT was far from certain. Skepticism and some outright opposition toward the treaty simmered within the executive branch as well—for reasons that had beset the CTBT during the years it had been a work in progress. Many military officers, several important Pentagon civilians, and quite a few scientists at the national laboratories felt that a comprehensive ban would tie their hands in perfecting existing weapons and developing new ones, and they continued to question whether the Russians, even now that the Soviet Union had collapsed, would ever fully comply.

The treaty was in additional trouble because of a bizarre provision in its own small print. To win support from Russia and China—the two established nuclear powers that were most reluctant to stop testing—the United States and other proponents of the comprehensive ban agreed to make its entry into force conditional on signature and ratification by all states that were considered "nuclear-capable." That meant states that were supposed to remain non-nuclear under the NPT but that had covert nuclear weapons programs, nuclear power plants, or other infrastructure required to build a bomb. Since India and Pakistan were in that category, either of them could prevent the CTBT's entry into force simply by refusing to sign and ratify it. Somehow, if there were ever going to be a truly comprehensive test ban, India and Pakistan had to be brought on board. Even though the entry-into-force provision gave the Indians a virtual veto over the CTBT, it also meant they would come under increased pressure to sign.[14]

So THE CLINTON administration and the wider community of nonproliferation advocates had a real dilemma, somewhat of our own making. In an effort to elicit advice and support from outside the U.S. government, I suggested to Leslie Gelb, the president of the Council on Foreign Relations in New York, that he set up a task force of distinguished and knowledgeable private citizens, including some with diplomatic experience, to come up with ideas on how to increase U.S. influence in South Asia, notably on the nuclear issue. The council's report, issued in January 1997, just before the second Clinton inaugural, concluded that India and Pakistan had become "de facto nuclear-weapons-capable states and show no sign today of reversing course." They should be encouraged to establish "a more stable plateau for their nuclear competition" in the form of an agreement not to test any sort of nuclear explosives (including ostensibly peaceful ones), deploy nuclear weapons, or export nuclear and ballistic missile technology. The United States would stand a better chance of getting India to accept those constraints if Washington proposed a "closer strategic relationship" that recognized India as having "the potential to emerge as a full-fledged major power."[15]

In other words, the United States should cut the Indians some slack on the NPT—that is, stop pressing them to renounce nuclear weapons—in order to enlist their acquiescence on the CTBT, and hope that if India moved in that direction, Pakistan would do the same.[16]

That advice from outsiders jibed with the recommendations of an internal study that the National Security Council staff produced in mid-1997. The NSC study also recommended that Clinton make the first presidential visit to South Asia since Jimmy Carter's two decades earlier.

THE SECOND TERM saw some turnover in the ranks of officials working on relations with India. Frank Wisner left government to work for the American International Group, a New York–based global insurance and financial services company. Clinton appointed as his successor in New Delhi Richard Celeste, a former director of the Peace Corps and governor of Ohio, who had worked as a special assistant to Chester Bowles when Bowles was ambassador to India during the Johnson administration.

The assistant secretary of state for South Asia during the first term had been Robin Raphel, a foreign service officer who had known Clinton since Oxford.* She had a rough tour of duty as assistant secretary, especially during her numerous visits to New Delhi. The Indians never for-

---

*Robin was the first person to hold that post. Before the Clinton administration, South Asia had been covered by the Near East bureau of the State Department. A separate South Asia bureau was mandated by Congress in 1992.

gave her for making statements they believed perpetuated the American tilt toward Pakistan, especially on the issue of Kashmir, and for publicly urging India to "cap, roll back, and eliminate" its nuclear weapons capability.[17] That phrase—which reflected the administration's fealty to the NPT—fueled Indian anger and gave ammunition to the nuclear hawks. Robin became ambassador to Tunisia; and Madeleine Albright, the new secretary of state, made Rick Inderfurth, who had been one of her deputies at the UN, the assistant secretary for South Asia.

Rick traveled to the region in September to prepare the way for a trip by Madeleine in November 1997—the first by a secretary of state in fourteen years. In press conferences and speeches in India, Inderfurth emphasized the need for "enhanced engagement," "sustained interaction," and a "new basis for confronting common problems."

As it happened, Madeleine had to cut short her visit to India and fly back to Europe for an emergency meeting on Iraq's ejection of weapons inspectors. Some Indian commentators grumbled at what they saw as yet another reminder that India was low on Washington's list of strategic priorities, while others accentuated the positive: the secretary of state had taken the trouble to come.

IN SEPTEMBER 1997 Clinton made the annual presidential pilgrimage to New York for the opening meeting of the United Nations General Assembly. That event brings leaders from around the world to several square blocks of Manhattan, creating a frenzy of diplomatic networking and monumental traffic jams. Within the U.S. government, preparations for the General Assembly meeting touch off months of jockeying over how many "bilaterals" (small, informal meetings with other heads of state) the president should cram into his visit to New York. The first round of the struggle takes place within the State Department, where each regional bureau pushes its own constituents. Then the department negotiates with the National Security Council over which meetings should have priority. Finally, the struggle pits the foreign policy officials of the administration against the president's schedulers, whose thankless and often impossible job is to keep him from being run ragged.

That particular year, it was Clinton himself who insisted on spending time with both Inder Gujral, who had assumed the prime ministership of India, and Nawaz Sharif, who had replaced Benazir Bhutto as prime minister of Pakistan after an election a few months earlier. The reason, said Clinton, was that he wanted to show that South Asia was high on his agenda for his second term.

The meeting with Gujral, which took place in Clinton's suite at the Waldorf-Astoria on September 22, was not particularly substantive, in part because Gujral spoke so softly that everyone on the U.S. side had trouble hearing what he was saying. He had come to the meeting expecting tough questions and harsh demands on Kashmir and nuclear weapons. To Gujral's immense relief, Clinton wasn't interested in dealing with sensitive and weighty matters so much as setting the right tone for the relationship. He showered Gujral with bonhomie, spoke about "the great feeling in our country for India," expressed regret about having "let too many opportunities to deepen our relations go by," and gave him a glimpse of bright vistas ahead. He raved about a book he was reading—*India from Midnight to the Millennium*, by Shashi Tharoor, then a senior aide to UN Secretary General Kofi Annan—and sought Gujral's advice on a reading list to help him further prepare for the trip he hoped to make to the subcontinent the following year.

The only piece of real diplomatic business done in the meeting was an agreement to launch "a comprehensive and sustained dialogue" between India and the U.S. on issues of disarmament and nonproliferation.

This was modest but promising progress in the vocabulary of the relationship. For fifty years the word *dialogue* had rarely appeared in the context of the U.S.-Indian relationship, except in complaints on both sides that it was a dialogue of the deaf. However, nothing came immediately of the initiative, since Gujral's government fell two months later, plunging India into electoral limbo. In March 1998 a BJP-led alliance soundly defeated the Congress Party and formed a coalition government with other opposition parties after a campaign in which the BJP vowed to "induct" nuclear weapons into India's arsenal.* Vajpayee moved back into the prime minister's residence, this time for what was likely to be a much longer tenancy.

---

*The Indians' use of this verb seemed to be another case of ambiguity, intended in part to confuse outsiders, especially Americans. The vow to "induct" the bomb left open the possibility, at least as understood in Washington, that India might declare itself a nuclear weapons power without testing.

FOR VIRTUALLY ALL of us in the Clinton administration who followed events in India, the emergence of the BJP as India's ruling party was unsettling. Americans had grown used to dealing with the Congress Party, and not just for reasons of familiarity. Congress represented continuity with Gandhi's and Nehru's commitment to secularism and pluralism as the basis for Indian statehood. On the nuclear question, the combination of restraint and ambiguity that had marked Indian policy since Indira Gandhi's time, while hardly ideal, was better than the alternative that was now staring us in the face.

At the same time, we knew that the ascendancy of the BJP was a development to which we would just have to adjust. Indian democracy has always been a mystery bordering on a miracle, not so much because of how it works as because it works at all. In many respects, India seemed destined, even designed, never to be a democracy, or to fail if it ever tried to become one. For centuries it was a victim of invasion from the northwest. Then it was the large colony of a small island off the coast of Europe. Its independence coincided with a bloody and divisive conflict over partition. Its hierarchical, caste-based social order was—and will be as long as it lasts—at odds with the very idea of political equality. Its economic order permits the acquisition of fabulous wealth alongside abject poverty on a massive scale. Add to those factors the uninspiring record of other countries that broke free of colonialism after World War II only to wallow in authoritarianism for decades afterward, and Indian democracy would have seemed far from a sure bet in 1947.

Yet India adopted a democratic constitution, a parliamentary system with multiple parties, a free press, an independent judiciary, and a vigorous civil society. To be sure, all those institutions were marred by shortcomings, excesses, and deformations, notably corruption. But unlike such developing countries as Indonesia, Brazil, Nigeria, Thailand, Korea—and Pakistan—as well as more developed ones like Portugal, Spain, and Greece, India nurtured a democratic political culture that proved resistant to lapses into dictatorship. The only exception—Indira Gandhi's so-called "Emergency" in the mid-1970s—proved the rule, since it was a failed experiment in the suspension of basic liberties and it lasted less than two years.

It was, above all, this sturdiness and resilience of India's democracy that created a bond with the United States, however frayed those ties had become during the last half century. Here, after all, was a nation based, like the United States, on the idea of inalienable and universal rights—a melting pot society whose motto could just as well have been *E Pluribus Unum*, with the difference that the melting process had been under way for millennia rather than merely a couple of centuries.

For exactly that reason, the ability of the BJP, with its ideology of Hindu supremacy, to beat the Congress Party at the game of electoral politics represented a vexing and paradoxical phenomenon. BJP politicians played by the rules of democracy. They acquired power in March of 1998 by tapping into popular grievances and frustrated aspirations. Insofar as they succeeded in substituting Hindu nationalism for the Gandhian-Nehruvian concept of a pluralist secular state, their victory might prove to be more than that of one party over another—it could become the victory of one idea of Indian statehood over another. For many Americans—as well as for many Indians—this was an ominous prospect. But only Indians could decide who would lead them and in what direction.[18]

How long the BJP would rule was anybody's guess. But one thing was clear: the interplay in the late 1990s between American and Indian democracies, both of which were influenced by passionate and powerful constituencies that favored the Indian bomb, augured badly for nonproliferation. The Clinton administration had its work cut out for it if it was going to keep the NPT and CTBT alive.

CLINTON HAD WANTED to make a trip to South Asia in mid-February 1998, but that would have put him in India just as the electoral campaign there was at a fever pitch, so he decided to postpone the trip until the fall. After the BJP victory, Clinton telephoned Vajpayee to offer his congratulations and propose sending Bill Richardson, the U.S. ambassador to the United Nations, to South Asia in April to prepare the way for Clinton's own visit later in the year.

Briefing the press on the call, Mike McCurry, the White House press spokesman, noted that the two leaders "look forward to a resumption of a strategic dialogue between their two countries to include many of the areas that we have pursued through high-level contacts in the past." It was a classically vague and anodyne "readout" of a presidential phone call, in this case one that had lasted only ten minutes. But for the Indian press, the big—and welcome—news was Clinton's failure to mention nuclear weaponry and testing. Indians hoped it was a deliberate omission meant to signal that the United States was finally getting over its hang-up about India's nuclear aspirations.

In fact, Clinton felt as strongly as ever that India should not test, but his instincts told him that it would be a mistake to begin his relationship with Vajpayee with a warning or a lecture.[19] At first, Vajpayee too seemed to be treading carefully. In his own public comments, he resorted to a variant of Indira Gandhi's mantra from two decades earlier about "keeping all options open."

Jaswant Singh acted as Vajpayee's public voice for dealing with the press and as his envoy for wooing coalition partners behind the scenes. He was suited to these roles since he had a reputation for being one of the party's leading moderates. But largely for that reason, militant Hindu nationalists—especially in the RSS—opposed his appointment to the cabinet, so Vajpayee made him his deputy on the Planning Commission, a government body that drew up India's five-year plans. (Traditionally, the prime minister reserved the chairmanship of the commission for himself.) Jaswant Singh quickly established himself as the principal spokesman on foreign policy while Vajpayee retained the title and portfolio of minister of external affairs.*

THE FIRST WEEK in April, Pakistan caught India off guard by testing a Ghauri missile, which could reach targets deep inside India. The result was a burst of angry protests and some saber-rattling from New Delhi and, behind the scenes, intensified pressure for India to come up with a surprise of its own.

A week after the Ghauri test, Bill Richardson arrived in New Delhi. Dick Celeste, the U.S. ambassador, took Richardson and his team on a round of appointments with the key members of the new Indian leadership. In addition to Prime Minster Vajpayee, they saw his principal secretary, Brajesh Mishra, a retired diplomat whose friendship with Vajpayee had led him to join the BJP in 1991. By 1998 Mishra was serving the new prime minister not just as chief of staff but as national security adviser—at first informally and later with the title.

---

*Most of Vajpayee's predecessors had appointed others to the foreign minister's job rather than keeping it for themselves.

The visiting Americans also met with George Fernandes—a former socialist and head of the railway workers' union who now led a small, labor-oriented party that joined the BJP-led coalition and, as a result, was made minister of defense—and Lal Krishna Advani, who held the powerful post of home minister, which made him the Number 2 figure in the government.

To a man, the officials who received Richardson said they wanted a better relationship that would be symbolized by a Clinton visit as soon as possible. They were agitated about the Ghauri test but gave no hint that anything was planned on the Indian side.

Treading delicately with the new Indian leaders, the Americans couched their questions about the government's nuclear intentions in terms of polite euphemisms. They recalled campaign promises about "inducting" nuclear weapons and inquired what that verb was likely to mean in practice. Their Indians hosts replied with even greater vagueness.

In a private conversation with Fernandes, Richardson went further than in other settings in seeking a direct assurance.

"George," he asked, "there aren't going to be any surprises on testing, are there?"

"Absolutely not," Fernandes replied.

AT THE END of the long day of meetings, Dick Celeste told Richardson that there was a last-minute, rather unusual, and potentially promising addition to the schedule. At Vajpayee's request, Richardson should meet with Jaswant Singh "off-line"—that is, in private. Dick arranged for the meeting to take place in the library at Roosevelt House, the ambassadorial residence that is part of an imposing Edward Durrell Stone complex of steel, concrete, and glass, replete with lacy grilles, indoor gardens, and fountains. Richardson included Dick, Bruce Riedel of the NSC, and Rick Inderfurth of the State Department in the session.

Jaswant Singh came alone. He said he was under instructions from Vajpayee to serve as a discreet—and if necessary, secret—channel to Washington, to be used for anything sensitive that the U.S. leadership wished to convey to the prime minister. Turning to Bruce as the White House official present, Singh asked that Clinton and Sandy Berger, the national security adviser, understand the utility of having such a channel. It would ensure prompt, high-level consideration of any matter that the

American president regarded as important for moving the relationship forward. The confidentiality of any exchanges that took place in the channel, he implied, would minimize the danger of leaks from an Indian bureaucracy that might otherwise obstruct progress or embarrass the leaders.

TWO WEEKS LATER, the senior civil servant in the Ministry of External Affairs, Foreign Secretary Krishnan Raghunath, came to Washington to meet with Tom Pickering, whom Madeleine Albright had made under secretary of state for political affairs, the Number 3 official in the department. From his previous stint in New Delhi, Tom knew Raghunath well and was on good working terms with much of the rest of the Indian diplomatic and political establishment. Following up on the idea that Clinton and Gujral had first discussed at the UN the previous September, Tom and Raghunath were supposed to initiate what both sides were now ready to call a "strategic dialogue" that was intended to elevate relations to a new plane. But there was at least one unpleasant possibility that would, in the American view, keep the dialogue from getting started, not to mention getting anywhere, so Tom probed Raghunath about whether the new Indian government would continue to pursue a policy of "nuclear restraint."

Raghunath replied that it would.[20]

Insofar as Fernandes and Raghunath, the two Indian officials most closely questioned, misled their American counterparts about Indian intentions, it was probably more out of ignorance than deliberate deception. Among the few who knew what was in the works at Pokhran were Vajpayee, Jaswant Singh, Advani, and Mishra.[21]

India's nuclear scientists and engineers were delighted that they finally had a political leadership that wanted to demonstrate the nation's nuclear weapons capability. They had been working for months to have a bomb test ready as soon as possible, before the politicians had second thoughts and before the United States could interfere. They had learned the lesson of December 1995, when Clinton, through Frank Wisner, prevailed on Rao to call off a test. This time, they kept telltale activity out of sight unless they were reasonably sure that no American spy satellites were passing overhead. Just in case, the civilians at the site wore camouflage fatigues so that, if spotted, they would appear to be military officers charged with ensuring the security of the facility.

Among the officials supervising the last-minute preparations was the nuclear and missile scientist Abdul Kalam. According to George Perkovich's history of the Indian nuclear program, Abdul Kalam had taken the alias Major General Prithviraj. He did so as part of the deception campaign to keep the test secret. The name was an in-joke that associated him both with one of the missiles he had developed—the Prithvi—and with the missile's namesake, the defender of Hindu India against Ghauri and other Muslim invaders from the north. As a Muslim much admired for his knowledge and appreciation of classic Hindu culture, Abdul Kalam must have savored the multiple ironies.

ON THE AFTERNOON of Monday, May 11, the scientists, officers, and officials in the command bunker felt a rumble beneath their feet as a timer simultaneously detonated three devices some three hundred meters underground. The explosions generated heat of about a million degrees centigrade, approximately the temperature of the sun. The explosion vaporized thousands of tons of rock, lifted an expanse on the surface the size of a football field several meters in the air, and sent shockwaves around the world, causing needles to jump on seismographs at more than sixty monitoring stations as far away as New Mexico, Antarctica, and Mt. Fuji.[22] In a haunting echo of Oppenheimer's expression of awe fifty-three years before, one of the scientists who saw the desert rise remarked, "I can now believe stories of Lord Krishna lifting a hill."

Shortly afterward, Vajpayee made a terse announcement at a hastily convened press conference outside his residence in New Delhi:

Today at 1545 hours, India conducted three underground nuclear tests in the Pokhran range. The tests conducted today were with a fission device, a low-yield device and a thermonuclear device. The measured yields are in line with expected values. Measurements have confirmed that there was no release of radioactivity into the atmosphere. These were contained explosions like in the experiment conducted in May 1974. I warmly congratulate the scientists and engineers who have carried out these successful tests.

A second set of tests followed two days later.

The reaction from the Indian press and public opinion was overwhelmingly favorable, and in many quarters ecstatic. "Explosion of Self-Esteem," read the banner headline in the *Pioneer*. "A Moment of Pride," declared a front-page editorial in the *Hindustan Times*, while one in the *Indian Express* hailed the government for putting the country on the "Road to Resurgence." There were rallies around the country celebrating the event, and the BJP called for a nationwide celebration. The Congress Party chimed in, calling the test a "milestone," and even the leftist United Front congratulated the scientists on their success. The Mahatma's grandson, Tushar Gandhi, issued an endorsement: "As an Indian, I am proud it was done in India and by Indians."

In the months that followed, devout and politically active Hindus, many wearing saffron robes, made pilgrimages to the test site in the Thar to gather sand, which they took back to their homes as sacred offerings.[23]

Many Indians were pleased that their country had not only pulled off a technological feat but had also blindsided the United States. "It's not a failure of the CIA," one Indian scientist remarked. "It's a matter of their intelligence being good, our deception being better."[24]

Since one of the CIA's jobs is not to be fooled, it was in fact a very serious intelligence failure, and a commission of experts headed by Admiral David Jeremiah, a former vice chairman of the joint chiefs of staff, was quickly impaneled to investigate. The report highlighted three factors: India's success in keeping the preparations secret, its use of diplomacy to lower suspicions of an imminent test (which the State Department spokesman Jamie Rubin publicly called "a campaign of duplicity"), and the relatively low priority that Washington assigned to South Asia at a time when Iraq, Korea, and the Balkans preoccupied policymakers and senior figures in the intelligence community. It only added to the CIA's humiliation to learn that the imminence of the test had been an open secret to Indian villagers in the Pokhran area. Their speculation about what was about to happen had even found its way into a Sikh community newsletter in Ontario, Canada, four days before the test occurred.

THIS TIME THERE were no coy references to the Buddha. The series of tests was dubbed *Shakti*, after the Hindu goddess of strength and energy, although it was widely known simply as Pokhran II, in part since that designation served as a reminder that India had been "going nuclear" for a quarter of a century.

As Vajpayee had acknowledged, the scientific purpose of the test included assessing the components of a thermonuclear, or hydrogen, bomb. Preliminary analysis by foreign experts suggested that the devices tested produced only a "boosted-fission" explosion—an intermediate stage between an atomic bomb and a hydrogen one that results from a fusion explosion. Some months later, American experts concluded that India had tested a true H-bomb, but the test had been only partially successful.[25] Just over a week after Pokhran II, Vajpayee proclaimed a moratorium on further testing, suggesting the test had been a complete success. But doubts remained among outsiders on that score.

The political purpose of Pokhran II was simpler and the results more immediate and conclusive: India had put the world on notice that it was now—unambiguously, unapologetically, and irrevocably—a nuclear-armed power, to be regarded as such by its historically and potentially antagonistic neighbors, Pakistan and China, and by its estranged fellow democracy half a world away.

THREE

THE MOUNTAIN TURNS WHITE

"WE'RE GOING TO come down on those guys like a ton of bricks," said President Clinton as he opened a meeting in the Oval Office. Twenty-four hours had passed since the news reached Washington, but his anger at India's leaders was unabated. In his view—and that of all his advisers—the BJP had increased the danger of nuclear war on the subcontinent, dealt a body blow to the global nonproliferation regime, and dimmed if not extinguished his hopes for improving U.S.-Indian relations.

It was not uncommon for Clinton to throw a volcanic fit when something went badly wrong in the world. When he vented his rage at the foreign leaders he felt were to blame, however, it was almost always behind closed doors, in the presence of trusted aides who he knew would tone down his reaction before conveying it publicly or through diplomatic channels. That happened in this case. When translated into the language of a statement released by the White House that day, presidential fury became "distress" and "displeasure." A few hours later, Sandy Berger modulated the official reaction further by noting that "there is an enormous amount of common interests that we have. I think [the United States and India] have a better chance at de-escalating or at least slowing these kinds of actions if we remain engaged than if we don't."

While the public rhetoric, in those first hours after Washington learned of the test, was relatively mild, the machinery of government cranked out an array of sanctions against India that reflected the requirements of the law and the intensity of the president's feelings. The measures included a halt to defense sales, export licenses for munitions, and military financing; denial of government credit and loan guarantees; U.S. opposition to loans or technical assistance from international financial institutions like the World Bank and International Monetary Fund; prohibition of most loans and credits from U.S. banks; a hold on Export-Import Bank loan guarantees and credits for U.S. exports to India; and termination or suspension of most assistance programs (the only exceptions were for food aid and other humanitarian initiatives because the sanctions were intended to influence the practices of the Indian government, not to hurt Indian citizens in need). The State Department undertook a review of scientific exchange programs, and the result was the denial, delay, or withdrawal of visas for Indian scientists visiting the United States.

All these were steps the United States could take on its own—and would do so in most cases three weeks after the tests, once all the relevant departments and agencies of the government had closed ranks behind a sanctions plan. Clinton also instructed the administration to encourage and coordinate condemnations of India by other countries along with every relevant international body we could think of: the United Nations, NATO, the NATO-Russia Permanent Joint Council, the Euro-Atlantic Partnership Council, the Organization of American States, the Gulf Cooperation Council, the Organization of Islamic States—and, crucially, the Group of Eight, or G-8, which included four of the five NPT-recognized nuclear weapon states (that is, all but China). The G-8 was about to hold its annual summit in Birmingham. Tom Pickering, the under secretary of state, was already on his way there to work with his counterparts from the other seven countries (Canada, France, Germany, Italy, Japan, Russia, and the United Kingdom) on a statement raking India over the coals.

PRIME MINISTER VAJPAYEE launched a diplomatic counteroffensive by sending personal letters to 177 heads of state. The one to Clinton pointed to India's two neighbors as reasons for the test: China, "an overt nuclear weapons state on our borders, a state which committed armed aggression against India in 1962"; and Pakistan, "a covert nuclear weapons state" that had committed aggression against India three times and that continued to sponsor terrorism in Kashmir.[1]

The Indians' anxiety about China was genuine, deep-seated, and long-standing, and their desire never to be subjected to nuclear blackmail by Beijing was understandable. Still, their effort to justify Pokhran II on that basis was not entirely logical, given the likelihood of consequences that would make India less secure. The Chinese, who had previously made a point of seeming unfazed by India's nuclear program, were riled at being identified as the reason for the test. Some Chinese officials hinted darkly that their government was more than prepared to run—and win—an arms race if New Delhi persisted in blaming China for the Indian buildup.

Part of the reason the Indians played up the threat posed by China was that it freed them from seeming excessively concerned about the one posed by Pakistan (even though Vajpayee included ominous references to Pakistan in his letter to Clinton). Many—probably most—Indians felt that their country was superior to Pakistan in all respects, including in its technical prowess. Nationalists of the sort who were ascendant under the banner of the BJP would have howled in protest at any suggestion that decisions on India's defense were motivated by fear of a country they disdained. China, by contrast, was a giant nation and an ancient civilization in its own right, a major player on the world stage, and therefore worthy of inclusion in India's strategic calculations as an arch-rival.

Many Indians believed that the United States had started to take China seriously when it conducted its own first nuclear test in 1964—long before the Chinese political and economic reforms of the late 1970s; it followed, according to this view, that the bomb must be, in American eyes, a certification of great-power status. It was easier to lament the lesson the Indians drew from that conclusion than to dispute their logic.

THE IMMEDIATE REACTION to Pokhran II from the U.S. Congress, including from members who were pro-India and anti-CTBT, was generally critical of India and supportive of the administration's response. Senator Sam Brownback, a Republican from Kansas, blamed India for the damage done to its "blooming relationship" with the United States. Senator Jesse Helms, the chairman of the Senate Foreign Relations Committee, went much further, thundering that India now "clearly constitute[d] an emerging nuclear threat to the territory of the United States." This was a charge no one in the administration made, since not even the most imaginative and paranoid war-gamers worried about Indian rockets being fired at the United States.

Helms then turned his guns on a target that he felt more confidence—and relish—in attacking: Clinton himself. He scorned the administration for "six years of cozying up to India," which had been "a foolhardy and perilous substitute for common sense." When Clinton heard what Helms had said, he snorted, "Ol' Jesse's got that exactly wrong. My mistake was not cozying up to India a lot earlier so that we might have had some leverage over those guys *before* they hit the button on that bomb."

A FEW MEMBERS of the American foreign policy establishment voiced some degree of support for, or at least open-mindedness about, what the Indians had done. Henry Kissinger made a statement at a supposedly off-the-record foreign policy conference in Europe that quickly reverberated in Washington: "If I were president of the United States, I'd deplore [the test]. If I were the prime minister of India, I'd do it."[2] When I learned what Kissinger had said, it seemed quite consistent with what I remembered as his inclination to accept Indira Gandhi's decision to conduct the Buddha's smile test twenty-four years before.

Pat Moynihan, the former ambassador to India who was now in his fourth term as a senator from New York, was less forgiving of American policy than Kissinger. When I called on him to get his advice about the test, he crisply told me that he had no patience for the administration's "righteous indignation" over having been blindsided by the Indians. "The BJP as much as told you they were going to begin testing," he said. "There's a tendency at the State Department to say, 'Gee, the CIA never told us.' So, yes, there was an intelligence failure here, but not in the sense that the spies fell down on the job. Your own analysts just weren't listening to the Indians, or you weren't listening to your analysts." The administration should "grow up and accept reality." The United States should welcome India into the ranks of nuclear weapons states, he said, in exchange for India's willingness to sign the CTBT—which would be proof of its being a "responsible grown-up in these matters."[3]

WHILE NEVER PREPARED to go that far, those of us working on the administration's response to Pokhran II were, in the first days after the test, thinking hard about how to get the Indians to accept the CTBT along with meaningful restraints on their nuclear and missile programs in exchange for our easing sanctions and throttling back on the campaign of international criticism we were orchestrating. In theory, a deal along those lines might be possible, since unlike the NPT, the CTBT did not distinguish between nuclear haves and have-nots and therefore was not inherently discriminatory against an India that had already tested. The CTBT, in that sense, was an equal-opportunity—and equal-obligation—nonproliferation treaty.

We knew, however, that this argument would be a very hard sell in New Delhi. The Indians had just made what they regarded as a clean and long-overdue break with an unfair regime of externally imposed constraints. Vajpayee had announced a unilateral moratorium on further testing shortly after Pokhran II, but he or a successor could resume testing at any time if the government's scientific advisers made a convincing case it was in India's vital national interest to do so.

There was another reason for sober realism if not outright pessimism about the administration's chances of persuading the Indians to join the CTBT. The fallout from Pokhran II had cast a dark new cloud over the prospect of the treaty's ever being ratified by the U.S. Senate. Jesse Helms and other Republicans opposed to arms control were quick to cite what the Indians had done as proof that the CTBT was worse than worthless. By sneaking their preparations for the test past American intelligence, said Helms, the Indians had provided yet another piece of evidence that the CTBT was unverifiable and one more argument for the United States to continue honing its own nuclear capabilities, unconstrained by treaties that other, less scrupulous countries would violate. In the politically supercharged atmosphere of those days, it did no good to point out that India could hardly be accused of cheating on a treaty it had never signed.

The practical effect of statements like Helms's was that they gave the Indians an excuse to bide their time and see how the American debate over the CTBT played out before plunging into one of their own.

WHILE ASSEMBLING A package of sanctions against India, the Clinton administration also set itself the more difficult and urgent objective of dissuading Pakistan from conducting its own set of tests.

A case could be made that, in theory, ought to have appealed to the Pakistanis' self-interest. They had, like the Indians, possessed the bomb for a decade even though they had never tested it. Now, because of what the Indians had done, the Pakistanis suddenly had a chance to occupy the high ground in the eyes of a nervous world. They could, literally, cash in by showing restraint. Virtually every dollar of aid that donor countries like the United States and Japan would withhold from India could be offered to Pakistan as a reward for resisting the temptation to test.

Pakistan desperately needed the money. Its economy was in terrible shape. The government was on the edge of default; foreign and domestic investment had all but dried up; unemployment was rising. On top of these troubles, Pakistan had been living for years under the Pressler sanctions that the U.S. Congress had imposed in the early 1990s because of its nuclear program. Those sanctions cost Pakistan about $600 million a year in military and economic assistance. The mood on Capitol Hill had shifted after the Indian test in a way that might allow the administration to offer the Pakistanis considerably more relief than I had offered them in 1994 if they had been willing to accept internationally supervised controls on their nuclear program.

In the midst of all that Secretary Albright was doing to keep the Middle East peace process alive, she went to work enlisting support from key members of Congress for the release of the sanctioned F-16s if we could get the Pakistanis not to conduct a nuclear test.

Clinton telephoned Nawaz Sharif, the Pakistani prime minister, to whet his appetite for the planes, huge amounts of financial aid, and a prize certain to appeal to Sharif—an invitation for him to make an official visit to Washington.

Sharif was not swayed. "You can almost hear the guy wringing his hands and sweating," Clinton said after hanging up. The lure of money, praise, and gratitude from around the world, with a few long-in-the-tooth warplanes thrown in for good measure, was far less powerful than the Pakistanis' fear of what had happened just across their border. India, in their view, had just ratcheted up its fifty-year-old campaign to humiliate, intimidate, and perhaps even eradicate their country. For that reason, any Pakistani prime minister would have been under virtually irresistible pressure to test.

Still, we had to keep trying. Our best chance was an emergency dose of face-to-face diplomacy. It was decided that I would fly to Pakistan and make the case to Nawaz Sharif. Since I would also see General Jehangir

Karamat, the chief of the army staff, who had replaced the sulfurous General Wahid as chief of the army staff two years before, I would be joined on the mission by Anthony Zinni, a Marine four-star general who was in charge of the U.S. Central Command that covered the Middle East, the Persian Gulf, Afghanistan, and Pakistan.*

ON THE AFTERNOON of Wednesday, May 13, 1998, two days after the Indian test, a small group of colleagues and I flew on an Air Force executive jet to Zinni's headquarters at MacDill Air Force Base outside Tampa, Florida, where we were supposed to make a quick transfer to his plane for the long flight to Islamabad. The Pakistanis appeared to be having second thoughts about whether to let us come, so we had to cool our heels in the VIP lounge at McDill. We watched C-SPAN's reruns of Rick Inderfurth's testimony before the Senate Foreign Relations Committee earlier in the day, then tuned in CNN's coverage of a joint press conference Clinton gave in Potsdam with Helmut Kohl, the chancellor of Germany. The president was experimenting with a variation on a theme that he had used in other contexts—the opportunities and responsibilities that came with modern statehood:

> I hope the Indian government soon will realize that it can be a very great country in the 21st century without doing things like this. . . . I think they've been under-appreciated in the world and in the United States. They're a very great country. . . . But to think that you have to manifest your greatness by behavior that recalls the very worst events of the 20th century on the edge of the 21st century, when everybody else is trying to leave the nuclear age behind, is just wrong. It is just wrong. And they clearly don't need it to maintain their security, vis-à-vis China, Pakistan, or anybody else. So I just think they made a terrible mistake. And I think that we, all of us, have a responsibility to say that, and to say that their best days are ahead of them, but they can't—they have to define the greatness of India in 21st century terms, not in terms that everybody else has already decided to reject.

---

*General Zinni was responsible for twenty-two countries. The Central Asian states would later be added. India, by long-standing practice, was assigned to the Pacific Command, headquartered in Hawaii.

Meanwhile, Tom Simons, our ambassador in Islamabad, was trying desperately to get through to his usual contacts in the foreign ministry and prime minister's office. When his efforts proved unavailing, General Zinni put in a call to General Karamat, reaching him right away. Karamat professed astonishment that there was any obstacle to our departure and cleared the matter up in a matter of minutes. It was further evidence that the civilian leaders were in a state of confusion, perhaps discord, and that the military called the shots in Pakistan.

It was about 3 a.m. when we finally boarded the plane, an ancient military version of a Boeing 707. The craft seemed better suited for a place of honor in an aeronautical museum than continuing service as a state-of-the-art airborne command center for the sole superpower's top general responsible for the most volatile region on earth. The cabins were outfitted like those of an old yacht, with analogue clocks in wooden nautical frames. The twenty-two-hour flight was one of the most turbulent I had ever experienced, made all the more exciting by three midair refuelings.

Since sleep was nearly impossible, we used much of the trip to hone the arguments we would make on arrival. Pakistan had a choice: it could join the rest of the world in isolating India, or it could follow India down a foolish, backward-leading, and dangerous path. Here was a chance for Pakistan to break free of the decades-long pattern of reacting to what India did and thus letting India manipulate Pakistani policy. India was larger, economically more vibrant, and politically more stable than Pakistan. Therefore even though both countries would be sanctioned if both tested, Pakistan would be the net loser.

"Restraint and maturity"—that was the phrase we planned to use at every opportunity with the Pakistanis. Restraint would allow us to put the Pressler amendment forever behind us and solidify a post-cold-war relationship with Pakistan as a moderate, democratic, and above all *responsible* Islamic state. Clinton would make that theme a centerpiece of a visit that he would make to Pakistan later in the year, perhaps in November.

On arrival in Islamabad, we had about an hour to freshen up at a hotel before our first official meeting, which was with the foreign minister, Gohar Ayub Khan, and the foreign secretary (the senior civil servant in the ministry), Shamshad Ahmad. During this brief interval, Secretary

Albright phoned from Washington to tell me she was making progress with previously pro-India members of Congress who were now prepared to support tough measures against New Delhi and support rewards for Pakistan if it did not test. I also talked to Tom Pickering in Birmingham, who said that the G-8 would soon be releasing a strong statement in the name of the assembled leaders.[4]

When we got to the foreign ministry, we found that the Pakistani civilian leaders had finally figured out how to handle our visit, and the result was a bracing experience. Gohar Ayub fidgeted during my opening courtesies, then unleashed a broadside that went on for nearly half an hour. It began with a history lesson featuring the perfidy of India going back to 1947 (a "habitual aggressor and hegemon") and the inconstancy of the United States ("a fair-weather friend"), whose various cutoffs of military aid had deprived Pakistan of its "qualitative military edge."

When I finally had a chance to reply, I ran through a medley of the arguments we had rehearsed on the plane. My two hosts rolled their eyes, mumbled imprecations under their breath, and constantly interrupted. They accused the United States of having turned a blind eye to the BJP's preparations for the test. Unlike us, they had taken seriously BJP campaign promises of a test. And unlike the CIA, they had noticed the speculation in the Sikh newspaper in Canada that something big was about to happen in the Thar.

Gohar Ayub remarked acidly that he had sensed from Bill Richardson's visit to the subcontinent four weeks earlier that, despite the BJP's rise to power, the U.S. administration was "more enamored than ever" with India, which he found explicable only because "you don't understand the Indian psyche."

I started to reply and got as far as mentioning the NPT when Shamshad Ahmad cut me off and said that the NPT was dead. So was the CTBT. Those treaties had been sick before—now India had "murdered" them.

As for the carrots I had brought, the Pakistanis gave me a version of the reaction I had gotten from General Wahid five years earlier: offers of Pressler relief and delivery of "those rotting and virtually obsolete airplanes," said Gohar Ayub, were "shoddy rugs you've tried to sell us before." The Pakistani people, he added, "would mock us if we accepted your offer. They will take to the streets in protest."

I replied that Pakistanis were more likely to protest if they didn't have jobs.

Gohar Ayub and Shamshad Ahmad waved the point aside. What Pakistan needed for its physical survival—and what Nawaz Sharif's government needed for its political survival—was proof that the leadership would "not stand idly by" while India thumbed its nose at the world.

I tried out another argument: Pakistan should not share "the ugly spotlight" now focused on India. "India is isolating itself," I said, "and should be allowed to stew in juices of its own making."

The two Pakistani officials were dismissive. The current burst of international outrage against India would dissipate rapidly, they predicted. India would get away with the test and the sanctions would wither away. In fact, India would end up benefiting politically as well as militarily for having tested. "Mark my words," said Gohar Ayub, his lips pursed and his fists clenched, "now that India has barged its way into becoming the world's sixth nuclear power, it will not stop there. It will force itself into permanent membership of the UN Security Council."

The clear implication was that when—not if—Pakistan tested, it too would quickly be forgiven.

Gohar Ayub was equally contemptuous of my claim that Pakistan already had the ability to deter its enemies without testing since the Indians knew it had nuclear bombs. "As any military man knows," he said, "before a weapon can be inducted into military service—even a water bottle—it must be tested." He meant the comment to carry particular weight, since he was the son of Mohammad Ayub Khan, the first in a series of generals to rule the country.

"The people of Pakistan," added Shamshad Ahmad, "will not forgive those in this room if we do not do the right thing."

When the meeting ended, my colleagues and I were given a bum's rush out a side door while the foreign ministry's spokesman, Tariq Altaf, briefed the press waiting at the main entrance. The American visitors, he reported, had been "good listeners." The translation, understood and reported by the press, was that my team and I had come a great distance to have our heads scrubbed.

WE SET OFF with police escort, sirens blaring, to General Karamat's headquarters in Rawalpindi. Somewhat to our surprise, it was a much less

contentious meeting. That was partly because Tony Zinni and Karamat
had worked together closely and had a no-nonsense, soldier-to-soldier
relationship. Karamat, who was soft-spoken and self-confident, did not
waste time on polemics. He heard us out and acknowledged the validity
of at least some of our arguments, especially those concerning the danger
that, by testing, Pakistan would land itself, as he put it, "in the doghouse
alongside India."

His government was still "wrestling" with the question of what to do,
he said, which sounded like a euphemism for civilian dithering. There
was more generally, in the way Karamat talked about his country's political leadership, a subtle but discernible undertone of long-suffering
patience bordering on scorn. For example, he noted pointedly "speculation" that Pakistan was looking for some sort of American security guarantee, presumably a promise that the United States would come to
Pakistan's defense if it was attacked by India, in exchange for not testing.
"You may hear such a suggestion later," he added, perhaps referring to our
upcoming meeting with Nawaz Sharif. I should not take such hints seriously, he said, since they reflected the panic of the politicians. Pakistan
would look out for its own defense. What it needed from the United
States was a new, more solid relationship in which there was no "arm-
twisting" or "forcing us into corners."

By stressing this point, Karamat made clear that our arguments against
testing did not impress him. In a calm, respectful manner, intended to
invite us to join him in thinking through the choices he now faced as a
military man, he ran through a set of questions. Why had India decided
to test? Why wasn't India content to continue relying on the universal
and unchallenged assumption that it had the bomb? Was the Indian
demonstration of a few days before just for political effect, or was it
intended as the first in a series of tests that would, over time, substantially
increase the potency and utility of India's bombs? If the latter, he implied,
Pakistan would need to play catch-up. And since it probably *was* the
latter, playing catch-up meant that preparations for a Pakistani test were
most likely proceeding apace even as we spoke.

Karamat considered it especially menacing that the explosion at
Pokhran had come when the government in New Delhi was dominated
by militant nationalists who were, by his reckoning and that of many
other Pakistanis, also rabid anti-Muslims. India's ruling parties, he said,

had always tried to "cut Pakistan down to size," but the BJP was a "special case." Its leaders might be calculating that Pakistan was "at its weakest" economically and therefore vulnerable to pressures of exactly the sort that the United States would apply if Pakistan tested. Put all this together, he concluded, and it had to be assumed that the Indian test was "the logical first step" in a BJP strategy of using nuclear intimidation to "solve the Kashmir problem once and for all" by forcing Pakistan to give up all claims to the disputed territory.

In conclusion, he assured us that given "the political, military, historic, and economic stakes" involved, the Pakistani government was carefully weighing what to do. He knew that his country was widely regarded as one "that is full of corrupt politicians, drug smugglers, and terrorists"—a perception he did not go out of his way to dispute—"but the majority of Pakistanis are hard-working and interested in security and the basic amenities of life. So we will not take this decision irresponsibly, as it will affect everyone's life in Pakistan."

I shared a car back to Islamabad with Bruce Riedel and Tom Simons. We agreed that we had gotten the same answer to our entreaties in both our meetings: a bombastic "no" from the foreign ministry and a polite one from the cool customer in Rawalpindi.

WHAT WE GOT from Prime Minister Nawaz Sharif was a Hamlet act, convincing in its own way—that is, I think he was genuinely feeling torn—but rather pathetic. I knew him a bit from earlier encounters. Diminutive and roly-poly, he had a pleasant round face and a diffident, eager-to-please, even fawning manner. It was hard to see how he had come out on top of a rough-and-tumble political system. Surely family money and connections had something to do with it—probably a lot. But my colleagues who knew him far better told me there was another side to Nawaz Sharif, a political persona that exuded street smarts, confidence, and a sense of command, at least in some settings. In my dealings with him, I always felt there was something I was missing even though I was looking for it: a core of ambition, toughness, and determination that he suppressed during encounters with the president of the United States and his envoys.

On this occasion he seemed nearly paralyzed with exhaustion, anguish, and fear. He was—literally, just as Clinton had sensed during their phone call—wringing his hands. He had yet to make up his mind, he kept telling us. Left to his own judgment, he would not test. His position was "awkward." His government didn't want to engage in "tit-for-tat exchanges" or "act irresponsibly." The Indian leaders who had set off the explosion were "madmen" and he didn't want "madly to follow suit."

But pressure was "mounting by the hour" from all sides, including from the opposition led by his predecessor and would-be successor, Benazir Bhutto. "I am an elected official, and I cannot ignore popular sentiment."

Sharif was worried that India would not only get away with what it had done but profit from it as well. When international anger receded, the sanctions would melt away, and the BJP leadership would parlay India's new status as a declared nuclear weapons state into a permanent seat on the UN Security Council along with "the other big boys."

Having heard a version of this scenario from Gohar Ayub, I did my best to refute it. India had violated international norms, I said; it had flouted the NPT, fallaciously equated great power status with nuclear weaponry, and thereby done grave damage to its reputation as a responsible steward of the capability it had now demonstrated. Far more likely candidates for permanent membership on the Security Council were Germany and Japan, which had remained non-nuclear-weapons states.

I went through what was by now a well-practiced litany of arguments, stressing the danger that India was trying to goad Pakistan into a test of its own that would prompt economic sanctions and political isolation harder for Pakistan to bear than for India. I laid out all that we could do for Pakistan, although this time I tried to personalize the list a bit more: Madeleine Albright was making progress with key members of the U.S. Congress in ensuring relief for Pakistan from the Pressler sanctions; General Zinni's presence in the delegation was an indication of U.S. determination to bolster security ties with Pakistan; I had been on the phone with Tom Pickering, who was in Birmingham negotiating a G-8 condemnation of India that would "amplify in the strongest terms" the one that had already been passed by the UN Security Council; Clinton had told me two days before that he would use Sharif's visit to Washington and Clinton's own to Pakistan in the fall to "dramatize" the world's gratitude if Sharif would just refrain from testing.

This point aroused the first flicker of interest I'd seen. Nawaz Sharif asked if Clinton would promise to skip India on his trip and come only to Pakistan. There was no way I could promise that. I had heard enough from Clinton about his desire to engage with India to be sure that, upset as he was with the BJP government, he was not about to bypass New Delhi on a trip to South Asia. Sooner or later, he would want to find a way to get past the rift caused by the test. All I could tell Nawaz Sharif was that Clinton would "recalibrate the length and character" of the stops he made in New Delhi and Islamabad to reflect that Pakistan was in favor with the United States while India was not.

Sharif looked more miserable than ever.

KASHMIR CAME UP repeatedly during the meeting. If only India would adhere to the fifty-year-old UN resolution calling for a plebiscite giving the Kashmiris a chance to decide their own future, said Nawaz Sharif, it would be easier for him to resist pressure to test. It was Kashmir, not the nuclear issue, that was at the core of the tension between India and Pakistan.

Shamshad Ahmad, who was sitting in on the session radiating wariness toward host and guest alike, added that if the United States would just commit itself to mediating in the Kashmir dispute, the nuclear issue could, over time, be resolved "bilaterally"—that is, between India and Pakistan directly.

Toward the end of the meeting, Sharif asked everyone but me to wait outside. Shamshad seemed miffed. He glanced nervously over his shoulder as he left.

When we were alone, I gave the prime minister a handwritten note from Secretary Albright urging him to hold firm against those clamoring to test and warning about the economic damage, to say nothing of the military danger, Pakistan faced from an escalating competition with India. Sharif read the note intently, folded the paper, put his head in his hands for a moment, then looked at me with desperation in his eyes.

At issue, he said, was his own political survival. "How can I take your advice if I'm out of office?" If he did as we wanted, the next time I came to Islamabad, I would find myself dealing not with a clean-shaven moderate like himself but with an Islamic fundamentalist "who has a long beard."

He concluded by reiterating that he truly had not made up his mind about whether to test. "If a final decision had been reached," he said, "I would be in a much calmer state of mind. . . . Please believe me when I tell you that my heart is with you. I appreciate—and would even privately agree with—what you are advising us to do."

I told him I noted the importance he attached to the Kashmir issue and promised that I would impress that point on the president and the secretary of state. Sharif gave me a wry smile and said what he would really like would be to hear from General Zinni an American offer to station U.S. troops along the Line of Control between the Indian- and Pakistani-controlled parts of Kashmir.

I could not offer that, I said, and neither could Zinni, but I could assure him that Clinton would, in a phrase the president had made one of his trademarks, "focus like a laser" on the Indian-Pakistani dispute.

As soon as my colleagues and I boarded our aircraft for the long flight to an air base near Birmingham, where the G-8 summit was already under way, I asked if there wasn't some way we could raise the American profile on the Kashmir issue as a way of holding the Pakistanis back from testing. Bruce Riedel and Rick Inderfurth would have risen out of their seats if they had not been strapped in. Yes, they said, we should be doing more on the Kashmir issue. But they warned me in the strongest terms against entertaining any idea of drawing Clinton into the Kashmir problem at Pakistan's request—which the Indians would interpret as meaning on Pakistan's terms. Clinton was naturally attracted to the role of mediator, as we were currently seeing in the Middle East and Northern Ireland. We would be doing him no favor, Bruce and Rick said, to tantalize him with the possibility of brokering a solution to Kashmir, especially now. The Indians were dead set against any outside mediator, whether it was the UN or the United States. By offering our services, we would only provoke New Delhi and bring false hope to the Pakistanis.

The more fundamental problem, as they saw it, was that the Pakistanis, while claiming to want American arbitration, would have great difficulty accepting the most obvious solution, which was to make the Line of Control a mutually recognized international border and give the Kashmiris a significant degree of autonomy within the Indian state. The Indians, conversely, might actually someday accept that territorial solution, since it would be a ratification of the status quo, and they might even be willing to accept special governance arrangements for Kashmir. They would never do so, however, if it were foisted on them by an outside power. Therefore I should just brace the president for the Pakistani test, which our hosts, each in his own way, had made clear was both inevitable and imminent.

"At least they didn't set the thing off while we were there," remarked Rick.

"I wouldn't be too sure," said Bruce. "Let's see what news awaits us in Birmingham."

BY THE TIME we arrived in Birmingham on Sunday, May 17, there was buzz in the corridors that the Pakistanis had in fact set off a bomb just hours after we had taken off from Islamabad. The epicenter of the rumor was the Russian delegation. President Yeltsin's entourage, which was checking regularly with Moscow, heard from General Anatoly Kvashnin, the chief of the general staff, that Russian military intelligence had detected a "seismic event" that it believed to be a test. American and British experts, who were monitoring the situation closely, could not confirm that judgment. Within hours, the story was being widely treated as a glimpse into the jumpiness and unreliability of the Russian spy services.

I went straight into a briefing that Sandy Berger and other White House aides were giving Clinton in preparation for his meeting with Yeltsin. Seeing me slip into the room, Clinton waved the others to silence and gave me an inquiring look.

"Not good, Mr. President," I said. "They're not buying what we're selling. It's only a matter of time before they pop one off."

Often when I would report bad news to Clinton, he would make some jaunty comment about how our work had just become all the more interesting.

Not this time. He scowled, looked down at the floor, and was silent for what seemed like a very long moment.

"That's bad," he finally said, shaking his head, "real bad. Those folks have got a kind of genius for making a bad deal worse." He was referring to both the Indians and the Pakistanis. "I've wanted to get into that situation out there, but it's going to be a whole lot harder now. And a whole lot more dangerous."

THE CRISIS IN South Asia was still gnawing at Clinton when he sat down with Yeltsin a short time later, but he had already begun to sublimate his anger at the Indians, putting the Pokhran II test into a broader perspective that made it easier for him to comprehend and even to forgive.

"I think India has made a terrible mistake," he told the Russian president. "But I also think India should get credit for fifty years of democracy. We need to help them see that they should not define greatness in a way that gives everyone else headaches. The ruling party there seems particularly to feel that earning the full respect of the world depends on India's being a nuclear power."

Out of the blue, Clinton suggested that he and Yeltsin coordinate their approaches, since both were planning trips to New Delhi in the fall. Yeltsin, who always welcomed demonstrations that the United States and Russia were joining forces to solve the world's most daunting problems, eagerly assented. Later in the session Clinton returned to his proposal, this time with the added notion of inviting China to join the United States and Russia. Why didn't he and Yeltsin both talk to Jiang Zemin, the president of China, and work out a "joint approach toward the problem of India and Pakistan"? The goal would be to persuade the two wayward South Asian states to sign up to the CTBT and "reinvigorate the peace process for Kashmir. Both countries have a lot of poverty. They can't afford this constant tension and conflict. If we could help them reconcile some of their differences, it would be a huge thing for your security, Boris. It would spur economic growth in Russia and China."

Yeltsin loved it. "A troika!" he proclaimed, spreading his arms. "Together with China, we will bring our influence to bear on India and Pakistan!"

Clinton suggested their aides who were present in the room—Sandy Berger and myself; Andrei Kokoshin, the Kremlin national security adviser; and Georgi (known as Yuri) Mamedov, my principal counterpart in the Russian foreign ministry—be assigned on the spot to develop a plan so that the two presidents could coordinate their dealings with Jiang Zemin later in the year.

"This is a big deal, Boris!"

"It sure is," said Yeltsin, still beaming. He especially relished the prospect of "drawing China into our U.S.-Russian orbit. It's truly a task for the next millennium! We'll be in retirement when this comes to fruition. Maybe we'll set up a club or a foundation for former heads of state. I don't think either of us wants to spend his retirement planting potatoes in the garden."

The meeting ended with a warm and prolonged embrace.

During this burst of presidential brainstorming, Sandy Berger and I exchanged knowing glances. So did Mamedov and I. Presidents are entitled to have their own ideas, and even to raise them unrehearsed with their fellow leaders. But this particular inspiration of Clinton's would definitely have benefited from some discussion in advance. The Chinese would either dismiss it as a harebrained scheme, suspect it as an attempt to subordinate their strategic priorities to those of the United States and Russia, or see it as an opportunity to consolidate their own influence over the Pakistanis while scoring points against the Indians.

As for the Indians, they would see the plan as an egregious example of what they most objected to about the NPT: three members of the nuclear club ganging up on India to protect their monopoly.

As the meeting broke up and we were heading to a press conference, Clinton grabbed me by the arm and pulled me close. Didn't I think he and Boris had cooked up a great plan?

I felt like the pusillanimous editor in Evelyn Waugh's novel *Scoop* who, when asked by his bumptious publisher whether he agrees with a truly cockamamie idea, always answers, "Up to a point, Lord Copper."

"Well, Chief," I said—that was what I called him in private throughout the eight years I worked for him—"I think it needs some more thought.. You've got a lot of people involved here with a lot of different agendas and hang-ups, so it may be kind of difficult to bring off without making things even more complicated."

Clinton, who was now in a good mood after his meeting with Yeltsin, said, "In other words you think it's a crock of shit. Well, ol' Boris liked it." Then he let out a big laugh. "Come to think of it, maybe that *proves* it's a crock of shit."

YELTSIN DID INDEED like it. When I met with Mamedov the next day at a hotel in London to review the presidential meeting and look ahead to next steps, he told me, with a touch of exasperation, that Yeltsin was "absolutely taken with this troika thing" and was leaning on the Russian foreign ministry to get to work on the project immediately. He added that when he sent word back to Moscow about what Clinton and Yeltsin had in mind, it "landed like a bombshell." Particularly aghast were members of Russia's "India lobby"—Soviet-era diplomats and security officials who remembered (and in many cases, no doubt, longed for) the good old days when India had been closely aligned with the USSR. Putting Kashmir on the troika's agenda would, said Mamedov, guarantee a debacle, since "that issue is absolutely hopeless."

I suspected that Mamedov's boss, Foreign Minister Yevgeny Primakov, whom I knew well, had an especially jaundiced view of the Clinton-Yeltsin idea of a troika. Primakov, a wily survivor who had served at high levels of Kremlin administrations going back to the Brezhnev era, was far from romantic about the much-ballyhooed partnership between the United States and Russia. He saw the relationship as still highly competitive—and fundamentally disadvantageous to a Russia that was no longer a superpower. Primakov was always on the lookout for ways that a weakened, post-Soviet Russia might join other countries in offsetting (or as he sometimes said, with a wry smile, "containing") American preeminence. From time to time he floated the idea of Russia, China, and India forming a "strategic triangle" to counterbalance the United States—a troika quite different from the one that Clinton and Yeltsin had in mind.

Mercifully, nothing came of either version. Clinton and Yeltsin's resolve to concert American, Russian, and Chinese influence on India and Pakistan made so little sense that it fell of its own weight. Primakov's idea of playing Russia, India, and China off against the United States resurfaced from time to time in later years, but never as much more than a rhetorical jab at whatever was seen as the latest instance of Uncle Sam throwing his massive weight around.[5]

IN A PHONE CALL on May 27, a timorous-sounding Nawaz Sharif apologized to Clinton for "disappointing" him, but Sharif simply had no choice but to go ahead with the test.

Meanwhile, members of his government put out the story that the test would be an act of self-defense since Israel, in perfidious collusion with India, was about to attack Pakistan. They claimed Israeli planes were poised on runways at Indian airbases ready to take off. The story was utter nonsense but had to be scotched nonetheless. Bruce Riedel called the Israeli ambassador in Washington, Eliahu Ben-Elissar, and asked him to put Amnon Shahak, the chief of staff of the Israeli Defense Forces, on the phone to Riaz Khokhar, the Pakistani ambassador in Washington, so that Khokhar could hear an authoritative denial.

It was too late. Within hours, the Pakistanis detonated what they said were five devices in a tunnel under the Ras Koh mountain range in the Chagai region of Baluchistan. The blasts dislodged dirt that had accumulated over the millennia and exposed the mountain's carapace of black granite. When the radiation hit the surface, the rock underwent rapid deoxidation, producing an effect like bleach removing rust from metal. The mountainside turned white.

Striking a tone quite unlike what I had heard in private in Islamabad and what Clinton had heard over the telephone a few hours before, Nawaz Sharif appeared on television. "Today," he proclaimed triumphantly, "we have settled the score!" A government statement claimed that Ghauri missiles were "already being capped with the nuclear warheads to give a befitting reply to any misadventure by the enemy." Joyous citizens poured into the streets, many firing guns into the air and offering each other congratulatory sweets. Hundreds of children danced to drums in Karachi, and thousands of worshipers poured into the Faisal mosque, Pakistan's largest, where the imam led them in prayers of thanks for the development of the first bomb in the hands of Muslims.

All political parties, including those associated with Benazir Bhutto's opposition, praised the government. The *Pakistan Observer* exulted that "five nuclear blasts have instantly transformed an extremely demoralized nation into a self-respecting, proud nation of 140 million people, having full faith in their destiny."

IMMEDIATELY AFTER THE Pakistani test, I spoke to Primakov. Usually his reaction to an unexpected development—or, as in this case, an expected but highly unpleasant one—was to act as though he had seen worse and this too would pass. We usually spoke a mixture of Russian and English with each other, and he enjoyed making wisecracks in both languages. On this occasion, however, both his sang-froid and his willingness to speak English deserted him. He was deeply rattled at what he saw as the very real possibility of nuclear war on the subcontinent.

There was no question that as he contemplated the two potential belligerents, Primakov was more worried about Pakistan. In part, that was because of Russia's long-standing friendship with India. But there was another factor in his thinking. "All these years, we've been worried about an Islamic bomb," he said. "Now there is one." Our governments must try anything that would, as he put it, "stop this craziness"—even if it meant plunging together into the "accursed issue of Kashmir," with or without China.

"I know what you mean," I said, then ventured what for me was a rare pun in Russian: *Kashmir—kashmar.* "Kashmir is a nightmare."

"Yes," said Primakov. "*Our* nightmare, not just theirs."

TWO DAYS LATER, Pakistan tested another device, bringing the total number of declared explosions in the two tests to six—and thus trying to convince the world that it had one-upped India for Pokhran II (or evened the score if Pokhran I were counted).[6]

Soon afterward, in an effort to exploit the popularity of the test, the government began running newspaper ads emblazoned with the slogan "NEW-CLEAR Vision, Marching toward a Better Tomorrow" and illustrated by a collage featuring a Ghauri missile blasting off from its launching pad with the now-familiar silhouette of the Ras Koh mountain in the background and a smiling Sharif shaking hands with a bearded elder meant to represent a devout and grateful nation. Floodlit fiberglass models of the Chagai test site began sprouting up in Pakistani cities.

FOUR

JASWANT'S VILLAGE

News of the muffled explosion in the mountains of Baluchistan reached New Delhi just as the lower house of the parliament was debating the implications of India's own test in the desert of Rajasthan a fortnight earlier. Many in the hall were stunned, which was itself surprising, given the virtual certainty that Pakistan would not let the Indian test go unanswered. Some members of the opposition shook their fists and shouted reproaches at the government for having set off a new spiral in the arms race and put the safety of the nation in jeopardy.

S. Jaipal Reddy, a leader of one of the opposition parties, Janata Dal, summarized what we in Washington saw as a strategic flaw in his government's action: "India had a decisive military edge over Pakistan. We must remember that an atom bomb is a great equalizer. With [the Pakistani] test, the edge that India had has been wiped out."

That, however, was a minority view. Other influential voices reacted with a degree of calm and satisfaction that was much more representative of public and elite opinion. "We can heave a sigh of relief," wrote Shekhar Gupta, the editor of *The Indian Express*. "Now Pakistan's Western friends have no choice but to impose on it the same sanctions that they have inflicted on us."[1]

While Pakistan was sure to be sanctioned, India, as the first to test, remained the principal target of American and international wrath. Hard-liners in the BJP urged that the government ride out the sanctions in stoic defiance rather than launch a diplomatic initiative that would suggest a willingness to compromise and subject India to more American rebukes and demands.

Vajpayee resisted this advice. India had made its point—now it should set about mending relations as much as possible with a country that was key to India's integration into the world economy. He decided to reach out to the Clinton administration by dispatching a personal envoy who would explain India's position, explore areas where the two countries' interests still coincided, and hasten the day when Clinton might be willing to resume progress toward what would meet the Indian definition of a better, more broad-gauge, and more equitable relationship.

Vajpayee assigned this mission to his friend and adviser Jaswant Singh.

THE MOOD IN Washington was still far from conciliatory. On June 3 President Clinton and Secretary of State Albright appeared together before the White House press corps in the Rose Garden. The president was sending Madeleine to Geneva for a meeting the next day of the foreign ministers representing the so-called P-5—the permanent five member states of the United Nations Security Council: the United States, Russia, China, the United Kingdom, and France. These were also the only countries allowed, under the NPT, to possess nuclear weapons. The Geneva meeting was convened for the sole purpose of excoriating India and Pakistan for the tests and laying out what those two nations would have to do to work themselves back into the good graces of the international community. China, which held the rotating presidency of the Security Council, would be in the chair.

In his remarks in the Rose Garden, Clinton called the tests "self-defeating, wasteful and dangerous" and said they would make the people of India and Pakistan "poorer and less secure." He bore down harder on India than Pakistan, accusing the BJP government of betraying "the ideals of nonviolent democratic freedom and independence at the heart of Gandhi's struggle to end colonialism on the Indian subcontinent."

He applauded China's willingness to chair the Geneva meeting of the P-5, citing it as "further evidence of the important role China can play in meeting the challenges of the twenty-first century and the constructive Chinese leadership that will be essential to the long-term resolution of issues involving South Asia." Clinton was about to visit China and was therefore making the most of Beijing's cooperation with the United

States in order to ensure a successful trip and to counteract criticism he was getting from Congress for improving relations with a country that had a poor record on human rights.

When Madeleine followed the president to the microphone, she called on India and Pakistan to "cool it—take a deep breath and begin to climb out of the hole they have dug themselves into." The world, Madeleine went on to say, would now have to "re-examine options for easing the underlying political problems between India and Pakistan, including Kashmir"—another red flag to the Indians, since it seemed to suggest intensified and unsolicited diplomatic intervention.

WHILE THE PUBLIC rhetoric, especially from Washington, was scorching, the joint communiqué that emerged from the meeting of the P-5 foreign ministers on June 4 was actually quite modulated in tone and reasonable in content. It established a trio of what India should have been able to embrace as unexceptionable objectives compatible with its decision to become a nuclear weapons state: the prevention of an arms race in the subcontinent, the bolstering of the regional and global nonproliferation regime, and the encouragement of peaceful resolution of differences between itself and Pakistan.

On the nuclear issue, the P-5 statement was based on the premise that no matter how much the rest of the world protested and demanded, it was not going to get India and Pakistan to undo or apologize for what they had done. The best that could be hoped for was that they might promise never to do it again—that is, they might accept a permanent prohibition on further testing, preferably by joining the CTBT. In addition, the communiqué called upon them to take three other steps. One was to cooperate with the United States and other countries in bringing to a rapid conclusion a negotiation that had been going on fitfully for three years on a treaty that would end the production of fissile material (weapons-grade plutonium and highly enriched uranium). Another was to refrain from putting nuclear warheads on their missiles or bombers, thereby somewhat reducing the danger that the pistols India and Pakistan held at each other's heads would, in a crisis, be not just loaded and cocked but on hair trigger as well. The third was not to export equipment, materials, or technology that could help other countries acquire nuclear weapons or ballistic missiles of their own.

The P-5 statement affirmed the desirability of universal adherence to the NPT, but it did so in a separate paragraph from the one that laid out more immediate and practicable goals.

The statement was crafted principally by Bob Einhorn, who accompanied Secretary Albright to Geneva. Bob spent hours talking the Chinese out of their preference for more India-bashing and harsher demands in the document. The P-5 communiqué would become the template for Washington's dealings with the Indians for the next two years.

THE SAME DAY that Clinton and Albright were giving India hell in the Rose Garden, George Perkovich, a leading American expert on India and nonproliferation who was highly respected in New Delhi, telephoned Jaswant Singh to interview him in connection with the book Perkovich was writing about the Indian nuclear program.[2] In response to Perkovich's questions, Singh stressed that Vajpayee had already declared that India would observe a unilateral moratorium on further testing and, furthermore, that he was prepared to consider joining the CTBT.

However, Singh added, "We need to talk to the Americans first. We have concerns that must be addressed. The United States, in its pique, seems to want us to sign first and talk later. . . . If you hold a gun to a country's head and say, 'Sign on the dotted line!,' then it makes things very difficult. This country has had a long history of colonial domination. It's only fifty years free from it. Now, fifty years down the line, we are not prepared to accept another form of colonialism. If you say first I must crawl—India must crawl before we can talk with you—then it reminds us of Amritsar." He was referring to an infamous episode in 1919 when the British commander in that Punjabi city ordered Indians to crawl past the place where two Englishwomen were allegedly molested.[3]

Singh said he was "ready to sit with an American of equivalent rank and address these issues and the CTBT"—as long as the United States entered the talks without preconditions. If, however, he came to Washington and was confronted with more demands of the kind that Clinton and Albright were making in public, "then I'm coming on a suicide mission—I'll have my throat cut."

MEANWHILE, THE INDIAN embassy in Washington took quiet soundings on whether official contacts might be resumed. The ambassador, Naresh Chandra, was so concerned about being rebuffed that he did not dare call anyone in the administration. Instead, he phoned Perkovich and asked his view about whether the administration would be willing to receive a visit from Singh. Perkovich passed the question along to Bruce Riedel at the NSC. Bruce, who had been impressed by Singh during the informal meeting in Ambassador Celeste's library in New Delhi four weeks before the test, told Perkovich he could tell Chandra that the emissary would be received "appropriately," and that while tempers were still pretty hot in Washington, an Indian initiative to rebuild bridges would be treated in a reciprocal spirit.

Bruce did not say who Singh's host would be, since that decision required further thought within the administration. Even though Singh had among his titles that of senior adviser on defense and foreign affairs to the prime minister, he was not Sandy Berger's counterpart in the Indian system. Also, it was deemed too early to give the Indian envoy direct access to the White House.

Madeleine had crossed paths with Jaswant Singh in the 1980s, when she had taught at Georgetown University and he had participated in a program for foreign visitors there. But for her to receive him now would signal undue eagerness to return to normal with a government that had done severe damage to the cause of nonproliferation.

Nor, for that matter, was Singh likely to be eager to begin his reconnaissance mission with Madeleine, who had an undeserved reputation for being pro-Pakistani and therefore anti-Indian. Her father, Joseph Korbel, had been a Czechoslovak diplomat assigned to the United Nations commission that tried in vain to broker a settlement of the Kashmir issue in the late 1940s. With Madeleine's help, Korbel, who emigrated to the United States and became a professor at the University of Denver, wrote a memoir of the experience. Pakistanis considered the book relatively sympathetic, while Indians regarded it—and therefore her—as tilting in Pakistan's favor.[4]

Madeleine's travel schedule offered a solution to the awkwardness of how to deal with Jaswant Singh's visit to Washington. She was due to be in Europe the second week in June to participate in a meeting of G-8 foreign ministers, who would issue yet another condemnation of the tests following up on the one that the leaders had released in Birmingham. Since I was acting secretary when Madeleine was abroad, I could receive Singh in that capacity. Moreover, since I was a deputy cabinet secretary and he was the deputy chairman of the Indian government's Planning Commission, he would have established a counterpart "of equivalent rank."

ON THE WEEKEND of June 6–7, Brooke and I, along with our parents, who had known Clinton since the late 1960s, drove from Washington through Maryland to Camp David in the Catoctin Mountains. Visits to the presidential retreat were supposed to be recreational for all concerned, particularly for the president. Clinton spent a good deal of time breaking in his new Big Bertha golf club on the driving range and chatting about sports, movies, politics, and the biographies and thrillers he was reading. I stayed away from any subject having to do with work unless he raised it himself.

At lunchtime that Saturday, as we were working our way through a buffet line in the main dining room in Laurel Lodge, Clinton vented his worries about the latest turn of events in South Asia. Once we had our plates, we went off into a corner to talk. He was still fuming at the Indians. By being the first to test, they had set exactly the wrong kind of example for the rest of the world, especially Pakistan. That was partly because, as Clinton put it, India was "the Rodney Dangerfield of great nations"—convinced that it was never getting enough respect.[5] "But that's all the more reason we can't give up on trying," he added. "I'd like to find a way in on this one."

While India was more to blame for the current perilous situation than Pakistan, it was also more likely to be part of the solution. Somehow we had to persuade India, as the larger, politically more stable, economically more dynamic of the two countries, to set a positive example for Pakistan by putting the brakes on its acquisition of nuclear weaponry.

Clinton was drawn to the idea that he might help bring India and Pakistan together, or at least establish for the United States a relationship with both so that American diplomacy might better be able to influence them in a crisis. He had been frustrated at not having made much of a dent in U.S.-Indian relations during his first six years in office. With only two years to go in his presidency, the nuclear tests gave him a powerful incentive to make up for lost time. Heading off an Indian-Pakistani arms race, and perhaps something much worse, was a compelling goal in itself. Beyond that, the very act of trying might give the United States a degree of traction with India that it had never had during the cold war.

Therefore he wanted South Asia to remain "front and center" in our diplomacy for the rest of his administration. The stakes justified a huge American investment, including, if it became useful, an investment of his own time and political capital.

"I want us to be bold and in the lead on this one," he said. The American people would "viscerally support" whatever we did because there was a threat of nuclear war.

He went on to tell me he had had a call a few days before from Robert Strauss, a Washington power broker and elder statesman. Strauss recommended that Clinton make Sam Nunn—the well-regarded former Democratic senator from Georgia, who was especially expert on nuclear weaponry, arms control, and international security—his special troubleshooter for India-Pakistan. Strauss was proposing a role for Nunn comparable to the one that Strauss himself had played for Jimmy Carter in the Middle East peace process back in the 1970s.

For the second time in a matter of weeks, I felt I had to talk my boss out of a bad idea—only this time I was more blunt than I had been in Birmingham about the U.S.-Russian-Chinese troika. It would be a mistake, I said, to pick someone of Nunn's prominence for an assignment that would be as delicate and protracted as this one. A celebrity might be welcome to the Pakistanis, since they made much of wanting high-profile American mediation. But for just that reason, the Indians would be all the more resistant. Also, precisely because Nunn was a public figure in his own right, he was likely to insist on a high degree of independence and would chafe at taking direction from the administration.

I reminded Clinton of the last time he had given Nunn a diplomatic mission. It had been four years earlier, in 1994, when Nunn along with Colin Powell and Jimmy Carter went to Haiti to give the leaders of the military junta that ruled the country a final chance to step aside and permit the restoration of the democratically elected president, Jean-Bertrand Aristide, whom they had overthrown and driven into exile three years before. While the three Americans were negotiating the details of the dictators' surrender, twenty thousand U.S. soldiers and Marines were boarding troop transports and helicopters and preparing to invade. Nunn, along with Powell and Carter, felt Clinton was taking too hard a line on several demands and asked him for some last-minute flexibility. What they considered to be face-savers for the junta looked more like loopholes to Clinton and his aides, myself included. In the end, Clinton ordered the three envoys to come home and sent in the troops. My memory of that incident made me all the more wary of delegating the India-Pakistan account to a distinguished former senator rather than keeping it in more traditional diplomatic channels.

I made these points to Clinton and urged that he give the job to someone who was part of the administration's own foreign policy apparatus. Preferably, I said, it should be someone at just below cabinet rank who would have clout in our own bureaucracy and sufficient standing to deal with ministers—and, at times, prime ministers—on the Indian and Pakistani sides.

"I agree with that," said Clinton, smiling. "And I guess you just volunteered."

He was right: I was by now deep enough into the assignment to be intrigued by the prospect of seeing it through.

"Just call me a glutton for punishment," I said.

"I'll call you anything you want—as long as you don't screw it up.'"

THAT DAY, SATURDAY, June 6, the UN Security Council unanimously passed Resolution 1172. In the flurry of drafting, the U.S. delegation to the UN, which did not include Bob Einhorn or anyone else who had been at the P-5 meeting in Geneva with Secretary Albright, let the Chinese reinstate some of their preferred tougher language and impossible demands. Alerted to the problem, Madeleine tried, at the last minute, to get Bill Richardson to back the Chinese off, just as Bob Einhorn had done in Geneva. But it was too late: the diplomats at the UN had already agreed on a text calling for India and Pakistan "immediately to stop their nuclear weapon development programs" and to join the NPT as non-nuclear-weapons states.

These exhortations were equally aimed at India and Pakistan and equally unwelcome to both. But the resolution also "encouraged" the two countries to "address the root causes" of the tensions between them, "including Kashmir." This formulation pleased the Pakistanis, who had been trying for decades to lure the United Nations and the United States back into mediation. Largely for that reason the resolution was all the more infuriating to the Indians, not just in the BJP but across the political spectrum.

With his envoy already en route to the United States, Prime Minister Vajpayee called the UN resolutions "unacceptable."

THE NEXT DAY, Jaswant Singh arrived in New York ostensibly to participate in a conference on narcotics at the United Nations. He used the occasion to take counsel from Frank Wisner, who was widely regarded by Indians and Americans alike as a wise head on the perennially troubled relationship. Scheduling the meeting proved difficult, so the two ended up having their conversation in the back seat of a limousine on FDR Drive. Singh was careful to betray no anxiety about what awaited him in Washington, although he probed Frank in a low-key fashion about the mood in the U.S. government and about me as his interlocutor.

In his previous job as ambassador to India, Frank had doggedly argued for the long-standing American policy of uncompromising opposition to India's nuclear weapons program. After the tests, however, he felt that the United States must find a way of living and working with a nuclear-armed India. Frank believed that to continue treating India as an outcast or probationer would be a huge mistake. Somehow a way had to be found to bridge what he saw as "the chasm of history and estrangement." Frank believed that, paradoxically, the tests might make it easier to revitalize the relationship. Perhaps Pokhran II had "unshackled the diplomacy" in the sense that neither the United States nor India could hide any longer behind the ambiguity of past Indian policy; they would now have to deal with the issues—and with each other—head-on.

As a private citizen Frank could say all that, and Singh, as the Indian official assigned the task of bridge-building, took considerable encouragement from hearing it.

WHILE IN NEW YORK Singh laid out for several interviewers a strategic justification for the tests. India, he said, was filling the nuclear security vacuum left by the collapse of the USSR:

If you examine the stretch from roughly Vancouver to Vladivostok, you have a kind of a nuclear security paradigm that has come into existence through the dissolution of [the] Warsaw Pact. The Asia Pacific is covered in part. China is an independent nuclear power in its own right. It is only Southern Asia and Africa that are out of this

protective pattern of security arrangements. Therefore, this, in our
assessment and strategic evaluation, is an area uncovered and is a
vacuum. If we have the kind of neighborhood that India has, which
is extremely troubled, and if we have two declared nuclear weapons
powers in our neighborhood, the basic requirement is to acquire a
balancing deterrent capability.[6]

In other press events and a speech at the Asia Society, he said that by
testing and thereby offering a nuclear counterweight to Chinese power,
India had corrected a "disequilibrium" in the Asian nuclear balance. That
was not just a favor India was doing the world—it was something India
had to do in the face of its own most formidable potential enemy: "Large
parts of the world today enjoy the benefit of the extended deterrence of
nuclear weapons powers . . . [but] missing in the flood of comment on
India's decision to test nuclear weapons . . . are informed assessments of
India's own security predicament."[7]

He went public with what he had told Perkovich over the phone: India
was "willing to discuss the [Comprehensive Test Ban] Treaty, but not sign
it when a gun is put to our head and we are informed that either you sign
this paper or else."

He also let it be known that Madeleine Albright's comment in the
Rose Garden several days before that India had "dug itself into a hole"
smacked to him of a cultural insult: "I must point out that, civilizationally,
we, in India, do not dig holes to bury ourselves, even metaphorically
speaking [Hindus do not bury their dead—they cremate them]. Therefore
this observation exemplifies yet another fundamental lack of comprehen-
sion about the Indian state and about addressing Indian sensitivities."[8]

I was watching on the television in my office, in part because I wanted
to get my first look at the man who would be coming to my office two
days later. I concluded it was just as well that he and Madeleine would
not be meeting this time around. I was also struck by his locution, slightly
orotund yet elegant, more affecting than affected. Anyone who used the
adverbial form of "civilization" must take the qualities associated with the
noun seriously.

JASWANT SINGH ARRIVED at the State Department mid-morning on
Friday, June 12. The meeting began in my outer office, which I used

mostly for large gatherings and ceremonial occasions. Bruce Riedel came over from the White House to attend, and Singh was accompanied by Ambassador Chandra, along with note-takers from the State Department and Indian Ministry of External Affairs. This was the normal procedure for a diplomatic encounter of this kind, especially since the visitor and I were meeting for the first time on behalf of our leaders and on a matter of great contention between two governments that had rarely been in harmony.

In an attempt to rise above a stilted exchange of set pieces, I arranged with Bruce in advance that as soon as Singh and I had dispensed with opening pleasantries, I would invite him to join me alone in my back office. A one-on-one, without note-takers, would, I hoped, permit us to probe each other's official positions more deeply, range more widely, and test how we might get along with each other. Bruce was fully in favor of this departure from the usual form. Chandra, unsurprisingly, was not. Singh nodded but otherwise remained poker-faced.

Once we were alone, I offered him a comfortable wing chair, although he did not look in the least comfortable sitting in it. Singh always carried himself like the soldier he had once been. His ramrod posture gave him an air of severity accentuated by his dark blue *sherwani*, which Westerners often call a Nehru suit, the collar buttoned tight at the neck. He spoke in a sonorous baritone and measured, often rather complex sentences. On the occasion of our first meeting, both his body English and his spoken English conveyed an extra degree of caution.

Perhaps overcompensating a bit, I lounged on a couch opposite him and suggested that we shift from addressing each other by our titles to using our first names. He agreed, but in the substance of the conversation that followed about the nuclear issue, we both stayed close to our prepared briefs, each reviewing, politely but firmly, our government's positions.

India regarded the Pokhran test as an exercise of its sovereign rights and an act of military necessity, while the United States regarded it as an irresponsible and dangerous provocation. The principal American concern was that other countries with the capability and aspiration to have nuclear weapons would see India as having provided them with a tempting precedent.

Jaswant asked me to look at what I had said from the Indian point of view: India was still excluded, as it had been for "the fifty wasted years" of U.S.-Indian relations, from "its rightful acceptance" as a normal, mature power; it had long been subjected to a double standard, denied the right to defend itself against its enemies. Foremost among those was China—"the principal variable in the calculus" of Indian foreign and defense policy.

As for India's decision to go forward with the Pokhran II test, the United States bore its own share of responsibility for that development, "complicating as it may be." India might have been able to live with nuclear weapons merely as an "option" and not felt it necessary to proceed with "overt weaponization" had it not been for the indefinite extension of the NPT and Washington's obvious intention to universalize the CTBT. The NPT in particular made a mockery of the goal of universal disarmament to which India had long subscribed since it legitimized nuclear weaponry. What gave the United States the right to say that there was anything *illegitimate* about India's desire to guard its own security, including against nuclear powers like China?

WE FAIRLY QUICKLY exhausted our briefs on this subject. As it turned out, the most time-consuming and heated issue between us was not nuclear weaponry but Pakistan. When that topic arose, which was only when I raised it, Jaswant would either sigh or shake his head wearily, as though I had diverted us into an area that was neither pleasant nor germane—nor, for that matter, suitable for lengthy discussion between representatives of two "major powers," a category that, for him, did not include Pakistan. As far as India was concerned, Pakistan was not just India's sibling but its twin—"we are born of the same womb," said Jaswant. However, from the moment of its birth, Pakistan had gone terribly and permanently wrong. He did not take seriously—or at least he did not want me to think he took seriously—the chance of nuclear war between India and Pakistan, a relatively small, incurably troubled, and incorrigibly troublesome country that dreamed of a parity with India it would never attain or deserve. China was a power and a threat worthy of India's strategic attention, not Pakistan.

I remarked that since Kashmir had already been the casus belli for two wars between India and Pakistan, and very nearly several more, that issue too would have to be on the agenda if U.S.-Indian diplomacy were to resume.

Jaswant, whose expression was deadpan most of the time, pulled a sour face. Kashmir, he said, should be regarded as an issue of "closed history" and a "case study in the rather fraught psychology of our neighbors." It was not "fitting" as a topic for international diplomacy. We should not let the Pakistanis' obsession with Kashmir make the hard work of improving U.S.-Indian relations all the harder. Americans must be especially careful not to fall into the trap of seeing Kashmir as a flash point because that would only play into the Pakistanis' game of trying to lure us onto their side of a tiresome and pointless argument. The Pakistanis kept talking about Kashmir as something that was "stolen or lost," when in fact it was neither. Pakistan's fixation with Kashmir should be understood as an objectification of Pakistan's predicament as a lost soul among nations, an ersatz country whose founders' only real legacy was a permanent reminder of what a tragic mistake partition had been.

After I had referred several times to "India-Pakistan" relations, Jaswant registered a complaint with the phrase and especially with the hyphen, since it encouraged the world to think of the two countries as locked in a deadly embrace. "Why do you Americans keep hyphenating us with Pakistan?" he asked, "These linkages are unwarranted—they are deeply resented in my country. 'India-Pakistan' is a false equation."

I pointed out that the United States had been, in recent years, moving toward delinkage of the kind he wanted. Since the end of the cold war, Americans had been thinking about India more in its own right, as a major regional power with the potential of becoming a global one as well. It was India's nuclear test, along with the totally predictable consequence of Pakistan's, that had refocused everyone on the extent to which the two countries' fates were, like it or not, interlocked. So the hyphen was not inserted between India and Pakistan by outsiders. Rather, the two countries put it there themselves. It symbolized the way they prosecuted their relentless and seemingly endless animosity. They were, I said, like a pair of boxers, either throwing punches in war or, when ostensibly at peace, snarling at each other in a clinch.

SCHEDULED TO LAST an hour, the meeting stretched for more than two and a half, nearly causing me to be late for my son Adrian's graduation from high school. Toward the end Jaswant and I returned to the nuclear issue. We agreed that however far apart our positions, there was still an overriding need to reconcile India's security concerns with Washington's nonproliferation agenda.

For Jaswant, reconciliation required the United States to accept India's nuclear weaponry as a fact of life.

From the American point of view, India would have to accept that the United States would not do anything that diluted the NPT. That meant Washington could not grant India an exception that gave it the privileges and benefits of NPT membership. Because India would remain outside the NPT, it would be ineligible for certain forms of assistance available to non-nuclear member states. Principal among those was help in developing nuclear power for peaceful purposes, primarily the generation of electricity.

As long as India understood those parameters, I said, it might be possible for the United States to find ways of easing sanctions. But for that to happen, I said—remembering what Clinton had said during our conversation at Camp David—India, having made itself part of the problem of proliferation by testing, should now find ways of making itself part of the solution. First and foremost, that meant never testing again. The best way of providing such a pledge would be to join the CTBT.

Jaswant replied that it was further evidence of unequal treatment that the established nuclear powers would insist on India's signing the CTBT after only one test, while they had carried out some two thousand.

Nevertheless, he continued, India was prepared to "find a modus vivendi with the U.S. and with the global nuclear order" through participation in a number of arms control agreements, as long as none of them required India to renounce either what it had already done or what it might feel necessary to do in the future to ensure its security. He affirmed his government's "de facto adherence to the spirit" of the CTBT and repeated what he had told Perkovich: in exchange for the lifting of American sanctions, India might take the next step, "de jure formalization of our position and acceptance of the letter of the treaty."

The possibility of attaining this goal seemed to be the most concrete and promising thing Jaswant had said and might be the basis for further talks between us. We agreed that each of us would assemble a team of experts and hold a series of meetings. To increase the chances of success, we would keep the substance of our discussions confidential, since leaks would only stir up trouble from those on both sides who opposed compromise.

Jaswant agreed. He asked that we be careful not to characterize our talks as a "negotiation," since that word implied retreat from "basic and immutable national positions." Instead, we should conduct a "dialogue," the term that had already been applied to the exchanges that Foreign Secretary Raghunath had come to Washington to begin with Tom Pickering thirteen days before Pokhran II.

However we explained our diplomacy in public, he said, "people will demand of me, 'Why are you even talking to the Americans about matters that are none of their business?'" That question, he said, would come from the parliament and from the press. It would also come, I suspected—though he didn't say so—from his more hard-line colleagues in the BJP.

How would he deal with that challenge? I asked.

He gave me a wan smile and replied that he would merely quote a proverb from his native Rajasthan: "Don't ask the way to a village if you don't want to get there."[9]

Like many of Jaswant's utterances, this one took some unpacking. I hoped it would throw off his critics back home as effectively as it stumped me when I first heard it. But once I had sorted out the double negative, I got the point: since India and the United States both had an interest in finding a way out of the dead end they had reached, there was no harm, and maybe some good, in their representatives talking about how to do so.

REFERENCES TO JASWANT'S village became a staple in our banter over the next two years, in part because it suited the itinerant nature of the enterprise. When we got together for yet another round in yet another city, one of us would ask the other, was this finally the village? Well, no, we would conclude after a day or two of hard slogging. Instead of celebrating an arrival, we would have to settle for agreeing on where we would meet next.

Even after the story told in this book came to an end, Jaswant's snippet of Rajasthani folk wisdom remained for us a verbal memento of the dialogue. There is, on the windowsill next to my desk at the Brookings Institution in Washington, a framed photograph of the two of us as we strolled smiling, side-by-side, into one of the many joint press conferences at which we dodged and weaved to avoid providing much information about what was going on between us in private. The inscription, written in Jaswant's neat italic hand, reads, "In memory of a journey we took together to a village called 'Better Tomorrow'" (an unintended echo of the Pakistanis' triumphant slogan after their test). A copy of the same photo sits on a credenza in his office in New Delhi. My scrawled message to him reads, "A couple of guys on their way to a village."

In Jaswant's own occasional public reflections on the dialogue, such as one contained in an interview he gave to the *Indian Express* in 2003, around the time of the fifth anniversary of Pokhran II, he recalled using the proverb "the first time I met Strobe at his lovely office in the State Department. . . . This journey was guided by a sense of power and pride that India is not subservient to anyone and we speak as equals."[10]

Thus, even at the beginning, we saw our destination differently. For Jaswant, the village was a place where India and the United States would put behind them not just the estrangement of the cold war but our dispute over nuclear issues in the post-cold-war era as well. We would get there, he believed, once the United States finally accepted India as a major power with an internationally recognized right to bear nuclear arms.

There was, however, no such place on the American map. Since India had left the land of the NPT forever, my job was to try to induce Jaswant and his government to meet us halfway, somewhere in the land of the CTBT.

FIVE

STUCK ON THE TARMAC

On June 18, the week after my first meeting with Jaswant, I made a relatively rare appearance in the State Department briefing room to announce the administration's "rollout" of the sanctions that went into effect that day. This battery of punitive measures was the big stick we were carrying while we spoke softly in the dialogue, and I felt I had to brandish that stick myself. I didn't want to look like the administration's good cop, searching for compromises in back rooms while the U.S. government was publicly beating up on India and Pakistan.

Sanctions have had, at best, a mixed record as an instrument of American foreign policy. They tend to work best when imposed in conjunction with other governments and sustained over a long period of time. Sanctions that met that standard hastened the end of apartheid in South Africa in the 1980s. By contrast, the unilateral restrictions on U.S.-China trade that Congress enacted after the Tiananmen massacre in 1989 did little to improve human rights in that country, and Fidel Castro has used the American embargo to justify repression and blame Cuba's economic hardships on a giant external enemy.

Sanctions are least controversial in the United States when the target country is widely regarded as beyond the pale—a brutal dictatorship that threatens war against its neighbors and supports terrorism. If such countries are nuclear proliferators to boot, U.S. sanctions are applied with all the more vigor. But that still does not mean they work. In recent years, under both Republican and Democratic administrations, the United States has tried, without much success, to use sanctions to stop Iran, Iraq, and North Korea from going ahead with nuclear weapons programs in contravention of their obligations under the NPT. In the case of Iraq, the second Bush administration gave up on sanctions altogether and resorted to the much blunter instrument of war and regime change.

The most difficult cases are those where a country that provokes American sanctions because of a specific action or policy is one with which the United States wants nonetheless to maintain overall decent relations. India and Pakistan were in this category.

Sanctions had already failed as an effective tool of American nonproliferation policy in South Asia even before a battery of new ones came into force on June 18, 1998. The legal restrictions on Washington's willingness to help India develop nuclear power, going back to the mid-1970s, had not had any decisive effect on Indian policy, nor had U.S. pressure and punishment kept Pakistan from pushing ahead with its own nuclear weapons program. In May 1998 the leaderships in New Delhi and Islamabad knew that by testing they would be bringing additional sanctions down on their heads. Not only were they undeterred—they tested largely to demonstrate that they rejected American (and international) admonitions, and that they were confident they could survive the consequences.

Our best hope was that, having made their point with regard to the NPT, India and Pakistan might now be more willing to curb the development and deployment of their nuclear weapons, starting with acceptance of the CTBT. If so, we could reward them by easing the sanctions we had imposed.

Yet to achieve even that relatively modest goal, the executive branch, which has responsibility for the conduct of diplomacy, needed the full cooperation of the legislative branch, which has a crucial say over when sanctions must be imposed and when they could be waived or lifted. Maintaining firm congressional support for a tough policy toward India was going to be hard, given the pro-Indian sentiment in both parties on Capitol Hill. Getting approval from the Republicans on CTBT was going to be even harder, given the party leadership's fierce opposition to the treaty.

A LITTLE MORE than a week after sanctions were announced in Washington, Clinton was in Beijing and issued a joint statement with President Jiang Zemin lambasting India and Pakistan for the tests and suggesting that the United States and China were looking for additional ways of applying the screws to both countries.[1]

Within hours, I received a blistering e-mail from a close friend, Nayan Chanda, the editor of the *Far Eastern Economic Review* in Hong Kong and the son-in-law of Amarjit and Bhagwant Singh, the Indian couple with whom Brooke had lived during the summer of 1968. Nayan and I had come to know each other during my reporting forays to Asia in the 1980s. I regarded him as an astute observer of his native country. He was often critical, both in print and in conversation, of the Indian government and its decision to test a nuclear weapon. But he thought Washington's attempt to play the China card against India was bad poker and boneheaded diplomacy. The Beijing statement would serve only to validate India's long-held suspicion about Sino-U.S. collusion against India. Nayan predicted it would be all the harder for me to accomplish anything with Jaswant.

He was right, and I faulted myself for not having seen in advance the complication we were creating for ourselves. The incident was a classic example of what can happen when the U.S. government pursues, as it does every day, multiple and often conflicting objectives with rival, if not hostile, countries. By issuing the joint statement with Jiang Zemin, Clinton was trying to strengthen ties with China and encourage its cooperation on nonproliferation. Moreover, the administration was throwing everything it could lay its hands on at the BJP government, and the presidential statement in Beijing was the kitchen sink. Still, while that was an explanation for what the president did, it was no excuse. Our goal with the Indians was to change their policies and attitudes, not to insult, embarrass, or frighten them, since the effect was sure to be a hardening of their position in the dialogue we had just begun.

A DAY OR TWO later, Jaswant sent word that we had better hold a fairly high-visibility meeting as soon as possible to counter the perception that the relationship was in free fall and that he had made a mistake in coming to Washington. We agreed to get together, this time with our experts, the second week in July in Europe.

In preparation, I convened a series of meetings with the team that had been working on India and Pakistan for the past several years, a mixture of regionalists and functionalists from the key departments and agencies of the U.S. government. The core members from State were Bob Einhorn and Rick Inderfurth, along with Rick's senior adviser, Matt Daley; Walter Andersen, a career South Asia analyst in the Bureau of Intelligence and Research; and Phil Goldberg, a versatile foreign service officer on my staff who had the unenviable job of meshing the many moving pieces of the process and managing my role in it.

The National Security Council was represented by Bruce Riedel, his deputy Don Camp, and Gary Samore, a veteran nonproliferation specialist. The principal participant from Treasury was Karen Mathiasen, a specialist on the effect of sanctions on our economic assistance programs. Depending on the agenda of the moment, we often included officials from the intelligence community, the Justice, Commerce, Energy, and Defense Departments as well as officials from State and the White House who handled relations with Congress.

These gatherings became a regular, often daily feature of our lives for the next two years. We would talk through the disparate and often competing goals we were trying to advance and, to the extent possible, hammer out approaches that balanced the various interests involved. If disagreements remained, I would make the call rather than trying to split the difference. Those who lost the argument would know they had participated in the debate and understand why the decision had gone the other way. It was an extraordinarily collegial process, and it helped keep to a minimum the personal backbiting, bureaucratic warfare, and mischievous leaks that too often accompany policymaking.

THE FIRST FULL-CAST session of the U.S.-Indian dialogue took place July 9–10, 1998, at Frankfurt Airport, in a drab conference room in one of those soulless hotels that cater to weary, often stranded travelers.

Jaswant had assembled a flying squad that lined up well with mine. Bob Einhorn's opposite number, Rakesh Sood, was a veteran of UN disarmament negotiations in Geneva and a master of the technical aspects of our agenda. He was a formidable debater, even-tempered but relentless. He had a knack for making his government's position seem like sweet reason and any contrary view illogical. He took subtle though unmistakable pleasure in exploiting the weak spots in his opponent's argument. When dealing with Americans, that meant pointing out the injustice of our insistence that India must refrain from doing, even on a relatively modest scale, what the United States had been doing massively for half a century: developing, testing, and deploying hydrogen bombs and threatening, in the name of deterrence, to obliterate its principal adversary.

Over dinner that first night in Frankfurt, when conversation turned from the business of the day, Rakesh expounded at length and with great enthusiasm on his principal hobby—astrology, a subject he seemed to know and care about as much as the technology of nuclear weaponry and the theory of nuclear strategy. With obvious satisfaction at the incredulity it caused among the Americans around the table, he predicted that the success of our dialogue would depend not just on the brilliance of our statesmanship but on the movements of the moon, the planets, and the stars. He promised to keep an eye on the charts in case they offered any guidance on when and where we should hold future meetings.

Rick Inderfurth's primary counterpart was Alok Prasad, who was responsible for the Americas division at the Ministry of External Affairs. In manner and appearance, Alok came across as milder than Rakesh, but not in the positions he took or in the firmness with which he argued them. He had spent hundreds of hours standing up to representatives of a superpower that was, in his view, far too used to getting its way and far too inclined to take India for granted. At the same time, he genuinely wanted to see the opening of a new, positive chapter in Indo-U.S. relations, and he worked tirelessly and pragmatically to help make that happen.

Ambassador Naresh Chandra and Foreign Secretary Krishnan Raghunath were also regular and courteously combative participants. In his long career Chandra had served as cabinet secretary (the highest ranking civil servant in the government), chief secretary in Rajasthan, adviser to the governor of Kashmir, a member of India's Space and Atomic Energy Commissions, and governor of Gujarat. His brother, Girish Chandra Saxena, was a former spymaster, national security adviser to Rajiv Gandhi, and two-time governor of Kashmir. Naresh's background and connections made him a figure of considerable weight in the Indian political and foreign policy establishment.

Perhaps in part because of this assemblage of institutional memory, the session at Frankfurt Airport served little purpose except to show the world that the long-promised dialogue was now actually under way and that, at least geographically, the two governments were prepared to meet each other halfway. The Indians' objective and their strategy for attaining it was the obverse of ours. We were trying to convince them that the best way to get sanctions lifted and put U.S.-Indian relations on a favorable course was for them to adopt the restraints urged upon them by the Permanent Five members of the UN Security Council in the Geneva communiqué. For their part, the Indians were trying to persuade us that the best way to create a climate for cooperation, including on the issue of nuclear weaponry, was to lift sanctions; then, once the two sides were dealing with each other as equals, *maybe* something could be worked out on nonproliferation.

Two points that came up in the Frankfurt session bear recalling in light of what did, and did not, happen later. The first involved Kashmir. In a low-key fashion, almost in passing, Jaswant mentioned that he was willing to lift the virtual taboo on discussing that topic, if only for purposes of "clarifying" the Indian view on potential solutions to the problem. As a preview of what he was prepared to talk about, he mentioned that his government might consider converting the Line of Control, which was based on the 1949 cease-fire line between the Pakistani and Indian portions of the territory, into an international boundary—a significant departure from the long-established BJP position that India should persist in seeking the integration of Pakistani-occupied Kashmir.[2]

The other noteworthy element in the Indians' position in Frankfurt was the relish with which they professed to believe that the tests in May would usher in an extended period of nuclear stability in South Asia comparable to the one that had preserved the peace between the United States and the USSR throughout the cold war. In the months that followed, we would hear this sanguine view from the Pakistanis as well. It was as though the two South Asian adversaries saw nearly fifty years of U.S.-Soviet brinkmanship in the twentieth century as something for them to emulate in the twenty-first.

All of us on the American side had lived in the shadow of the mushroom cloud and did not recall the experience with nostalgia. We urged the Indians (and, later, the Pakistanis) to take another look at the record, not with the consolation of knowing that the cold war never turned hot, but with a sober appreciation that the superpowers had come close to thermonuclear catastrophe over Berlin and Cuba. India and Pakistan had far less margin for error. The Americans and Soviets never shed a drop of each other's blood in direct conflict on the battlefield, while the Indians and Pakistanis had already fought three wars.

We also suggested that before India and Pakistan set about replicating the U.S.-Soviet nuclear competition, they consider the price tag. Maintaining the American nuclear capability had, by some estimates, cost the United States more than five trillion dollars.[3] On the other side of the Iron Curtain, the crushing expense of the struggle against the West contributed to the disintegration of the Soviet system and state. The cost of developing nuclear weapons is only a fraction of what is required for safely managing even a modest capability. Tensions on a nuclearized subcontinent would drive up military budgets, which neither India nor Pakistan could afford, and drive away the foreign capital that both countries desperately needed.

Jaswant and his colleagues listened to these arguments with polite indulgence, then replied with unshaken confidence in their own position and undisguised satisfaction that they had finally gotten the Americans' full attention. I had the impression that the very fact that we were finally sitting down together was, for the Indians, in and of itself a vindication of the Pokhran II test.

Ten days later, we met again, this time in New Delhi. The American team was augmented by a ringer—Joe Ralston, an Air Force four-star general and the vice chairman of the joint chiefs of staff. His participation was intended to demonstrate the Pentagon's commitment to nonproliferation and to give the Indians a foretaste of military cooperation that might be possible if the relationship could be put on the right footing.

Joe provided an airplane for the trip, a military version of a DC-10 that was outfitted in its giant hold with a Winnebago-like VIP cabin, known as "The Silver Bullet." Unlike the turbulent flight my team and I had taken with Tony Zinni to Islamabad in May, this one was smooth except for an incident that occurred as we were refueling over Saudi Arabia. The automatic pilot of the tanker to which we were connected by a twenty-foot boom suddenly ceased to function, causing the tanker to dip suddenly. Only because the pilots on our plane were watching carefully and had their hands on the controls were we able, by a fraction of a second, to go into a sharp dive and avoid plowing into the underbelly of the tanker.

The laptop on which I was typing rose three feet in the air and remained suspended for a long moment as though we were in a space capsule. Joe, an unflappable ex-fighter pilot, got out of his bunk and allowed as how he was going to "check up front." When he returned, he said there was nothing to worry about. He waited until we were on the ground to add that we had "just missed a fireball."

THE SETTING FOR the meetings—Hyderabad House, once the New Delhi residence of the ruler of that former Mogul kingdom and princely state—was as exotic as the Frankfurt Airport hotel had been dreary.

The discussion focused on what the United States was asking India to do in the wake of the tests. Using the P-5 joint communiqué of June 4 as a basis, the American team had come up with five conditions—or benchmarks, as we called them—that we wanted India to meet. If India made demonstrable progress, the United States would lift post-test sanctions and President Clinton would proceed with the visit that had been scheduled to take place in November 1998 but that was now on hold.

First on the list of steps we wanted India to take was its signature on the Comprehensive Test Ban Treaty. Prime Minister Vajpayee was due to attend the United Nations General Assembly in September, and we hoped he would use that occasion to declare that India would sign the treaty within a year. Second was Indian cooperation in negotiating a permanent ban on the production of fissile material and, in the interim, a freeze on further production. Third, we pushed for a "strategic restraint regime" that would limit the types of ballistic missiles in India's arsenal to the two it already had, the Agni and the Prithvi. Under a strategic restraint regime, the Indians would also agree not to deploy missiles close to Pakistan and also not to mount warheads on rockets or store them nearby. Fourth, we called on India to adopt stringent, "world-class" controls on the export of dangerous material, technology, or know-how that would, if it got into the wrong hands, make it easier for other countries to manufacture nuclear weapons and ballistic missiles of their own. The fifth benchmark used language from UN Security Council Resolution 1172 passed in early June in calling on India and Pakistan to "resume dialogue to address the root causes of tension between them, including Kashmir."

From the American standpoint, the benchmarks seemed realistic and reasonable. We were not demanding that India give up its nuclear capability and join the NPT. That goal had, for years, been an object of little more than lip service. While we were not about to concede that the Indians were right or wise to have tested—we reminded them continually that we thought Pokhran II had been unnecessary, dangerous, and irresponsible—we did not make our objection to what they had already done the basis for our proposal on what they should do next.

Moreover, the nonproliferation benchmarks were designed to coincide as closely as possible with what India had publicly identified as its own intentions and needs. Signing the CTBT was, as Jaswant had said, a matter of formalizing the unilateral moratorium Vajpayee announced after the test. Joining an international cutoff of fissile material should not have been a problem because India would have stockpiled plenty of fissile material by the time a ban went into effect. Strategic restraint was intended to be consistent with India's policy of requiring nothing more than what was necessary to deter others from using nuclear weapons first. Acceptance of high-standard export controls should have been especially easy, since India had every reason to want to keep its hard-won capabilities to itself. In fact, India already had a record in this regard better than two NPT states, Russia and China, which were, respectively, helping Iran and Pakistan acquire dangerous technology, not to mention Pakistan itself, whose national hero, A. Q. Khan, was peddling nuclear wares around the world.

As we saw it, if the Indians really wanted to move quickly to repair relations with the United States while retaining the capability they had already demonstrated, they could have done so simply by accepting the benchmarks and collecting the reward in the form of sanctions relief and a rousing presidential visit in the fall.

THE INDIANS, HOWEVER, saw it all differently. They bridled at the very notion that their country had to do anything at anyone's behest. They found the word *benchmark* objectionable, since it implied that Americans saw themselves as stern schoolmasters who would be grading their performance.

Another difficulty was that three of the benchmarks—on the CTBT, fissile material, and strategic restraint—were based on American judgments about Indian defense requirements. The Indians themselves had not reached judgments of their own about how many nuclear warheads to have and how to deploy them.

Our urging that India sign the CTBT posed an especially acute political problem. Indian politicians, especially those associated with the BJP, had spent the last several years vituperating against the treaty as an example of America's attempt to protect the monopoly of the five NPT-approved nuclear weapons states. It would, we were told, take time to "de-demonize" the treaty sufficiently for the parliament and public opinion to accept Indian accession.

That much Jaswant told us candidly. He did not say, but we assumed, that in addition to overcoming popular and parliamentary distaste for the CTBT, he would have to find allies in the military and scientific establishment who would certify that Pokhran II had provided enough data to obviate the need for further testing.

For all these reasons, Jaswant fended off my attempts to elicit his agreement on a September 1998 deadline for an Indian promise to sign the CTBT coupled with a deadline a year later for signature itself. The most he would commit himself to was a timetable for his own efforts to move his government "in the right direction." First, he said, would come a "national statement" that would extend the testing moratorium indefinitely. That statement would be approved by parliament in August. A month later, it would be circulated—presumably to universal applause—at a summit in Durban, South Africa, of the Non-Aligned Movement (which still existed, even though its very name had become an anachronism). When Vajpayee came to the United Nations in late September, he would deposit the national statement with Secretary General Kofi Annan. This sequence, Jaswant hoped, would "negate what is most invidious about the CTBT and favorably alter the context in which the treaty might be looked at anew."

These carefully chosen words had a hopeful ring, but they did not really carry matters very far. The United States wanted India to *sign* the CTBT, not "look at it anew." When I told Jaswant that the plan fell well short of what would allow the United States to ease sanctions and go ahead with the Clinton trip, he said that he understood, but that "the art of the possible" as practiced in Indian politics was a matter of taking small steps slowly. "We are conducting diplomacy within the arenas of two great democracies," he said. "That makes our task both more complex and more noble."

BY TRYING TO persuade the Indians to adopt, quickly and with some specific assurances, a strategic restraint regime, we were, in effect, urging them to address the question of sufficiency—how much is enough?—that had dogged the United States and the Soviet Union for decades during the cold war. There were still nuclear abolitionists in India, but they had been losing the debate for a long time, and they lost it irrevocably with the test in May. Still in the game were the minimalists, who argued that India already had enough bombs (even if they did not know exactly how many that was). But from what we could tell, they, too, were on the defensive. Then there were the maximalists, who wanted India to have an arsenal on par with those of the United Kingdom, France, and China. The majority of opinion was probably somewhere in the middle.[4]

Several Indian officials and strategists, both inside the government and out, would have had us believe that they were simply having their own version of the nuclear debate that we Americans had conducted back in the 1970s and 1980s.

We tried to point out that as dangerous, preoccupying, and expensive as the cold war had been, at least the United States had been able to focus on only one major adversary and calculate its needs for deterrence accordingly. The Indians had to worry about both China and Pakistan, even if they claimed to take only China seriously. China had a head start in the acquisition and deployment of nuclear weaponry. If the Indians tried to play catch-up with China, the Chinese would do whatever it took to maintain their lead, while Pakistan would rush to stay abreast of India. Unlike the face-off between the United States and the Soviet Union, which had settled into a rough and durable sort of balance, a three-way dynamic such as the one developing among India, China, and Pakistan would be inherently unstable.

By refusing to give us an answer about what they felt they must have and what they would be prepared to forgo, the Indians were not keeping any secrets from us. Quite simply, they did not know what sort of nuclear forces would ultimately constitute their deterrent; they were making it up as they went along. We tried to persuade them that not having a coherent nuclear doctrine could be even worse than having a bad one, since the result could be to increase the degree of uncertainty and ad hoc decision-making on both sides in a crisis during which the slightest misunderstanding or miscalculation on either side could be catastrophic.

Our Indian interlocutors were not just impervious to these arguments—they were offended by them. To their ears, American preachments called into question their right to make momentous decisions in their own time, in their own way, and by their own lights—and thus constituted further evidence of our arrogance, hypocrisy, and refusal to accept them as a mature power.

I HAD A glimpse into Jaswant's domestic arena when I paid courtesy calls on various members of the political leadership, including Vajpayee. Dick Celeste, who accompanied me to the session, warned me in advance that I should concentrate on listening—and not be in a hurry to fill the long silences that marked Vajpayee's side of the conversation: just because the prime minister stopped talking did not mean he was finished speaking; I should wait patiently for him to continue.

Even with that warning, I was not prepared for what awaited me. Vajpayee's pauses seemed to last forever. Even when his thoughts were ready for delivery, he spoke slowly and softly. I had never met a politician so laconic. In Vajpayee's case it was all the more surprising, since I knew that on the hustings, in parliament, and in Hindi, he was admired even by his opponents as a spellbinding orator.

On the subject of the CTBT, Vajpayee's silence was absolute; he simply left my own statements and questions unanswered. If he flatly refused our request for him to sign the treaty, he would lose the Clinton visit, which would expose him to the charge that he had mishandled relations with the United States. But would that be worse than appearing to have given in to American pressure? My sense was that Vajpayee was reserving judgment while letting Jaswant see how much he could get from us—and how little India would have to give in return.

I also spent some time with two members of Vajpayee's inner circle— his experienced, taciturn principal secretary, Brajesh Mishra, and the home minister, Lal Krishna Advani—both of whom were cool to the very idea of the U.S.-Indian dialogue insofar as it entailed any suggestion of compromise on anything. There was certainly no echo from them of Jaswant's talk about "harmonization" or "reconciliation" of the U.S. and Indian positions. When I floated those words in my own presentation (principally to see how they would react), Advani arched his eyebrows, pursed his lips, and abruptly changed the subject; Mishra was more poker-faced but no more willing to endorse anything that implied mutual accommodation.

I could see that Jaswant had his work cut out for him within his own government.

The session with Advani was unnerving for another reason as well. He mused aloud about the happy day when India, Pakistan, Sri Lanka, Bangladesh, and Myanmar (formerly Burma) would be reunited in a single South Asian "confederation." Given India's advantages in size and strength, this construct, especially coming from India's highest-ranking hard-line Hindu nationalist, would have been truly frightening to all its neighbors, most of all Pakistan.[5]

In passing, Advani mentioned that at the time of the Indian test, he had "looked forward to" the Pakistanis following suit, thus confirming a suspicion we had tried to impress on the Pakistanis: they were sucker-punched.

In keeping with the common practice that an official visitor from Washington pays a courtesy call on the leaders of the parliamentary opposition, Dick Celeste took me to see former prime minister Inder Gujral and Sonia Gandhi, the Italian-born widow of Rajiv Gandhi and the president of the Congress Party. Both of them were gracious in welcoming me, generous with their time, but wary about being drawn into discussing matters of substance, particularly the one most on my mind.

When I conveyed to Gujral my government's hope that he and other opposition leaders might support a fresh, positive look at the CTBT, he was visibly embarrassed, then lapsed into a rambling reminiscence about his own handling of the "nuclear dilemma" when he had been prime minister. He concluded by expressing what I found to be strangely detached curiosity about what Vajpayee would do—but that was it.

As for Sonia Gandhi, she was all charm, some diffidence, and no give. Joined by two senior colleagues, Natwar Singh, who had earlier been a senior official in the ministry of external affairs and active in the Non-Aligned Movement, and Manmohan Singh, a former finance minister and the mastermind behind India's liberalizing economic reforms, she listened with patience, apparent interest, and even sympathy while I explained how strongly President Clinton felt about the need to improve U.S.-Indian relations while strengthening nonproliferation. When I finished, she didn't even make a pretense of replying. Instead, she asked me to give her warmest personal regards to Hillary Clinton (who had called on her in 1995) and said she hoped I enjoyed the rest of my stay.

So much for any chance that the BJP's principal opposition was going to provide Vajpayee with political cover for progress in the dialogue with the United States. Knowing how popular the tests had been and with her eye on the next election, Sonia Gandhi was not about to open herself to the charge that if she were prime minister, she might be any less stalwart than Vajpayee in standing up to American pressure.

She accompanied me outside to my car, chatted with me while a large crowd of photographers clicked away, then bowed slightly while I got into the car. As I was being driven out of the courtyard and waiting for the gate to open, I looked out the rear window. She was still standing there, waving and smiling serenely. I found myself thinking about the few glimpses I'd had of her mother-in-law, Indira Gandhi, who started it all with Pokhran I, back in 1974, the year of my first visit to India. Sonia was an altogether softer-seeming figure, but on the issue of the Indian bomb, they were very much in sync with each other, and with Vajpayee as well.

THAT EVENING, AT an elaborate reception and dinner that Jaswant hosted for our delegation, the visiting Americans, all of us by now bleary-eyed, had a chance to meet an array of Indian politicians, media figures, and scientists. They treated us with a combination of courtesy and curiosity. They communicated undisguised pride at what their government had done in Rajasthan two months before and, in many cases, did little to disguise their smugness at the upset the test had caused in Washington.

Among the guests were several members of the family with whom my wife, Brooke, had lived in New Delhi thirty years before. Seated next to me was Malvika Singh, the rambunctious columnist and editor of the magazine *Seminar*, known for her zest for good-natured conversational combat. Mala, as she is called, teased me about how hard it must be for the United States to get used to dealing with India as a fellow nuclear power. Suddenly, to the astonishment of everyone at our table, she burst into song. In a comically broad American accent, she belted out a Tom Lehrer number from 1965:

First we got the bomb and that was good,
'Cause we love peace and motherhood.
Then Russia got the bomb, but that's O.K.,
'Cause the balance of power's maintained that way!
Who's next?

France got the bomb, but don't you grieve,
'Cause they're on our side (I believe).
China got the bomb, but have no fears;
They can't wipe us out for at least five years!
Who's next?

She ran through the remaining three verses, in which Indonesia, South Africa, Egypt, Israel, Luxembourg, and Monaco all get the bomb. Her point was that India had not even made the list of countries whose nuclear ambitions were worth laughing at.

DURING MY VISIT in New Delhi, Jaswant and I made several brief appearances together before the press. I let him do most of the talking, not just because he was the host, but because of his ability to keep the substance of our talks confidential while creating the impression that the two of us were getting along famously. He was a master of public statements that made up in panache what they lacked in content and sometimes even in discernible meaning. Two of my favorites were, "The totally moral has become the realistically moral," and "If strategic deterrence is not on the negotiating table, how can you have a missile-development program on the table?"

The journalists dutifully scribbled down these oracular utterances, never asking for clarification or amplification, and then reported them to their readers as though they provided insight into what was going on in the talks.

These positive though insubstantial reports in the Indian press fanned suspicions and anxiety in Pakistan. When my team and I flew from New

Delhi to Islamabad, we found our hosts there convinced that they were getting second-class treatment. For one thing, we had gone to India first. Moreover, the publicity from New Delhi suggested that something good was happening between Jaswant and me, and that had to be bad for the Pakistanis. They tried every means they could think of to get me to tell them what was going on in the U.S.-Indian channel. I told them little, lest they leak what they learned in ways intended to embarrass the Indians. That would only further complicate Jaswant's end of the dialogue.

Part of what drove the competition on the subcontinent was Pakistan's chronic fear of being left behind by its large neighbor. India was the first of the two to develop a nuclear device, the first to test a weapon, and now the first to enter into intense diplomacy with the United States. In each case Pakistan scrambled to close the gap. Sartaj Aziz, who was finance minister in July 1998 and later became foreign minister, once remarked to me, "Pakistan is the dependent variable in American reckoning about this region, and India is the independent variable."[6] Rick Inderfurth saw a pattern in Pakistani behavior that he called "keeping up with the Joneses."

Traveling between the two capitals was always a bit like passing through the looking glass. Both countries had suffered from colonialism and racism. Both feared big neighbors. Both felt alternately pushed around and taken for granted by the United States. There was an eerie similarity to Indian and Pakistani complaints about historical injustices, infringement on sovereignty, insensitivity to legitimate security concerns, and insufficient appreciation of how domestic politics made what Americans were asking difficult if not impossible. Yet the difference between the two mind-sets was profound. The Pakistanis seemed to wear on their sleeve an insecurity about the cohesiveness and even the viability of their own state, not to mention the durability of its democracy. After more than half a century, Pakistan was still grappling with questions of identity and survival, and these were heightened in the late 1990s by the seismic shifts in the geopolitics of the region that came with the collapse of the Soviet Union, the emergence of new states in Central Asia and the Caucasus, and the ongoing turmoil in the Greater Middle East. Pakistan's neighbor, Afghanistan, was under the obscurantist rule of the Taliban, which Pakistan had done much to nurture and which was now creating a blowback into Pakistan itself, contributing to radicalism there. Where, exactly, did Pakistan fit in the strategic calculations of its big neighbors

China and Russia? Or in those of Iran? Or in those of Pakistan's far-off, inconstant protector, the United States?

Then there was, as Sartaj Aziz might have put it, the one, steady constant—the glowering presence of India, whose government now included people like Advani, with a glint in his eye when he talked about a South Asian confederation under Indian hegemony.

ANOTHER DIFFERENCE WAS personal. In India, my designated counterpart was a senior figure who was close to the prime minister and who had standing of his own in the eyes of the parliament, the press, and the public. In Pakistan I was to deal with Shamshad Ahmad, the foreign secretary, whose primary role in May had been to blame the Indian test—and therefore the Pakistani one as well—on the United States. He was not just below Jaswant in the pecking order but in a different category—a civil servant rather than a member of the leadership. While Jaswant's team was highly disciplined in every respect, some of Shamshad Ahmad's colleagues tended to be querulous, surly, and sometimes abusive. On one occasion, early in our dealings, a member of the Pakistani delegation exploded at our observation that his country seemed always to react in knee-jerk fashion to Indian moves. He rose out of his chair and lunged across the table as though he were going to strangle either Bruce Riedel or me, depending on whose neck he could get his fingers around first. He had to be physically restrained.

In general, our sessions with the Pakistanis, while occasionally more exciting than those with the Indians, lacked a comparable degree of intellectual engagement. Shamshad Ahmad and his colleagues did not enjoy anything like the latitude from their prime minister that Jaswant had from Vajpayee. Largely for that reason, they rarely ventured beyond their briefs.*

---

*A notable exception was Riaz Muhammad Khan, who headed the foreign ministry's policy planning unit. He was an urbane and erudite professional diplomat, married to a U.S. foreign service officer, and the author of a highly regarded book on the negotiations that ended the war in Afghanistan titled *Untying the Afghan Knot*. Over a working dinner for the two delegations the night my team arrived in Islamabad, he marshaled his considerable knowledge of history and culture to argue that the Indus River constituted a "civilizational divide." He later sent me a reading list of works by scholars that supported that thesis, which underscored the rationale for separation between Pakistan and India. In August 2002, Riaz Muhammad Khan became Pakistan's ambassador to China.

For all these reasons, my team had to shift gears when we traveled from New Delhi to Islamabad. The danger with the Indians was that they would wear us down. They had their game plan and would stick with it, waiting for us to lose congressional support for the sanctions and give up on even the modest demands we were making with the benchmarks.

The Pakistanis had no game plan. They always seemed to be either hunkering down, lashing out, or flailing about.

Thus, it was apparent from the outset that the Indians were going to be hard to move, while the Pakistanis were going to be hard to help. And far more than the Indians, the Pakistanis needed help. Their economy had sunk even deeper into crisis. Exports had fallen precipitously. The country was spending seventy-five percent of its budget to service interest repayments on its debt and military expenditures. Foreign investment and remittances from Pakistani workers in other countries were in sharp decline, prices were on the rise, and rampant unemployment fueled unrest and political and religious militancy. A collapse of the banking sector and a national default were possible, perhaps imminent.

The Clinton administration wanted Pakistan to devote its energies to developing its economy, consolidating its democracy, and modernizing its society, especially its educational system. Pakistan's economic stability was a security issue for the United States as well as a humanitarian one, since the meltdown of the Pakistani economy would pose a threat to American interests in the region. The ensuing political chaos might spread to neighboring countries, including those in the former Soviet Union. Within Pakistan itself, an upheaval might offer a target for exploitation by homegrown and external radical elements—a prospect rendered all the more serious now that Pakistan had the bomb.

But for the United States to help Pakistan, its government had to make hard decisions—and follow through on them. Even if all sanctions were lifted, the Pakistani government would have to undertake sweeping and painful reforms of a corrupt, hidebound system in order to attract foreign investors and qualify for assistance from the International Monetary Fund. Economic reform was possible only if Pakistan stopped prosecuting a nuclear rivalry with India that it could never win and only if it stopped pursuing a fantasy about recovering Kashmir.

Pakistanis responsible for the economy did not want to hear these messages. They seemed to think that the sheer desperateness of their situation gave them leverage over us rather than the other way round. They were betting that since the United States could not afford for Pakistan to become a failed state, we would cut them the slack they needed to protect themselves against a nuclear-armed India.

American officials like Rick Inderfurth of State and Karen Mathiasen of Treasury who had to deal with the Pakistanis on economic matters sometimes compared the experience to being mugged by someone who was holding a pistol to his own head and threatening to blow his brains out if you didn't give him your wallet. The Pakistanis, said our ambassador Tom Simons, were "adept at bullying from weakness."

WHILE RICK AND KAREN were getting roughed up at the finance ministry, I met with Nawaz Sharif at his residence. Just as during my first encounter with him in May, the prime minister was uneasy having any of his own advisers around, and he quickly shooed an unhappy Shamshad out of the room.

What Sharif said when we were alone reinforced my awareness of a fundamental problem I was up against: Pakistani diplomacy was so reactive and ineffectual in part because Pakistani democracy was so fragile. The country had, for long stretches, been ruled by unelected leaders, including three generals. The United States bore substantial responsibility for the shakiness of civilian control of the military even when there was a prime minister in charge of the country, since successive American administrations found it easier to deal with the army than with the politicians and the foreign ministry. It was not unnatural or unreasonable that elected leaders in Islamabad tended to look over their shoulders and worry about what was going on up the road in Rawalpindi.

Nawaz Sharif had to look over his other shoulder as well—at the militant Islamists who were a powerful force in Pakistan and, it seemed, permanently enraged at the United States. It was this political threat, more than the one posed by the military, that had seemed to obsess Sharif in May 1998 and that still preyed on him when he and I had a long private meeting two months later, on July 22. Early in the conversation, he remarked that the election that had allowed him to replace Benazir Bhutto in 1997 pitted him not just against her but against what he called "right-wing radicals" who advocated an Islamic revolution like the one that had swept the ayatollahs into power in Iran in the late 1970s. When he read a letter I had brought to him from Clinton, he took issue with a sentence that referred to the Pakistani nuclear test as a mistake: "If I had not made that 'mistake,' as the president calls it, someone else would be sitting in the prime minister's house right now. That someone probably would be a fanatic. We have no dearth of those." Then he added, "Either that, or the country would have gone to the dogs."

I could not imagine hearing something similar in New Delhi.

Our only chance of getting the Pakistanis to accept the nonproliferation benchmarks was to play upon their insecurity and, more specifically, their fear of being left behind by the Indians. If Nawaz Sharif believed that Vajpayee might come to New York and announce a commitment to sign the CTBT within a year, he might do the same. Therefore I used my one-on-one with him to sketch out a scenario in which both leaders, having brought down sanctions on their countries by conducting back-to-back tests in May, might earn sanctions relief by making back-to-back pledges to sign the CTBT in September.

Sharif went into the same sort of apologetic but stubborn sales resistance I had seen in May. He was reluctant—for domestic political reasons, he said—to make any promises about the CTBT. However, he added, it might make it easier for him to overcome the opposition of his enemies if the United States sweetened the pot with some additional favors. What he was driving at was elaborated by his colleagues in the foreign and finance ministries: the Pakistanis were trying to make their signature on the treaty contingent on our granting them a multitude of concessions and restitution for past injustices. They wanted not just the complete and permanent lifting of all sanctions, but a massive bailout of their sinking economy; a resumption of military assistance suspended in the past (including delivery of the F-16s); and sweeping new security assurances, including a theater missile defense system to protect them against Indian Agnis and Prithvis. In addition, they asked for renewed loans for the purchase of armaments and a U.S.-led diplomatic offensive to convince the Russians, French, and Israelis not to sell arms to India.

The reason why all these requests should meet with American favor, Sharif asserted, was that "a nuclear Pakistan must be very close to the United States." In other words, having done exactly what we had tried so hard to dissuade him from doing (that is, testing), his country was feeling all the more vulnerable—just as we had warned.

It was hard for Sharif to admit the dilemma in which he now found himself, he added, since the United States "has not always been a steadfast friend and, worse, it discriminates against us in favor of India."

ONE MORE ITEM loomed large on the Pakistanis' wish list. It was their version of the fifth benchmark: the need for American intervention to "solve" Kashmir once and for all. Nawaz Sharif and Shamshad Ahmad both hammered away at this point every time we met. If the United States would just devote ten percent of the energy to Kashmir that it was giving to the Middle East peace process, the prime minister kept saying, the world could "rest easy" about India and Pakistan having nuclear weapons, since the most likely cause for a war would be removed.

Sharif's proposal had two major problems. The first was the only one I mentioned to his face: in the case of the Middle East, both parties, the Israelis and the Arabs, wanted the United States involved; in South Asia, only Pakistan wanted to "internationalize"—and, more specifically, to Americanize—the process. The other more fundamental problem was that American mediation—or, as Sharif sometimes characterized it, "binding arbitration"—probably would not work, since the Pakistanis themselves seemed unlikely to accept the obvious solution that any outside mediator would probably recommend: the conversion of the Line of Control into an international boundary. Jaswant had already hinted at Frankfurt Airport that India might go for this idea, as long as it emerged from direct Indian-Pakistani talks and was not "imposed" by outsiders. Some Indians might hold out for "recovering" Pakistani Kashmir as well, and incorporating it into India, but they were on the fringes. In Pakistan, however, the paramountcy of righting what was perceived to be the historic wrong done both to Pakistan and to the Kashmiris was an article of faith. India's needs could be met by retention of what it had gained at the time of partition, while Pakistan had to recover what it had lost.

I did my best, with both Nawaz Sharif and Shamshad Ahmad, to dissuade them from linking progress on the CTBT to any other issue, especially Kashmir. Knowing how conscious the Pakistanis were of comparisons between their dialogue with the United States and the one that was under way with the Indians, I noted pointedly that Jaswant had assiduously avoided hinting at linkage; he had not even initiated discussion of sanctions relief in our sessions to date.

Stung, Shamshad replied, "We're *not* linking—we're just telling you our requirements if we are going to be able to do what you want."

BEFORE LEAVING PAKISTAN, Joe Ralston and I made the motorcade journey to Rawalpindi to see General Karamat. As in May, Karamat seemed more thoughtful and realistic than the civilians. He told us signing the CTBT and agreeing with India to limit missile deployments made sense. He barely disguised his exasperation with the government.

Nonetheless, he wanted us to face up to the extent to which the United States had squandered its influence with Pakistan over the past decade. The cutoff of spare parts for American-made aircraft, not to mention new planes, for Pakistan's aging air force was costing lives: there had already been eleven crashes so far that year. Another victim of the Pressler sanctions was a military training program that had for many years brought promising young Pakistani officers to the United States. Part of the purpose, in addition to teaching the students the art of war, was to inculcate in them a respect for American political values. Karamat himself had studied at the U.S. Army's Command and General Staff College at Fort Leavenworth in the early 1970s. He predicted that because of the suspension of the training program, he was probably its last Pakistani graduate who would rise to the position of chief of the army staff. His successor was less likely to be imbued with as much good will toward the United States or with as much respect for democracy and civilian rule.

It occurred to me at the time that perhaps one reason Nawaz Sharif appeared less worried about a military coup than other Pakistani prime ministers was that Karamat did not seem eager to leave the barracks and try his hand at running the country. In fact, he commented privately to Joe Ralston that he was sick of politics and would much rather be commanding troops along the Line of Control.

Joe and I rejoined our delegation at the airport and headed home with a stop in Tbilisi, the capital of Georgia. While we were holding meetings with President Eduard Shevardnadze and ministers of his government downtown, the sweltering July heat started to melt the tarmac and nearly trapped our Air Force jumbo jet at its parking slot. Fortunately, the crew—yet again ready for anything—saw what was happening and, much to the entertainment of ground staff and passengers waiting for commercial flights, had the aircraft towed up and down past the terminal for several hours so that it would not get stuck in the goo.

When our delegation returned to the airport and witnessed this scene, several of us had the same thought: our plane had to keep moving even while it was on the ground if it was going to have any chance of taking off. Much the same could be said of our diplomacy with India and Pakistan.

SIX

SOFT STONEWALLING

POPULAR AS POKHRAN II was with the Indian people, the government knew that it was in trouble with much of the rest of the world. One of the first chances to gauge whether the furor was dying down was the annual meeting of a group called the ASEAN Regional Forum (known by the infelicitous acronym ARF), to be held in Manila on July 26–27. Once the foreign ministers of ASEAN's own member states had met among themselves, they invited counterparts from around the Pacific rim to join them for another two days of discussion on regional security, trade, drug trafficking, human rights, and democratization. *

Early in 1998, before the nuclear tests in South Asia, India had been asked to join as a regular participant in the ARF, an important acknowledgment of India's influence and interests beyond its own region. After the tests in May, the ARF added nonproliferation to the agenda for the Manila meeting at the insistence of the Americans, Japanese, Australians, New Zealanders, and Chinese.

It fell to Jaswant Singh, as India's de facto foreign minister, to go to Manila. He knew he was in for a rough time, including from Secretary Albright.

---

*ASEAN stands for the Association of Southeast Asian Nations, which was then made up of Brunei, Cambodia, Indonesia, Laos, Malaysia, Myanmar (formerly Burma), Philippines, Singapore, Thailand, and Vietnam. The ASEAN regional forum included Australia, China, Japan, New Zealand, Russia, South Korea, and the United States, along with a representative of the European Union.

Jaswant had another reason for dreading the assignment. The ARF had a tradition that was intended to promote bonding among the participants and inject a bit of levity into their otherwise serious, often tedious, and sometimes tense proceedings. Every year, during the dessert course at the final dinner, each delegation was expected to put on a skit, replete with goofy costumes, silly hats, sillier songs, ukuleles, castanets—whatever it took to invoke hooting and hollering from a roomful of normally staid diplomats and politicians.

Jaswant, whose defining characteristic in public was a Spartan brand of dignity, was aghast at the prospect of having, literally, to sing for his supper. He knew that I had had some experience with the ARF, so during our talks at Hyderabad House in the third week of July, Jaswant asked for reassurance and advice. I could give him none of the former and only a bit of the latter. Four years earlier it had fallen to me to appear in one of these skits when I had to fill in for Warren Christopher at an ARF meeting in Bangkok. It had been one of the more indelible humiliations of my career. As judged by the applause meter, the American troupe, which was supposed to uphold the reputation of the world's sole remaining superpower (not to mention the land of Broadway and Hollywood), was runner-up for worst in show. The only bigger flop was a harmonica solo by the South Korean foreign minister, who, soon after he stood up and started to perform, either had an acute attack of stage fright or suddenly recovered his self-respect, and sat down.

With this memory seared in my brain, I urged Jaswant, in his own ARF debut, to avoid sobriety, hope everyone else did the same, and, even more important, avoid anything that smacked of *substance* in whatever stage number he concocted for the occasion.

He may or may not have done as I suggested on the first and second points but he definitely ignored my advice on the third. Perhaps he got a bit too much into the spirit of the evening, the highlight of which was a duet between Madeleine Albright and her Russian counterpart, Yevgeny Primakov, crooning to each other as Tony and Maria in *West Side Story*. It was a well-received encore for Madeleine, who had brought down the house the year before as Evita Peron with her rendition of "Don't Cry for Me, ASEANies."

When Jaswant's turn came, he took his place before the microphone, threw back his shoulders—very much a cavalry officer doing his duty on what he knew to be a ridiculous but unavoidable assignment—and dead-panned, a cappella, a patriotic hymn well known to all Indians (*"Yesterday's events are now a part of the past/ In the new era, we Indians will build a new future together"*), only with new lyrics, written by his staff for the occasion:

> Why such a fuss over a few crackers in the Thar?
> They weren't as loud as Nevada and Lop Nor.
> Sharif took his ones and joined the fun.
> Evita lost some sleep, Jiang proliferated in the sun.*

There were a few more verses, all rubbing it in: the rest of the world would just have to get over its hypocritical tantrum and learn to live with an India that had the bomb.

No one in the audience found Jaswant's performance amusing, least of all Madeleine. She had already spent much of her time in Manila fending off skeptical questions from her Australian, New Zealand, Japanese, and Chinese counterparts about what was really going on between Jaswant and me. They wanted to know whether, having led the charge in condemning the test in May, the United States was now going to let India off the hook. Fortunately, two members of my team, Bob Einhorn and Matt Daley, had flown out to Manila to brief the secretary on our meetings in New Delhi, so she was in a position to tell the other ministers that the American benchmarks were consistent with the P-5 and G-8 statements and that we were using the dialogue to maintain a solid front with the rest of the world.

IN A PRIVATE meeting with Jaswant in Manila, Madeleine, who was never one for pulling punches, decided to land one as soon as they sat down. "You lied to us," she said, "and democracies don't do that with each other." She was referring to the false sense of assurance Bill Richardson and Tom Pickering had gotten from George Fernandes and Krishnan Raghunath shortly before the test.

Jaswant's head snapped back in surprise. He took a moment to compose himself and said there was a difference between secrecy and deceit. Recriminations would only make it harder for India and the United States to find common ground. Madeleine should support his desire to remove the nuclear issue from the Manila agenda.

---

*As noted in chapter 1, the Thar, or the Great Indian Desert, is where Pokhran is located. Lop Nor was the Chinese test site; "Jiang" was Jiang Zemin, then president of China.

She refused. The Indian decision to test had been a "disaster," she said, and there was no use pretending otherwise. She added, however, that the United States would downplay its criticism in public and take a "forward-looking" attitude in the dialogue between Jaswant and me.

She also bore down on Kashmir and why, now more than ever, India and Pakistan had to get serious about finding a settlement—and so did the international community. Jaswant bridled. Everyone, he said, had to accept the reality in the region and stop trying to redraw the map.

When I heard about Jaswant's half of this exchange, it sounded like a combative expression of a potentially constructive position—and an echo of what he had said about Kashmir when he and I met in Frankfurt: accepting reality and no more redrawing of the map could mean conversion of the Line of Control into an internationally recognized boundary.

JASWANT AND I were next due to meet on August 23 in Washington. I hoped we would make enough progress for the president to travel to South Asia in the fall. But three unforeseen developments intervened.

The first was on August 7, when virtually simultaneous explosions tore through the U.S. embassies in Kenya and Tanzania, killing two hundred and thirty-four people, including twelve Americans. Retaliation was certain once the United States determined who, and where, the perpetrators were.

Ten days later, on August 17, Clinton went on television and admitted to having had a "relationship" with Monica Lewinsky. Republicans, who controlled both houses of Congress, demanded the president's resignation or, if he refused, his impeachment. The political damage to Clinton was immense and lingering. The personal effect on him was also, no doubt, profound and complex, but he kept it mostly obscured from his friends and aides. The day after Clinton's confession, I attended a meeting in the Oval Office about how the United States should respond to the bombing of its embassies. American intelligence services had put the blame on Osama bin Laden's al Qaeda network, headquartered in Afghanistan, which had declared a jihad "against Jews and crusaders." In assessing the evidence and deciding among the military options available to him, Clinton seemed completely focused on the task at hand.

Two days after that, on August 20, U.S. submarines and surface ships in the Arabian Sea launched a barrage of Tomahawk cruise missiles at al Qaeda training camps outside Khost in Afghanistan.[1] To reach their targets, the missiles had to fly over Pakistani territory. The administration tried to keep the Pakistanis in the dark about the plan, since their intelligence services were tied into the Taliban. The United States needed to catch bin Laden by surprise if there was to be any chance of killing him.

Joe Ralston had the awkward assignment of making sure that he was with General Karamat during the launch of the Tomahawks. That way, if the low-flying missiles showed up on Pakistani radar screens, Joe would be able to assure Karamat that they were not the first wave of an Indian sneak attack. Toward the end of a dinner at the VIP lounge at Islamabad airport, Ralston checked his watch and told Karamat that about sixty Tomahawks had just passed through Pakistani airspace en route to their targets in Afghanistan. Shortly after, he thanked his host for dinner, shook hands, and departed.

Karamat felt humiliated and betrayed. The next day his anger grew more intense when it was learned that one of the cruise missiles had gone astray and come down in Pakistan. Those that found their mark killed a number of Pakistani intelligence officers and trainees at the Afghan camps. These casualties were further cause for outrage in Pakistan, but they also confirmed Indian charges that Pakistan was officially supporting terrorism and the U.S. administration's need to keep the operation secret.[2]

The attack missed bin Laden by hours. Suspicions lingered for years afterward that even though the Pakistanis did not know exactly when the attack was coming, they may have known enough to tip off bin Laden.[3]

FOR THE REMAINDER of the administration, the U.S. government did constant battle against an enemy that waged a sporadic, hit-and-run war aimed primarily at Americans abroad. The United States undertook an array of offensive, defensive, and sometimes preemptive operations, many of them covert, often in concert with other governments.

Of the so-called functional bureaus in the State Department, the one dealing with counterterrorism virtually overnight became first among equals. From August 1998 on, the senior staff meetings that began my working day almost always included an update on terrorist threats and what we were doing to head them off.

Madeleine Albright was deeply involved in the day-to-day, White House–led effort to track bin Laden and stop him before he struck again.

That challenge shot near the top of the agenda of the Principals Committee, chaired by Sandy Berger and consisting of cabinet-level officials. Sandy also created a smaller group, dedicated to combating terrorism and consisting of senior officials from State, the Pentagon, the CIA and, occasionally, the FBI. During periods when intelligence showed an increased level of threat, this group met on a daily basis to ensure that the issue got the highest level of attention and coordination from all relevant agencies. Virtually whenever I went to the Oval Office or to the Situation Room in the basement of the White House, no matter what the principal subject—Russia, the Balkans, Iraq, or South Asia—the meeting was also used for an update on the hunt for Osama bin Laden and the steps the United States was taking to head off new attacks.

The new focus on terrorism had profound implications for South Asia policy. Al Qaeda was protected by an Afghan regime that was, in turn, supported by the Pakistani military and intelligence services. At the State Department, we now had to strike a three-way balance among the regionalists, who sought to maintain the best possible relations with (and thus the most leverage on) Pakistan; the nonproliferationists, who sought to curb the Pakistani nuclear program; and the counterterrorists, who wanted to use all available means of pressure and suasion to turn the Pakistanis against the Taliban and al Qaeda. Once again, the group of officials responsible for South Asia worked very much as a team. Rick Inderfurth threw himself into the task of impressing upon the Pakistanis that they must cooperate with the United States in stamping out al Qaeda and met with Taliban leaders at least twenty times in an effort to get them to expel bin Laden.[4]

As the division of labor among us was adjusted after the African bombings, I concentrated on trying to manage the Indian side of the equation. Indian officials had been telling us for years that the rise of bin Laden as a threat to the United States in the 1990s was the result of Washington's delusion in the 1980s that the Pakistanis and their jihadist protégés on the far side of the Khyber Pass could be U.S. allies in the cold war. Even before Jaswant came to Washington in August 1998, we knew that one of his messages would be "we told you so."

JASWANT ARRIVED JUST after the U.S. attack against the Afghan camps. The American media was in a frenzy of suspicion that the president was "wagging the dog" (manufacturing a national security crisis to divert attention from his personal and political troubles).

I invited Jaswant to my home on a Sunday afternoon so that we could talk alone for a couple of hours on the eve of the formal session with our teams the next day. I picked him up at the Watergate Hotel in Brooke's convertible sports car and brought him back to the house. The Indian reporters, who were conducting a stakeout in the lobby, went into a collective delirium over this latest indication of how splendidly Jaswant and I were getting along with each other. The truth, of course, had been more nuanced even before the multiple complications of recent days.

It was too hot for us to sit in the backyard, so Jaswant and I settled in the living room with cool drinks. He led off with a forty-five-minute disquisition on India's view of the world. The prelude was a history lesson that I had heard before, but never with quite so much intensity and detail. India, he said, had suffered the effects of radical Islam for fifty years, starting with the "vivisection of our country" (that is, partition) in 1947 and continuing through decades of Pakistani-backed incursions and acts of terror. Ninety-five percent of those incidents were carried out by foreign mercenaries from Afghanistan, the Arab world, and Sudan—the same gang, in other words, that was killing Americans in Africa and elsewhere.

Yet for all those years when India was under attack from Pakistan, the United States based its policy toward that country on "a grave error about its very nature": Pakistan had never really been a cohesive nation or a viable state and never would be; it was "an artificial construct, structured out of hate, a stepchild of Uttar Pradesh"—the Indian state where the pro-partition Muslim League had its roots.

Knowing of my own constant work with the Russians, he quoted something Yevgeny Primakov had told him at the ARF meeting in Manila: "The globe cannot live with a Talibanized Pakistan that has the bomb" (which was close to what Primakov had said to me the day after the Pakistani test).

Jaswant reminded me that India had warned the United States in the 1980s that by using Afghan holy warriors as proxies against the Soviet occupation forces, it was creating a "Frankenstein monster." Thus, the United States had already helped, however inadvertently, to generate the "malevolent energy" of the Taliban, which had already overrun

Afghanistan and was now on its way to overrunning Pakistan itself: "The Taliban is a creature of Pakistan, and now Pakistan is in danger of becoming a creature of the Taliban."

Why hadn't the East African bombings "made the scales fall from your eyes" about Pakistan as well? Why did the United States not abandon, once and for all, the dangerous notion of Pakistan as the linchpin of its policy in South Asia?

So as not to appear anti-Islam, Jaswant distinguished Pakistan from such moderate states as Malaysia, Morocco, Indonesia, and Bangladesh, with which India had relatively good relations.

As for India's own huge Muslim minority, Jaswant claimed that it had not been, since partition, either the source or the victim of systematic violence. Nor had homegrown Indian terrorism of any origin ever been directed against American diplomats. Yes, there had been "aberrations, tiny bubbles of irrationality" from time to time—which I took to be a reference to eruptions of sectarian bloodletting, some of them horrendous, such as the massacres of Sikhs in 1984. But India had maintained its "civilizational essence, its innate rationality, and its ability to absorb shocks."

I found myself thinking of Samuel Huntington's theory about the clash of civilizations.[5] Jaswant's variant was both ecumenical and Manichean. It posited the need for the Judeo-Christian West, secular India, and moderate Islamic states to make common cause against a single evil of global reach, rooted in radical regimes like Pakistan's and radical groups like al Qaeda.

WHILE JASWANT DID not come near the subject of the Lewinsky scandal and any concern about its impact on American foreign policy, he did refer pointedly to a pair of Republican senators who, during a recent visit to New Delhi, had publicly gloated about being able to thwart the Clinton administration on many issues, including its desire to get the CTBT ratified.[6] Jaswant said that these statements made it harder for him to steer his government toward a commitment to sign the treaty ("undoing the long-standing national campaign of demonization against the CTBT," he said, was like "trying to reverse the course of a giant battleship").

But the bigger problem, he continued, was America's refusal to recognize that the United States and India were on the same side in the war on terrorism—which meant we should be allies against Pakistan.

That was where Jaswant and I most sharply disagreed. For the United States to give up on Pakistan—to treat it as an enemy—would be to commit a folly far worse than the one he was accusing us of. Regarding Pakistan as no better than Afghanistan would increase the chances of it becoming so.

Jaswant protested that he had been misunderstood. Of course the United States must continue to nurture whatever chance there was of a moderate Pakistan—but it must do so in a way that was "realistic" rather than self-deluding.

While I was puzzling over exactly how that advice might translate into sensible practice, he shifted to a new, quite different critique of American policy. By depicting Osama bin Laden as Public Enemy No. 1, he said, "you have made an individual into an icon—a hero of Islamic militancy and radicalism." The U.S. military action had "utterly transformed the situation" in the region for the worse. We had "stirred up a wasps' nest" in South Asia. Violence, aggression, terrorism—these were all part of "a terrible evil visited upon our region that you in part helped come into existence." Then, after a pause, he added, "This is only the beginning."

Now I was totally stumped and told him so. It sounded as though he was *against* the U.S. attack on the al Qaeda targets in Afghanistan. Given his view of Islamic radicalism, I would have thought he would have approved of what we had done.

"Absolutely!" he replied. "You did the right thing, but you did it too late, and you did it without fully realizing the consequences or drawing the right implications." He acknowledged that the United States was in a Catch-22, but one of its own making.

Lest I miss the implications of all this for what he knew to be my hopes for the fall, he mentioned to me that Vajpayee had reached him by phone earlier in the day to stress that the "backdrop" of our dialogue had been "altered by what happened on August 20th at 11 p.m."—when the American cruise missiles slammed into their targets in Afghanistan. America's obtuseness about the organic bond between Pakistan and the Taliban, he said, offended and frightened many Indians. The idea of a broad-gauge commonality of views between the United States and India, to say nothing of a true strategic partnership, was now less plausible than before to those in New Delhi whose support Jaswant needed on the CTBT.

JASWANT HAD COME to Washington with a subliminal message in support of an overarching goal: to persuade the American government that unlike Pakistan, a democratic, socially cohesive, politically confident India could be trusted with the bomb. A nuclear-armed India was a natural ally of the United States in the struggle against Islamic fundamentalism, while a nuclear-armed Pakistan was a threat to both countries. Therefore the United States should back off its insistence on India's acceptance of the nonproliferation benchmarks—which he called the "four legs of the elephant"—and stop pestering his prime minister for a timetable that required a public commitment to signing the CTBT within a year.

All that was background for the letter from Vajpayee to Clinton that Jaswant had brought with him to Washington, which he showed me in my living room. Scanning it, I saw immediately the key sentence: "India will continue to engage constructively with key interlocutors with a view to arriving at a decision regarding adherence to the CTBT by the month of September 1999."

In short, there was no promise on signature. The Indian government had adjusted its strategy in the wake of the East African bombings: it was going to lie back and wait for the administration's suddenly heightened preoccupation with Islamic terrorism to replace its upset over the Indian nuclear program, even if that meant missing the opportunity for a presidential visit.

Concerned that the dialogue was turning sour and would be judged a failure, Jaswant suggested that we put the best face possible on our efforts by issuing a press statement or agreeing on an aide-mémoire that referred, vaguely, to "progress."

I replied that since there was no progress—indeed, there was backsliding—we should not try to kid the public or ourselves.

Jaswant's usual equanimity showed signs of cracking. I was being unfair and stubborn, he said. He referred again to the difficulties of Indian domestic politics. The United States was not helping by "overdoing" the linkage between the benchmarks and the presidential trip in the fall. A backlash had already begun. Now that American sanctions were in effect, Indian scientists in the United States were being expelled. Press coverage of their departures prompted day-in-day-out criticism of the Vajpayee government for not taking a tougher, more defiant line against the United States.

"If you try to make us move faster," he said, "everything we're trying to accomplish will come apart because of problems with our parliament."

"This is about leadership," I replied. "Your prime minister had no problem leading when it came to testing. Why can't he lead in dealing with the consequences of testing? Instead, we get a letter from him that is ambiguous, mushy, filled with weasel words—it sounds like a dodge more than a commitment; it amounts to one big 'maybe.' . . . This elephant can't walk. And it certainly doesn't deliver the mail."

I HAD ARRANGED in advance for Sandy Berger to join us toward dinner time. I wanted Jaswant to have a bit of direct (though off-site) access to the senior White House staff that he had not previously been granted. I also wanted Sandy to be able to assess, first-hand, what—and whom—we were dealing with on the Indian side. Sandy was my closest friend on the White House staff and the colleague there with whom I had the most frequent interaction. We were constantly on the phone with each other during working hours, often late at night as well, and no strangers to each other's homes on weekends. We often met for bagels and coffee on Sundays. We would watch the television talk shows and a Redskins game, talking a bit of shop during commercials or when the action lagged on the field.

The session with Jaswant at my house was both less casual and less pleasant than our usual Sunday get-togethers. After Jaswant summarized what he had told me, Sandy came down on him hard. Listening to Indians and Pakistanis talk about each other, he said, reminded him of dealing with the chronic crises in Northern Ireland and the Middle East: "Gerry Adams [the leader of Sinn Fein] wants to talk about David Trimble [the leader of the Ulster Unionist Party] and what the other guy has got to do to make peace; Netanyahu wants to talk about Arafat and what he's got to do, and vice versa. And now I find that all you want to do is talk about the Pakistanis. Let's talk about what *India* can do to make the situation better, both with Pakistan and with the U.S."

Jaswant replied with a shorter version of what he had said to me about Islamic radicalism. Sandy noted tartly, "Many people think there's Hindu radicalism in your country that's equally threatening," but he was careful not to depict India so much as a dangerous, unstable state as an otherwise admirable one whose government had made a dangerous, destabilizing mistake: Pokhran II had "loosened the moorings of the NPT regime at a time when irresponsible countries will use India's act as a pretext for them to test." As a result, the United States and India might lose the opportunity to make their relationship that of "two natural allies." Instead, he said, "we may be moving into a twilight zone."

It was in that context, Sandy continued, that Vajpayee's letter to Clinton was so disappointing: "I wouldn't even convene a meeting to discuss this proposal. From where I sit, the decision to pull the plug on the president's trip would be sad but easy. If the president decides to go anyway on the basis of what you've got here and because Strobe buys it, we'll call it the Talbott plan because I'm not taking any credit for it, and I promise you it'll be plenty controversial."

"Especially if it's called that," I interjected.

Jaswant, visibly taken aback by Sandy's vehemence, insisted that Vajpayee had made an "irreversible" decision to sign the CTBT—it was just a question of how and when to make that decision public.

"If he's made a decision," said Sandy, "then it should be easier for him to say it at the UN."

Jaswant urged Sandy not to look at the Vajpayee letter in a vacuum. The prime minister was constrained from going too far in public, but Jaswant was giving private assurances: "It would be ironic and tragic if the success of what we're trying to do all hinged on phraseology." The United States should make the most of what was the best India could do under current circumstances.

"We can't do that," said Sandy. "We can't take the vague words you've given us in writing and staple you to it and call that a commitment. The language has to stand on its own, and this language doesn't do that."

With Brooke joining us at the kitchen table for a dinner she had prepared, Jaswant and Sandy sought to lower the temperature and return to a more positive theme, which Sandy summarized: "We were, for fifty years, encumbered by defining the world in terms of communism versus democracy, applying the same template where it had no applicability—in effect putting India with the Soviets. Now we're liberated from all that. We've got a huge opportunity. Let's get on with it."

I'd said my piece and spent most of the meal listening.

THE NEXT DAY Jaswant and I met at the State Department with a small circle of our key colleagues. Yet again—as in Frankfurt and as in his first encounter with Madeleine Albright in Manila—Jaswant hinted that the one benchmark on which we might actually make some progress was the fifth: Indian-Pakistani relations, including Kashmir.

In preparation for his visit to Washington, the American team had put together a package of eight suggested confidence-building measures that would, if implemented, reduce tensions along the Line of Control and perhaps even lay the ground for direct negotiations on the terms of a settlement. To demonstrate my willingness to meet Jaswant halfway, I told him we might split the difference and include only four of the measures in the way we dealt with the fifth benchmark.

Jaswant waved this offer aside, saying, "We're beyond that. No need to play that game. We'll talk about Kashmir and we can do all eight steps at once."

He then repeated what he had told me in June about the possibility of making the Line of Control an international border.

I did not fully appreciate the significance of this statement at the time, mostly because I was focused on the lack of movement on the four nonproliferation benchmarks. What I did notice, however, was a point of contrast between this round and our first one, alone in my office three months earlier. On that occasion, he had not wanted to talk about Pakistan at all. This time it seemed to be the main thing he wanted to talk about.

AFTER JASWANT LEFT town, my colleagues and I flew to London to see Shamshad Ahmad. For the first time—and, as it turned out, the last—the Pakistanis seemed willing to move further and faster than the Indians on the nonproliferation agenda. Shamshad promised, on behalf of Nawaz Sharif, that Pakistan would "adhere to" the CTBT within a year. That verb form did not quite mean "sign," and Shamshad was cagey about how much Sharif would say in public at the UN.

Hoping to whet the Pakistanis' appetite for a presidential visit in the fall, Bruce Riedel told Shamshad that Clinton would like nothing better than to "show up in person and refute Sam Huntington—and his Hindu equivalents." He was referring to the line of argument we had heard from Jaswant and others that Pakistan represented a civilization-gone-bad with which India and the United States were both destined to clash.

While the meeting was far from conclusive, its tone and content were still more positive than what we had just heard from Jaswant. When I got back to my hotel just before midnight, I called Secretary Albright. Since we were on an open line and did not know who might be listening in, my report was brief and cryptic. I told her simply that the tortoise had caught up with the hare—and maybe even passed him; I added that her father (who had felt a certain sympathy for, and optimism about, Pakistan) would be pleased.

In early September, Jaswant and I were scheduled to cross paths at Kennedy Airport and arranged to meet in the departure lounge. I arrived first, straight off a transatlantic flight after a grueling trip with Clinton to Moscow, where the Russian economy and government were in apparent meltdown. I was so exhausted that I asked Bruce Riedel to take me on a brisk walk around the duty-free shops to keep me from falling asleep before Jaswant appeared.

When Jaswant showed up, he too was road-weary and a bit frazzled. Our meeting was strained and mercifully brief. For once, he had no desire to talk about the political or intramural challenges he was facing at home, and for just that reason I guessed that the difficulties he was coping with were even more complex and stressful than usual.

Jaswant was due to return to New York later that month to attend the UN General Assembly at which Prime Minister Vajpayee would be making his long-awaited statement on India's policy with regard to testing. I asked Dick Celeste to sound out Jaswant on whether we could hold another round of the dialogue in Washington.

Jaswant agreed, but with a barb. It was "convenient" for him to make a side trip to Washington, he said, since he wanted to pay a call on Jesse Helms, the chairman of the Senate Foreign Relations Committee. Even as Jaswant was imploring us to be sensitive to his government's dealings with its parliamentary opposition, he was, literally, going out of his way to meet with one of the administration's most powerful congressional adversaries—a senator, moreover, who scorned the CTBT.

Jaswant also asked Dick to pass directly to me what I took as an uncharacteristically peremptory message: "Tell Strobe that we must not quibble about the elephant's toenails while ignoring its four legs. . . . We have very different styles. You want everything in writing, I want to reach a general understanding."

Not surprisingly, that round of the dialogue, which took place the day before the Vajpayee speech, was a total bust, in part because Jaswant did not want to say anything in our channel that might undercut what his prime minister was about to tell the whole world.

NAWAZ SHARIF AND VAJPAYEE both gave speeches at the UN the last week in September, and they were just about what the administration had been led to expect. Using the same language I had heard from Shamshad in London, Sharif promised on September 23 that Pakistan would, within a year, adhere to the CTBT "in conditions free from coercion or pressure"—in other words, in exchange for the lifting of U.S.-led sanctions.

Vajpayee's formulation, when he went before the General Assembly the next day, was even more convoluted in its syntax and more conditional in its content:

> India, having harmonized its national imperatives and security obligations and desirous of continuing to cooperate with the international community is now engaged in discussions with key interlocutors on a range of issues, including the CTBT. We are prepared to bring these discussions to a successful conclusion, so that the entry into force of the CTBT is not delayed beyond September 1999. . . . These tests do not signal a dilution of India's commitment to the pursuit of global nuclear disarmament. Accordingly, after concluding this limited testing program, India announced a voluntary moratorium on further underground nuclear test explosions. We conveyed our willingness to move towards a de jure formalization of this obligation. In announcing a moratorium, India has already accepted the basic obligation of the CTBT.

Once again, like his letter to Clinton, this statement carefully avoided promising anything. It could even be read as a rationale for *never* signing the treaty, on the ground that in the absence of a binding international agreement, India's open-ended observance of its own moratorium discharged its obligation to be a responsible nuclear weapons state.

Without the hoped-for progress on the CTBT, there was no point in keeping open the possibility of a presidential visit to South Asia that fall.

Clinton wrote Vajpayee and Nawaz Sharif on September 30 informing them that the trip would have to be postponed.

The Indians were disappointed but not surprised. They found consolation in the U.S. Congress's passage of an amendment to the Arms Export Control Act, sponsored by Senator Brownback of Kansas, which technically allowed the president to waive a number of the sanctions but in fact encouraged him to do so. Brownback had no sympathy with the administration's attempt to use sanctions to induce progress on the CTBT, since he opposed the treaty. Besides, lifting sanctions would help farmers in his home state sell wheat, and it could earn him favor with the Indian American community as well.

THE CONGRESSIONAL FACTOR in U.S. policy toward India had changed dramatically. A few years before, the nonproliferationists on the Hill, led by Senator Glenn, had not only given the executive branch a big stick to use against India's nuclear weapons program—they had given us little discretion in how we used it. Now the combined forces of pro-India and farm-belt members of Congress, personified by Brownback, were taking that stick away from us.

We had heard reports that Vajpayee had gone ahead with Pokhran II confident that sanctions would start to erode after about six months because of congressional impatience to get back to normal. Here we were, approaching the six-month mark, and events were unfolding almost exactly as the Indians had hoped.[7]

I phoned Jaswant on November 5 to tell him that we would lift or waive some of the restrictions on loans and other financial assistance from U.S. commercial banks and government agencies (the Overseas Private Investment Corporation, the Export-Import Bank, and the Trade and Development Agency). Pressing his advantage, Jaswant asked why we weren't prepared to release our hold on loans from the World Bank and the Asian Development Bank as well. The reason, I said, was that we simply had not made enough progress in the dialogue. He replied, with a sigh audible over the phone, that he and I would just have to work all the harder in the weeks and months ahead.

There was another problem we would have to manage, I said: the United States was leaning toward using a one-year waiver of the Pressler sanctions that was authorized under the Brownback amendment to support emergency assistance to help Pakistan avoid a massive default on its debt and an implosion of its economy.

To my surprise, Jaswant said he understood that the financial collapse of Pakistan would be dangerous for everyone, including India, since it could lead to political instability. Especially after our heated disagreement over U.S. policy toward Pakistan in August, I took Jaswant's reaction as a sign that perhaps Indian policy might be shifting in a welcome direction.

A blast of protests out of New Delhi soon disabused me of that hope. Vajpayee and Foreign Secretary Raghunath denounced as "discrimina-tory" the U.S. decision to grant Pakistan more relief on sanctions than it was willing to give India. Ambassador Chandra told Rick Inderfurth and me that we should not be surprised by the drubbing we were taking from Vajpayee. State and local elections were imminent, and the Vajpayee gov-ernment had to be seen standing up to the United States.

Not for the first time and not for the last, Jaswant had gotten out in front of his government in his willingness to give the United States the benefit of the doubt.

IN THE WEEKS that followed, the overall tone of Indian public state-ments, including Jaswant's, began to turn tougher. The autumn issue of the journal *Foreign Affairs* carried an article by Jaswant called "Against Nuclear Apartheid." As the title implied, the piece charged the United States, along with the other NPT nuclear weapons powers, of practicing the geopolitical equivalent of racism in the name of nonproliferation.[8]

After consulting with Madeleine Albright and Sandy Berger, I decided to lay out our own side of the story. I picked up on a standing invitation from Richard Haass, the vice president for foreign policy stud-ies at the Brookings Institution who had worked on South Asia in the first Bush administration, to make a speech on policy toward the region. Both in the prepared text and in the question-and-answer period, I lim-ited myself to explaining the American rationale for the five benchmarks, all of which were public and derived from the various international reso-lutions passed after the tests in May. I stressed that while staying within the letter and spirit of the NPT, we had designed the benchmarks to be as consistent as possible with what India and Pakistan conceived as their rights and interests. I took care not to characterize the Indians' side of the dialogue or imply that they had accepted our proposals. I also sought to neutralize the argument that we were dictating terms to New Delhi and Islamabad or disregarding their security:

> We recognize that any progress toward a lasting solution must be based on India's and Pakistan's conception of their own national interests. We're under no illusions that either country will alter or constrain its defense programs under duress or simply because we've asked it to. That's why we've developed proposals for near-term steps that are, we believe, fully consistent with the security requirements that my Indian and Pakistani counterparts articulated at the outset of our discussions. . . . [W]hile universal NPT adherence remains our long-term goal, we are not simply going to give India and Pakistan the cold shoulder until they take that step.

The reaction to the speech in the Indian press was more or less what I had hoped for. A number of editorials and commentaries welcomed the glimpse I had provided into what was going on and expressed pleasant surprise that the Americans were not, as many Indians believed, dictating terms for unconditional surrender on the NPT.[9]

Whatever good the speech did in terms of public diplomacy was offset by the apparent damage it did to the effectiveness of our private channel—and perhaps to Jaswant himself. A few scattered press reports portraying what I had said as hectoring were exploited by his opponents, who claimed that the United States was waging a war of words. Vajpayee wrote a letter to Clinton complaining about what he characterized as a hardening of the U.S. position and a breach of the administration's agreement to preserve the confidentiality of the dialogue. Vajpayee's displeasure, I suspected, was stoked by those around him who were holding the line against any compromise on the CTBT and looking for evidence that the Americans were acting in bad faith.[10]

THERE WERE COMPARABLE suspicions on our side about what the Indians were up to. Since the first formal round of the dialogue, in Frankfurt in June, there had been skepticism about whether the Indian government had any intention of ever accommodating us on any of the benchmarks.

Between my sessions with Jaswant, Bob Einhorn led a team of experts in talks with their Indian counterparts. These so-called working groups were charged with trying to develop technically precise understandings on what it would take to jump-start the negotiations in Geneva over a fissile material cutoff treaty, what constituted the "minimum credible deterrent," and what India would have to do to bring its export controls up to world-class standards.

The Indians, however, were not trying very hard to make the working group worthwhile. After yet another fruitless round, Bob told me that, in his judgment, we were being subjected to "soft stonewalling."

There was a growing sense in Washington that Jaswant Singh's assigned role was to be the "smiling face" that the BJP was showing to the outer world, and that he was part of a campaign to divert attention from the party's hard-liners who were pursuing a nationalistic, even jingoistic and sectarian agenda, with all the ill that boded for religious conflict within India as well as more trouble with Pakistan.

I had another view of Jaswant. To me, the differences between him and BJP hard-liners like Advani were real, not tactical. Jaswant represented a more sophisticated, less militant, but no less firmly held view of Hindutva. I was supported in this belief by Frank Wisner and other India hands who pointed out that Jaswant came from Rajasthan, where a tradition of pride and independence coexisted with a willingness to reach a modus vivendi with others, rather than from the Hindu heartland, where Hindutva in its more aggrieved, vengeful, and vociferous forms had taken hold.

In his approach to diplomacy, Jaswant was a pragmatist, recalculating as he saw fit the trade-offs that might be necessary to achieve his goal. He would be prepared to push for progress on the nonproliferation agenda only if he became convinced that it was the most promising way to break out of sanctions, bring Clinton to India, and transform the relationship. Jaswant's principal goal was to see if he could get the United States to lift sanctions without India's having to meet any of the benchmarks. He was especially hoping to fend off pressure on the CTBT, since that benchmark was the most problematic for his government, as he had told me repeatedly. At the same time, he knew the CTBT was the benchmark of highest political value to the Clinton administration. If signing the CTBT turned out to be the price India must pay for an end to sanctions and a new era of good relations with the United States, I believe he would have risked his personal prestige and political capital to press for that outcome. Meanwhile, as we went from one round of the dialogue to the next, he would adjust the ratio of reassurance to caution in what he told me about the CTBT with several factors in mind: whether the United States was holding firm in its insistence on signature as a condition for major sanctions relief and for Clinton's trip to South Asia; what Jaswant's colleagues in the Finance Ministry were telling Vajpayee about the Indian economy's ability to withstand the effects of the remaining sanctions; and how much importance Vajpayee himself attached to a presidential visit.

At some point, Jaswant would decide whether to make an all-out push for CTBT signature. But we were not at that point yet, and therefore he was not going to make me any flat-out promises. When I pressed him on the need for a firm timetable on the CTBT, he would say, "At the end of the day, Strobe, you will not find us wanting." This refrain, like his proverb about not asking the way to a village if you did not want to go there, was an example of his predilection for double negatives that did not quite add up to positives.

I suspected that the end of the day, by his reckoning, was still several months off, probably in mid-1999, when Clinton would be looking to his own legacy, including a new opening to India. Jaswant probably hoped that when Clinton's desire to come to India was at its highest, the price India would have to pay for the trip would be at it lowest.

SEVEN

THE AVATAR OF EVIL

JASWANT SINGH AND I had to meet again, and relatively soon, if only to avoid the appearance that we were giving up on the dialogue and that U.S.-Indian relations were slipping back into their old rut. We arranged for our paths to cross the third week in November in Rome, where I had business to do with the Italian government. Jaswant could conveniently stop in Rome en route to London to see his publisher, Macmillan Press, who would be bringing out his latest book, *Defending India*, early the next year.[1] Accompanied by a few of our usual colleagues, we held a perfunctory plenary session at the Excelsior Hotel on November 19.

On the evening of November 20, Brooke and I met Jaswant for dinner in a rooftop restaurant in the Hotel Hassler just above the Spanish Steps with a spectacular view of St. Peter's, the Pantheon, and the Coliseum. Much of the conversation was about his book. He had completed the manuscript before Pokhran II and dealt with it only in a postscript, but the rest of the book reinforced India's defense of the test. Far from being a radical break with the nation's past or a betrayal of its traditional values, Jaswant wrote, the acquisition of nuclear weaponry was a logical next step in the evolution of India's sense of itself, its interests, and its "strategic culture"—a rite of passage, a loss of innocence about what it took to survive in a dangerous world. He traced the origins of BJP defense doctrine back to the earliest inhabitants of the Indus River valley through various kingdoms and sultanates that followed. The BJP's induction of nuclear weapons was an act of pragmatism and continuity; pacifism was aberrational and, in its own way, irresponsible.

One reason he had written the book, he said, was to make Hindutva, as the guiding idea of the BJP, more comprehensible and palatable to Western readers. As he saw it, Hinduism was not just the cultural bedrock of Indian civilization and identity but a big-hearted host to adherents of other religions as well. The Zoroastrians were welcomed in India when they were driven out of Persia (hence coming to be known as Parsees), and Jesuit missionaries, arriving in Goa and elsewhere along the west coast, were greeted by local Hindu rulers as "pandits," bearers of interesting new ideas about how to gain access to God.

This view of India's historic openness to the outside world clashed with recent headlines. Hindu militant attacks on Christians had increased in recent years, especially in Gujarat. Brooke, who had traveled in that state in the late 1960s, asked Jaswant how one should understand what was happening there and how it squared with his thesis.

The press reports, he replied, were a gross distortion of the facts. Besides, these were village feuds that happened to break down along religious lines—they were not religiously based killings as such. As for the communal massacres that attended partition in 1947, those tended to occur in the Punjab and areas directly under British rule, not in other regions, such as his native Rajasthan, which were ruled by local princes and therefore less contaminated by the divide-and-rule tactics of India's imperial masters.

This discussion was the most relaxed, open, wide-ranging, and intellectually stimulating of our encounters to date. Yet the more Jaswant elaborated on his thesis, the more resistant to it I became. There was, in what Brooke and I were hearing, either a denial of ugly facts, such as those she raised, or a resort to casuistry to blur their ugliness and call into question the accuracy of published reports. Insofar as the facts were indisputable, Jaswant assigned responsibility elsewhere—anywhere but to India and Indians. To wit, it was the Raj that had undermined the pluralism inherent in Hindu civilization; it was the Viceroy and the British government who were to blame for the bloodbaths of 1947–48.

I had heard others associated with the BJP revile Gandhi as a charlatan, an ambitious and angry man who fooled the world into thinking he was a paragon of serenity and love. Jaswant was far more subtle, but during our dinner in Rome and on other occasions, he did not disguise his impatience with the idea of Gandhi as the Mahatma. I suspected, though he never said so, that as much as anything, this was because Gandhi's name was associated with civil disobedience, turning the other cheek, peaceful resistance to brute force, and other ideas that were incompatible with the thesis of Jaswant's book and with India's decision to become a nuclear power.

I also found troublesome the way Islam fit into Jaswant's worldview— or, more to the point, the way it seemed to be inherently at odds with his concept of Hindu civilization. By implication, while Parsees, Christians, and others qualified as welcome additions to the Indian melting pot, Muslims did not. For example, in his paean to Hinduism, Jaswant noted how this most polytheistic of the world's great religions included a dizzy- ing array of female goddesses, thus proving itself egalitarian, in contrast to Muslim society, with its proclivity for male chauvinism and misogyny. Hinduism, over the millennia, had proved itself absorptive and hos- pitable, while Islam was all about conquest and conversion by the sword.

This sort of invidious oversimplification of Islam was—and would continue to be in the years that followed—an all too common feature of one side in the worldwide debate over the religious and cultural roots of terrorism. What concerned me, in hearing it from Jaswant, was what it implied about the BJP's ideology and therefore about the party's approach to governance. If someone as sophisticated as Jaswant saw Islam this way, it meant that there were surely many who held more primitive and virulent forms of his view.

The implications for India's relations with Pakistan were even more sobering. A number of Jaswant's patented phrases about Pakistan stuck in my mind for their vividness ("born of the same womb," for example), but one in particular stood out for its resonance with current events and its ominous ramifications for the future. On several occasions, including over that excellent meal with a glorious view of the splendors of Rome, he called Pakistan the "avatar" of all that was intolerant, aggressive, and terrorizing about radical Islam. India, by contrast, was the avatar of all that was benign, inclusive, and tolerant in Hinduism—and Hindutva.

Here was the stuff of which vicious cycles are made, especially now that both India and Pakistan had brought bombs out of their basements and were likely to brandish them at each other the next time there was a crisis.

THIS WAS THE second time Jaswant and I had delved into a nexus of subjects for which we had no talking points from our governments. The first had been in Brooke's and my living room and over our kitchen table in August. Strictly speaking, these conversations had no standing as part of the diplomatic business we were supposed to be transacting. Yet I sensed at the time, and certainly believe in retrospect, that our digressions from the subject of nuclear weaponry and nonproliferation were essential to whatever chance we had of fulfilling our original assignment, at least as broadly defined. Discussing, and debating, the core of the India-Pakistan dispute gave us a chance to break out of our official roles in a way that broadened and deepened what we—and our leaders—might be able to accomplish later on. When we were talking about nonproliferation, whether alone or in plenary, I was a spokesman for a U.S. administration that had a coherent policy that the Indians considered dogmatic and obnoxious. In that capacity, I had the job of scolding India for what it had done and setting the terms for what it must do to put the relationship on a better footing. Jaswant responded accordingly in his capacity as spokesman for an Indian government that felt an obligation to defend its sovereignty.

On the questions that dominated our talk over dinner in Rome, however, Jaswant was arguing from a position of advantage, not just by his own lights but by mine as well. He was, after all, an Indian and a Hindu who had lived all his life amid Muslims and next door to Pakistan, while I was from another country, another culture, and, for that matter, another civilization. For that reason alone, these informal, unofficial exchanges had political and diplomatic utility. After all, tensions between India and Pakistan were on our agenda in the form of the fifth benchmark, and those tensions were likely to get worse in the months ahead. When that happened, Americans might have a helpful role to play. And when *that* happened, the Indians' willingness to trust us would depend on their judgment about our motivations.

For fifty years, the working assumption in New Delhi had been that the United States was, for reasons of geopolitics, reflexive in its support for Pakistan. The purport of my end of the conversation in Rome was to persuade Jaswant that those days were over. Americans like myself had our disagreements with Jaswant and other Indians about political Islam (and, for that matter, misgivings about his concept of political Hinduism), and we certainly had our disagreements over how to handle Pakistan. But that did not mean we were still automatically on Pakistan's side in the zero-sum game of the subcontinent.

About two weeks later, Prime Minister Vajpayee made Jaswant minister of external affairs, a job Jaswant had been performing in all but title since the BJP took power nearly eight months earlier. Ironically, his promotion occurred in large measure as a result of a severe setback to the fortunes of the BJP. The party had been on the ropes through the fall, mostly because of popular discontent over such pocketbook issues as the skyrocketing cost of vegetables. On the hustings, BJP leaders kept trying to focus on national security, but to little avail. At a preelection rally in Jodhpur, in Rajasthan, when Vajpayee boasted that the nuclear tests had heightened India's prestige, angry voices in the crowd shouted complaints about the sevenfold increase in the cost of onions. At the end of November, the Congress Party's candidates trounced the BJP in a number of states where the BJP had been losing ground in recent years. With that setback behind him, Vajpayee concluded that he no longer had to indulge the BJP's right wing in its dislike of Jaswant, so on December 5, the prime minister formally turned over to his friend the ministerial portfolio that, until then, he had retained for himself.

But Jaswant's elevation did not enhance his willingness or his ability to push the CTBT through the government or the parliament. With him now formally in charge of India's foreign policy, militant members of the BJP were all the more on guard against any attempt he might make to reach accommodation with the United States. So were Sonia Gandhi and other leaders of a suddenly revitalized Congress Party. They wanted to remain on the side of the widespread popular sentiment in favor of India's continuing to stand up to the Americans.

In mid-December Jaswant gave a speech on the floor of the parliament defending the dialogue but promising that India would not move forward on the CTBT without a "national consensus." Ambassador Celeste cabled back to Washington that the Congress Party and public opinion would hold the government to that promise.

This latest obstacle to signature on the CTBT had, from our viewpoint in Washington, a look of artificiality. The BJP government had not felt obligated to seek a national consensus on testing. Our counterparts in New Delhi were selectively using their changing political fortunes as an excuse to keep the brakes on the sort of diplomatic progress the United States sought.

Now THAT JASWANT officially outranked me, I had some concern that the Indians' political sensitivities about our treating their officials as equals would require either that the dialogue be downgraded on the Indian side (that is, I would deal from now on with Foreign Secretary Raghunath) or upgraded on the American side (Jaswant would deal with Secretary Albright). However, when I called to congratulate him the day after his appointment was announced, he said, in effect, never mind protocol—we should carry on as before.

I checked with Madeleine to make sure she had no objection. She had her hands full with the Balkans, Iraq, and the Middle East peace process, and she assured me that she had no desire to take on another "problem from hell." However, she thought it might make sense to boost the level of American diplomatic attention that our government was giving to South Asia by accepting an offer Jimmy Carter had made to step in as a special envoy for the region.

This notion had come up during Nawaz Sharif's visit to the United States a few days before. During a conversation with Clinton in the Oval Office on December 2, Sharif renewed his long-standing appeal for Clinton to make an investment of personal energy in the search for a settlement to the India-Pakistan dispute comparable to the one he was making in the Arab-Israeli peace process. Clinton reminded Sharif of the salient difference: both parties in the Middle East wanted American involvement, while in South Asia, India adamantly rejected it. Clinton tried to get Sharif to focus on the nonproliferation agenda and on the need for Pakistan to get tough on the Taliban, al Qaeda, and Osama bin Laden.

During a trip to Atlanta the next day, Sharif asked Carter to volunteer as a mediator between India and Pakistan. Carter was tantalized. Madeleine, who went to Atlanta as well, thought the idea was worth pursuing. Carter, after all, had been the last president to visit South Asia twenty-one years before, in 1978, the same year he had brokered a peace agreement between Israel and Egypt. He had devoted his postpresidential career to numerous good causes—the eradication of trachoma, a preventable eye disease endemic in poor countries; the sponsorship of studies on how to prevent deadly conflict; and peacemaking missions that would earn him the Nobel Peace Prize in 2002. He had stepped up his diplomatic activity since Clinton assumed the presidency, partly because he expected Clinton, as a fellow Democrat, to be more welcoming of his help than Reagan or Bush had been, and partly because he felt the Clinton administration was too inclined to give up on negotiation and resort to military action as an instrument of its foreign policy.

In addition to the episode in 1994 (recounted in chapter 5), when Carter, along with Sam Nunn and Colin Powell, tried to cut a deal with Raoul Cédras, the military dictator of Haiti, the former president also volunteered, quite insistently, to talk sense to two other tyrants, Kim Il Sung of North Korea and Slobodan Milošević of Serbia.[2] In each instance, the view in the administration was that Carter's intervention, however well motivated, complicated a delicate and dangerous situation by giving Cédras, Kim, or Milošević hope for more flexibility in the U.S. position than we felt warranted. Carter had a noble but sometimes misplaced faith in the human capacity for redemption as well as an iron confidence in the powers of sweet reason and in his own powers of suasion.

Even though we had accepted some of his offers in the past, I felt it essential that we not do so in South Asia. A special emissary of great distinction and independent standing might favor a strategy and a set of criteria for what constituted a good deal that were different from those that guided the administration. But beyond that generic risk—the one I had stressed earlier in the year in talking Clinton out of the idea of making Sam Nunn the czar for South Asia—there was a more personal one: Carter did not altogether hide his lack of regard for Clinton's character and statesmanship, especially in the wake of the Lewinsky scandal. It was therefore even more questionable whether Carter would take direction from the president himself—not to mention, I added when discussing the idea with Madeleine, from the secretary of state.

She was not so sure. She felt the stakes were so high in South Asia that we needed to be open to bold ideas. Besides, she noted, her eyebrow slightly arched, we were not doing all that well in the Jaswant channel.

I couldn't dispute that. But whatever difficulties we had encountered to date were nothing compared to the uproar we would provoke from the Indians if we let Carter try his hand at peace brokerage between them and the Pakistanis—and at the request of Nawaz Sharif, no less.

There was one more reason for fending off the former president: the current one had made it plain that if an opportunity ever did arise for mediation between India and Pakistan, he had an interest in taking on that assignment himself.

That cinched it with Madeleine. "Okay," she said with a laugh, "the problem from hell is all yours."*

WITH THE RENEWAL of the mandate for Jaswant and me to keep talking to each other, I wrote him a letter on December 28 laying the ground for our next meeting, which was scheduled to take place in New Delhi about a month later. I had help from the India-Pakistan team in drafting the letter and made sure that everything I wrote had the support of the key agencies of the U.S. government (State, Defense, Treasury, and the National Security Council); but it was personal in tone, and Dick Celeste

*This was an all too common phrase in the Clinton administration, since we were dealing with many situations around the world that so qualified. It acquired a certain notoriety in 2002, when Samantha Power used "the problem from hell" as the title for her Pulitzer-prize-winning book on genocide.

While Sharif did not get his way on the appointment of Carter as a special presidential envoy with a mandate to mediate a settlement between India and Pakistan, he did get a consolation prize: two weeks after his visit to Washington, the United States finally resolved the issue of the F-16s by having the Treasury pay Pakistan $324.6 million in cash, plus millions more in agricultural goods and other items.

When the Indians learned through press reports that Carter's name had been floated as a special envoy, they expressed relief that nothing came of the idea. Several Indian commentators recalled that during his 1978 visit to their country, an open microphone picked up an exchange between him and Secretary of State Cyrus Vance in which Carter—a vigorous promoter of nonproliferation—said that as soon as they returned to Washington the United States should send a "cold and very blunt" letter to the Indians on the nuclear issue.

delivered it by hand, emphasizing its nature as an "off-line" communication. From my early days in the administration, I had found occasional communications of this kind helpful in giving my principal counterparts in foreign governments an idea of what to expect at our next meeting.[3]

The January session, I wrote, had "the potential to be a breakthrough, [but] it has the potential to be the opposite as well." I appealed for him to join me in imbuing the session with the spirit of a New Year's resolution: each of us would work within his own government to develop flexibility that might translate into "reciprocal and calibrated" progress on the nonproliferation issues that mattered to the United States and on further sanctions relief for India. Our goal should be an agreed timetable that linked Indian steps on the benchmarks with American alleviation of the sanctions. The pivotal point was still to be an announced commitment by Vajpayee to sign the CTBT. I concluded by alluding to the doubts within my own government about the Indians' good faith in continuing the nonproliferation dialogue:

> I sensed in Rome that there may be a belief on your side that Indian "patience," or "firmness" will translate into further American "concessions". . . . In other words, there may be a working assumption on your side that we, the U.S., don't entirely mean what we say about the four legs of the elephant being truly necessary for the animal to walk (at least with us on board)—that perhaps he can be mobile on two legs (CTBT and export controls). That is quite wrong: if we're still looking at a two-legged beast after the upcoming round in New Delhi, then we—both of us—will need to think quite differently about the challenge of the year ahead; we'll need to lower our sights and, instead of aiming for a breakthrough, aim at management of mutual disappointment. I stress *mutual* disappointment: we'll be disappointed at the prospect of India keeping all its strategic options open, and you'll be disappointed at the continuation of sanctions.

JASWANT, MEANWHILE, WAS on the defensive at home for having entered into the dialogue in the first place—and for having stuck with it in the face of American adamancy on nonproliferation. George Fernandes and others within the government made barbed comments in public to the effect that Jaswant did not have much to show for all his globe-trotting to meet with me. Others in the press and the vigorous pro-nuclear lobby accused him of worse than wasting time—he was, they suggested, giving in to American pressure.

In early January Jaswant gave an interview to *India Today* defending himself against both lines of attack. The dialogue had been more useful than might be apparent on the surface, he asserted, because it had given India a chance to "harmonize" its relations with "the world's great powers in areas wherever it is possible to do so." Besides, he added, "resolving presupposes conflict. Harmonizing denotes an understanding, an acceptance of the sovereign right of a nation to decide its national interest. . . . Let us not always have the worm's eye view—let us attempt to have the eagle's vision; after all, they both inhabit the world."

Asked if he had been disappointed at not getting the foreign minister's portfolio earlier, when, as the interviewer put it (accurately), "the RSS had your name knocked off Atal Bihari Vajpayee's original cabinet list," Jaswant answered:

I was not [disappointed]. My name was given to me by my parents. It doesn't get knocked off. Let me only say that the graveyards of the world are full of those who thought they were indispensable to the nation. I am not indispensable. . . . I might have shed my uniform but I am still a soldier, soldiering along. A soldier does what he is asked to do. I will be a soldier diplomat among other diplomats soldiering for India.[4]

Meanwhile, Indian newspaper columnists, often citing anonymous sources inside the BJP government, were chiding Jaswant for his frequent references in interviews to "my friend Strobe." The suggestion was that Jaswant had gone soft.

The charge was ludicrous. Jaswant was as hardheaded and tenacious an advocate for his government's position as I had ever encountered. He knew his brief inside out and he stuck to it. He had no use for glad-handing and happy talk, and he could be quite stern when laying down his bottom line or taking me to task for mine.

Jaswant may have played up the "my friend Strobe" line to give himself more room to maneuver both diplomatically and politically. It fit with his preferred depiction of what was going on between us as an exchange of views that was less formal and less binding than a traditional negotiation. Also, by accentuating the personal nature of his relationship with someone known occasionally to have the ear of the American president, Jaswant may have been trying to lend the channel a touch of mystique to shore up his influence with his prime minister. He probably needed all the reinforcement he could get for his position, given the extent and intensity of resistance to any deal within the bureaucracy, the BJP party apparatus, and the military and scientific elite. Far more than mine, Jaswant's task within his government was lonely, thankless, and difficult—that much I could see every time I went to New Delhi.

I suspect that Jaswant's insistence on continuing to refer to me as a friend in public, even if it made him a target for backstabbing, was a bit like his refusal to take guff from the RSS. He could be just as thick-skinned and stiff-necked with critical countrymen as with high-handed Yankees.

From my standpoint, Jaswant's talk about our being friends had the additional virtue of being true. I made no secret of feeling the same way about him. I occasionally took some ribbing from my colleagues, although it was rare, private, and good-natured. My comeback was simple: the task of engaging India was a lot easier if one had an engaging Indian to work with.

IN MID-JANUARY 1999, the United Nations' under secretary general for disarmament and nonproliferation, Jayantha Dhanapala, a Sri Lankan diplomat of great skill and perseverance on behalf of what often seemed a losing cause, called on me in Washington. He was worried that India was wearing the Clinton administration down and would get rewards in the form of sanctions relief that it did not deserve. That anxiety was widely shared among governments like Australia, Ukraine, Brazil, and South Africa that had forsworn nuclear weapons and were counting on the administration to hold firm in the dialogue.

They were right to worry. The administration's grip on the levers that allowed it to apply pressure on India was slipping. With every passing month, the U.S. Congress was more impatient to lift the remaining sanctions. The administration faced the same problem with several foreign partners, especially fellow nuclear weapons states. Of the seven governments in the G-8 that had the power to continue blocking international lending to India, the administration had solid support only from the Japanese and the Canadians.*

The French, in particular, were champing at the bit to reopen loans to India from the World Bank and other financial institutions, and they had some support from the Italians as well. In September 1998, during a visit by Vajpayee to Paris, President Jacques Chirac had announced that France would conduct its own "strategic dialogue" with New Delhi. Both France and India regarded this new channel as a way of tweaking Uncle Sam's nose. The French thought they had found, in India, a partner in their effort to build what they called a "multipolar" international system—that is, one in which a strong, largely French-led European Union would offer an alternative to the "unipolar" world headquartered in Washington. The Indians, who nurtured their own resentment at what they saw as American bossiness, did nothing to discourage the French strategy.

In addition to portraying themselves as more understanding of India's security concerns than the Americans, the French dangled the possibility that India might, with French help, become eligible for nuclear assistance of the kind forbidden to non-NPT states. If that happened, India would have hit the jackpot in the gamble it took with Pokhran II: not only would it have ridden out the sanctions imposed after the test and shattered the solidarity of international opposition to its recent action—it would have broken free of the restrictions that resulted from its long-standing refusal to join the NPT.

Seeing France and Italy breaking ranks, the United Kingdom and Germany showed signs of being tempted to step up the pace of restoring to normal their own relations with India. While not quite ready to let bygones be bygones, they seemed inclined to lower the bar for sanctions relief as much and as soon as possible, and to do so in return for the most modest of progress on the benchmarks.

Given the erosion of both domestic and international support for its position, the Clinton administration concluded that in order to keep the

*While the G-8 had formally come into existence at the Birmingham summit in 1998 with the admission of Russia as a full member, the G-7—Canada, France, Germany, Italy, Japan, the United Kingdom, and the United States—still existed, primarily at the level of finance ministers, for purposes of dealing with international economic and monetary matters and therefore for overseeing the multilateral development banks.

G-7 and the U.S. Congress from pulling the plug entirely, we had to maintain the appearance of progress in the dialogue. That meant being prepared to take some steps of our own toward sanctions relief if there was anything at all that could plausibly be called progress when Jaswant and I next met.

The Indians could see the administration's dilemma with great clarity and with high confidence that they could use it to their advantage.

I FLEW TO New Delhi on January 29 with a team augmented, as in our first trip there the previous July, by Joe Ralston, whose airplane this time provided no exciting moments en route.[5]

The three days that followed were tough going in all respects and in all settings—in the courtesy calls Dick Celeste and I made on Vajpayee and the two leading opposition figures, Sonia Gandhi and Inder Gujral, and in the appearances I made at think tanks, foreign affairs groups, and press conferences. Even more than in my first meeting with her six months before, Sonia Gandhi made clear that the Congress Party wasn't going to allow the appearance of any daylight between itself and the BJP on the nuclear issue. Previously, she had been merely diffident and evasive on the subject; this time she was steely—or, as I remarked to Dick, "almost Indira-like."

Even the one public ceremony I attended was, literally, chilling. Jaswant invited me to join him at the Beating of the Retreat, a lengthy and impressive feature of the annual Republic Day celebrations. It takes place on a mammoth square on the Rajpath, which runs from the President's (formerly the Viceroy's) Palace to the India war memorial near Hyderabad House. At dusk, against a backdrop of cavalry on camels arrayed with rigid precision along the walls of the palace, gloriously costumed honor guards and bands perform close-order drills and play a medley of martial music and patriotic hymns.

That particular January evening, it was all quite spectacular. So was the drop in temperature as the sun went down. I was dressed, stupidly, in a lightweight suit and had neither a sweater nor an overcoat. For more than two hours, I thought I might freeze to death in the service of my country. By the time I finally staggered back to the delegation's hotel, my body was putting me on notice that there was trouble ahead.

Fortunately, I was attended by a liveried twenty-one-year-old personal butler named Arun, who came with the VIP suite in the Maurya Sheraton. Dressed in his white tie, starched collar and tails, he was quick to clean and press my own considerably less classy wardrobe. This perk occasioned much hilarity among my traveling companions from the State Department, especially my chief of staff, Phil Goldberg. I put up with their merciless teasing on the condition that they not let word get back to Washington about the arrangement.

Truth be told, that night after the Beating of the Retreat ceremony, I was mighty glad to have Arun around. Instead of making me the usual cup of tea, he dosed me up with Thera-Flu and continued to do so over the days that followed. His ministrations spared me, I'm sure, a roaring fever to contend with during the hardest and most frustrating set of meetings to date.*

EXPLOITING THE OPPORTUNITY presented by the near-mutiny that the administration was facing both on Capitol Hill and in the G-7, the Indians shifted their tactics in a way that was intended to create the impression of progress but that had the effect, when judged analytically, of dramatizing the impasse between us on key issues. Rather than simply continuing to stall, they informed us of their willingness to take partial, conditional steps on two of the benchmarks. In return, they asked for a large, immediate, and irrevocable reward.

Jaswant said that India would sign the CTBT by the end of May. If this were actually to happen, it would be a significant development, but it would still leave ratification of the treaty for the indefinite future. When I pointed this out, Jaswant assured me that under the Indian system, signature was tantamount to ratification, which he called "a mere formality." Signing, he added, carried a "higher degree of finality" than was the case in the United States—a subtle but unmistakable dig, since even though President Clinton had signed the CTBT more than two years earlier, the U.S. Senate had so far refused to ratify it and might never do so.

---

*About the time I left government, in early 2001, I got an e-mail out of the blue from Arun wishing me well and updating me on his career: he had made his way to California and, despite the slump in Silicon Valley, had found a job in high tech.

The second adjustment in the Indian position was a statement that they might join the long-sought, elusive moratorium on the production of fissile material—but only on the condition that the other six countries (the P-5 plus Pakistan) that had tested did likewise. When I pressed Jaswant for an announcement of this intention, he demurred, saying that the parliament would "bay for my blood" if he accepted America's "counsel" in this regard, presumably because it would appear that he was beginning to crack under American pressure.

Indian promises were still voiced only in private, couched in the future conditional tense, and riddled with escape clauses. About halfway through the round, I asked to see Jaswant alone and told him that our diplomacy risked proving Zeno's paradox on the logical impossibility of ever reaching any destination—in this case, our village—especially if we moved by half-steps and sidesteps rather than full strides.[6]

In fact, however, it was a moment that dramatized the difference between the Indians' preferred destination and ours. It also underscored the quandary in which the Clinton administration found itself: political forces in both Washington and New Delhi were pushing in the same direction—toward a breakdown in sanctions without a breakthrough on nonproliferation.

THE JANUARY ROUND was most discouraging on the question of whether—and, if so, when and how—the Indians would limit their nuclear arsenal.

While India's signature on the CTBT was the benchmark of greatest symbolic value, a policy of moderation and predictability in their nuclear weapons and ballistic missile programs was the most important. If the Indians (and, in response, the Pakistanis) pulled out all the stops in developing and deploying the bomb, it would not much matter whether they adhered to a test ban. Nor would they probably do so, since they would likely conclude they needed to test new and improved bombs for all the different missiles they had developed.

What we had called at the outset of the dialogue the pursuit of a "strategic restraint regime" was, as Bob Einhorn put it, "the Big Biryani." It had also been, from the beginning of the dialogue, the biggest sticking point, and it would continue to be so until the end. Whenever the subject came up, the Indians would give us a runaround, even on what term to use. Early on, the Indians objected that "regime" sounded too coercive, so we started referring instead simply to "strategic restraint." They complained that "restraint" sounded too restrictive, so we switched to calling it merely "defense posture," on the grounds that we did not care as much about the label as the results.

In fact, the semantic dispute flagged an obstacle that was both theoretical and practical: if the Indians would not even *call* what they were doing the acceptance of a regime or the application of restraint, it was all the less likely that they would ever agree to act in a way that fit that description. The Indians did not want to say anything substantive about their long-term plans lest they appear willing to close off options for the future or to be negotiating with the United States on subjects of vital national interest. Nor, for that matter, did we Americans want to enter into a formal negotiation on how many bombs they would have, since that would be to abandon our own position of principle that the right answer was zero. Our goal was to get them to tell us in the dialogue, and eventually tell the world, about their defense doctrine and weapons development plans in a way that made good on Vajpayee's vow to his own parliament in August 1998, reiterated at the United Nations a month later, and reaffirmed to Dick Celeste and me when we called on him in January 1999: India aspired to having a "credible minimum deterrent." We constantly played this formulation back to the Indians and urged that they give the word *minimum* concrete—and, indeed, *credible*—meaning.

In a phone call to Vajpayee just before I went to New Delhi, Clinton stressed this point largely so that I could invoke his name when I made it to Jaswant. "As your prime minister heard directly from our president," I said, "our principal overall concern is defense posture. I hope you and your colleagues will take special account of the American view that failure to come to terms on this benchmark—or, worse, India's adoption of policies that are manifestly inconsistent with the concept of credible minimum deterrence—would bring our entire process to a halt and set us back to where we were last May."

On that occasion, and every other one when we tried to draw the Indians into a discussion of what their prime minister's three words meant, they either changed the subject or, in Jaswant's case, with exquisite courtesy, told us to mind our own business.

Occasionally, he did so in public. In his *India Today* interview on January 11, 1999, Jaswant said: "Minimum deterrence is not a physical quantification. It is not a fixity. It is the enunciation of a fixity. The principle is in contrast to cold-war phraseology. It is to be determined in accordance with the reality of an assessment of the security situation. And as the security situation alters with time, the determination of minimum deterrence also alters."

To some, that may have sounded like just another display of his gift for elegant obfuscation, but not to me, Bob Einhorn, or our colleagues who parsed everything said by any Indian of authority on these matters. Jaswant was reassuring his own watchful constituencies and putting us on notice that he would not let the outcome of the dialogue tie India's hands in any respect.

He said as much to me face to face in New Delhi: we Americans would have to be patient with our Indian friends; as with everything else we were talking about, India would come up with its own answers to questions about its security. In due course, the Indian government would produce a nuclear doctrine that would be consistent with what we were hearing.

It was the most pertinent example of soft stonewalling we experienced.*

STILL, AS BOTH Jaswant and I had known coming into the meeting, I had to give him something. I told him that the United States was prepared, in response primarily to the pledge of signature on the CTBT in the spring, to release forthwith its hold on a $210 million World Bank loan for the construction of several power plants in the southern Indian state of Andhra Pradesh. This would be the first time since the nuclear tests that the United States permitted money to flow to India for anything

*One ancillary area where we did make some progress during the January 1999 round concerned China. I suggested to Jaswant that I send to New Delhi the State Department's highest ranking China expert, Susan Shirk, a professor of Chinese studies who was on leave from the University of California at San Diego while serving as a deputy assistant secretary of state in the bureau of East Asian affairs. Her assignment was to meet with Indian government and academic experts and compare assessments on Chinese strategic capabilities and intentions. Consultations of the kind she would conduct were virtually unprecedented in U.S.-Indian relations, and they might help improve the atmosphere and perhaps also inject a bit of realism into India's exaggerated view of the Chinese menace. Jaswant took me up on the suggestion, and Susan's subsequent travels did seem to have a salutary effect. Asia hands in the Indian foreign ministry found that their analysis of what was going on in China and what it meant for the future was not that different from ours.

other than "basic human needs," primarily food and medicine. Once the Indians actually signed the CTBT, the United States would resume support for full-scope lending by the multilateral development banks; when the Indians went public with their still-private commitment on fissile material, we would shorten the list of Indian companies and other entities covered by U.S. unilateral sanctions; and when they implemented stricter export controls, we would permit the reestablishment of some government-to-government dealings and military collaboration.

Our Andhra Pradesh decision was substantial in value and immediate in effect. In exchange for the promissory note the Indians had given us with regard to the CTBT, we were giving them a down payment in cash. Yet the Indians turned up their noses and asked for more relief on a faster timetable with fewer strings attached. They seemed to think that rather than making any real concessions of their own they could simply wait for further erosion of support for sanctions in the U.S. Congress and in the G-7—and I feared they were right.

As WE FLEW to Islamabad to talk to the Pakistanis, we expected an even less productive round than we'd had in New Delhi, and that is exactly what we got.

In a working lunch at the prime ministerial residence, we tried to persuade Nawaz Sharif and his senior aides to accept a version of what the Indians had grudgingly agreed to: a promise of early signature on the CTBT in return for some international sanctions relief, plus a few Pakistan-specific sweeteners such as an easing of restrictions on official and military contacts. In one of the wilder and more frustrating diplomatic encounters I ever experienced, Nawaz Sharif agreed to this deal, only to let himself be talked out of it by Sartaj Aziz, the former finance minister who had taken over as foreign minister in August, and Shamshad Ahmad. By the end of the lunch (uneaten, in my case), Sharif was letting himself be used as a mouthpiece for a set of demands, clearly drafted by the foreign ministry, that the United States could not possibly meet: across-the-board sanctions relief and resumption of virtually all military sales.

It was another dramatization of both the difference between Shamshad Ahmad and Jaswant Singh as the American government's dialogue partners—and of Nawaz Sharif's weakness and malleability, even at the hands of his own subordinates. The experience left us more concerned than ever that any deal we might make with Sharif would be picked apart by his minders.

The stop in Islamabad was even more ominous in another respect: The Pakistanis dodged our efforts to stop their illicit import-export business in the most lethal technology. We had been, for several years, monitoring the activities of Abdul Qadeer Khan, the arch-proliferator who was lionized in Pakistan as the father of the country's bomb and the moving force behind its missile program. He made frequent trips to Pyongyang, and his laboratory at Kahuta was said to have contracts with various North Korean agencies. There was no question that North Korea had provided the No Dong missile to Pakistan, which the Pakistanis had converted into their own Ghauri. We suspected that there may have been a quid pro quo: in exchange for helping the Pakistanis acquire the missiles, North Korea may have gotten Pakistani nuclear weapons technology. Several years later evidence emerged that Khan was also involved in other countries' quests for covert nuclear weapons, including Iran, Libya, and Iraq.[7]

Clinton had told Nawaz Sharif on several occasions that this sort of activity had to stop, most recently during a visit Sharif made to Washington in early December 1998. Sharif did not so much deny what was happening as profess ignorance about it.

When I followed up with him in Islamabad, Nawaz Sharif replied with a carefully hedged promise: there would be no transfer of nuclear weapon or ballistic missile technology or data to the North Koreans. I pressed for termination of the full range of Pakistan's military transactions with Pyongyang, since otherwise we would end up haggling over what was permissible and what wasn't.

Sharif turned evasive. Once the North Koreans realized they were not getting access to useful Pakistani military secrets, he said, they would sever the relationship themselves and contacts would "ultimately" end. That wasn't good enough, I said: *ultimately* had to mean *immediately*.

Nawaz Sharif replied plaintively that he could not go that far. Pakistan, he said, had legitimate defense requirements with regard to its conventional weaponry that it could meet only through trade with North Korea. But the United States could rest assured that whatever interaction continued would not be in the area we were worried about.

Not good enough, I insisted. *All* interactions had to stop.

Sharif shrugged and lapsed into silence with that same cornered, hangdog look that I remembered from my first meeting with him in May.

AFTER ISLAMABAD, I stopped briefly in Paris to meet with Gerard Errera, a senior official of the Quai d'Orsay who was France's representative in its own dialogue with India. Errera's Indian counterpart was Brajesh Mishra, who seemed to be keeping a wary eye on Jaswant's dialogue with me and making sure that India made the most of its relations with the more lenient members of the G-7.*

Errera came close to confirming American suspicions about what France was up to. He all but rolled his eyes as I reviewed the American approach, then sighed heavily and recommended a more "realistic and mature" strategy: the United States should join France in cultivating India as a "strategic counterweight to China"—a breathtaking suggestion, given how obvious it was that France was offering itself to India (and many other countries around the world) as a commercial and diplomatic alternative, if not a counterweight, to *l'hyperpuissance*, a term that Foreign Minister Hubert Védrine had coined to deride what he saw as America's penchant for bossing others around.[8]

ON THE HOMEWARD leg of what felt by then like a very long journey, I wrote Madeleine Albright and Sandy Berger a memo with my assessment of where we stood. I frequently resorted to messages of this kind from the road. They were less formal and more candid than the dry, mostly verbatim cables that my staff or the local embassy drafted and that were widely distributed around the government back in Washington. My personal reports for Sandy and Madeleine were intended to give them the flavor and significance of the meetings, and composing them helped me sort out my own impressions and think through next steps. In this case, I let my exasperation show:

> Our three days of talks in Delhi, while more productive than the stop in Islamabad, reminded us that the Indians are moving slowly and crabwise, and on one of our benchmarks [strategic restraint], there's either no movement or movement in the wrong direction. . . .

*Four meetings of the Indian-French dialogue took place from September 1998 through 2000.

In addition to Indian and Pakistani stubbornness . . . , there are some complicating factors that put a bit of a dent in the purity and persuasiveness of our own position. There's China, which treats India with total contempt and shows no sign of making our work any easier. . . . There's our difficulty with the Senate on CTBT, which invites the Indians and Pakistanis to withhold ratification on their part if and when they do sign. There is squishiness on the part of several of our fellow P-5 and G-8 colleagues, especially (surprise!) the French, who are undercutting our South Asia diplomacy as part of their grand strategy of taming the mighty and obnoxious 'hyperpower.' . . . There are the rogues [Iran, Iraq, Libya, and North Korea], who are beavering away on their own nuclear and missile programs. There's Israel, which both the Indians and the Pakistanis mention pointedly from time to time, albeit from rather different perspectives and with different motives.

And then there's the uncertain state of domestic politics in both countries. In Delhi, our team had the distinct impression that we were dealing with a nearly lame duck government. The flip side is that when we met with Sonia Gandhi, we had the equally strong sense that we were dealing with one very confident lady—someone who treated the conversation as though it were a briefing for an issue she might deal with quite soon in another capacity.

As for Pakistani politics, they're a different sort of mess: a mix of fecklessness and fear—fear of each other, of us, of their neighbors (on several sides). At least in Jaswant we've got an interlocutor who's working the problem; in Shamshad I've got one who is fighting the problem.

Put all this together, and I guess we should count ourselves lucky that we have anything to show for eight rounds and eight months.

THE ONLY GOOD NEWS—which was very good indeed—was that, suddenly, the Indians and Pakistanis seemed to be doing well in their dealings with each other. During my stay in New Delhi, the Pakistani cricket team was playing in India for the first time in twelve years. When the Pakistanis won a match in Chennai (previously known as Madras), the Indian crowd gave them a standing ovation as they ran a victory lap around the stadium. Meanwhile, the two foreign secretaries, Krishnan

Raghunath and Shamshad Ahmad, were making headway on some procedural issues that might lead to institutionalized contacts, and Vajpayee
and Nawaz Sharif were talking by phone on a regular basis.

It was announced that Vajpayee would personally travel by bus to inau-
gurate a route between New Delhi and Lahore as the only road link
between India and Pakistan. In the region, Vajpayee's gesture was widely
hailed as comparable to Richard Nixon's trip to China in 1971 and Gorbachev's opening of the Berlin Wall in 1989, and it was universally seen
as a stunning symbol of Vajpayee's personal willingness to go the extra
mile for reconciliation.

To all appearances, Sharif was ready to reciprocate. He saw Clinton at
the funeral of King Hussein of Jordan on February 8, shortly after Vajpayee's intention to take the bus journey had been announced. Clinton
urged Sharif to be as responsive as possible to Vajpayee's extraordinary
initiative. Sharif promised to do so, but he hinted that he might face some
resistance from unnamed politicians back in Islamabad—or, more likely,
military officers in Rawalpindi.

On arrival in Lahore the third week in February, overriding the objections of BJP hard-liners, Vajpayee made a moving speech at a monument
commemorating the decision of the Muslim League nearly sixty years
earlier to commit itself to the creation of Pakistan. He held a summit
with Sharif, and the two released a joint declaration that sounded promising: "Recognizing that the nuclear dimension of the security environment
of the two countries adds to their responsibility for avoidance of conflict,"
India and Pakistan were committed to implementing "in letter and spirit"
the Simla Agreement of 1972, which had established the Line of Control in Kashmir.

Now there was what seemed to be dramatic progress on the fifth
benchmark. Moreover, India and Pakistan had embarked on this sudden
burst of promising developments on their own. That was the way the
Indians wanted it. It looked as though, just as they had so often said, they
would not need any help from the United States in dealing with their
neighbor.

EIGHT

FROM KARGIL TO BLAIR HOUSE

AMERICAN DIPLOMACY IN South Asia went into a hiatus for the first six months of 1999 while the BJP fought to stay in power and the United States went to war in the Balkans. For more than a year, the regime of Slobodan Milošević had brutalized the ethnic Albanian Muslim majority in Kosovo, a province of southern Serbia. From mid-January, when Serb forces carried out a massacre in the village of Račak, through early June, the foreign policy apparatus of the American government was busy mobilizing an international coalition against Serbia, shepherding the necessary decisions through the NATO political and military command structures, conducting a seventy-eight-day bombing campaign, coping with a massive refugee crisis in neighboring countries, and imposing a settlement that required Milošević to pull his forces out of Kosovo so that NATO and the United Nations could take control of the province.

My assignment was primarily to deal with the Russians. They were apoplectic over the war, but after much head knocking they agreed to use their influence to force Milošević to capitulate. For five months, I traveled to Europe on an almost weekly basis.

I was able to intersect with Jaswant only once, at the end of May. That meeting, held in the parlor of the Indian ambassador's residence in Moscow, was both in substance and atmosphere, our worst. Mercifully, it was also one of our shortest. I was by then in a chronic state of jet lag.

I was operating without the benefit of my usual India-Pakistan traveling team and had trouble shifting gears mentally from my negotiations with the Russians, which were, at that point, going badly.

Jaswant's mind, like mine, was on the Balkans, although he had an entirely different set of concerns. The U.S.-led air war against Serbia, conducted without a formal authorizing resolution by the United Nations Security Council (primarily because of the threat of a Russian veto), had aroused opposition in India and elsewhere to the perceived tendency of the United States to play self-appointed sheriff in High Noon–like face-offs with villains like Milošević. Jaswant used the occasion to give me a Dutch-uncle treatment on the need for the United States to show more respect for international opinion.

I was just as glad to debate Kosovo with him, since there was not much to talk about on our usual agenda—and for the usual reason: Indian domestic politics. The BJP-led coalition had collapsed in mid-April after narrowly losing a vote of confidence engineered by the Congress Party. Neither party had been able to form a new government, so the BJP hung on in a caretaker capacity until new elections could be held in late September. That meant parliament would not convene again until October.

So much for the possibility of Indian accession to the CTBT by September 1999, a prospect that Vajpayee had held out to the world in his statement of intent to the UN the previous year. More immediately, the political paralysis in India meant that there would be no Indian signature on the CTBT that spring.

For the first and only time in our dealings, Jaswant had made a promise that he would now not be able to keep. He told me in Moscow that he had made an honest and determined commitment on the CTBT, failing to anticipate "the vagaries of our democracy." I believed him then, and I still do. Nonetheless, his embarrassment and regret contributed to the grimness of his mood.

SO DID THE state of relations between India and Pakistan. The "spirit of Lahore" had given way to armed conflict in the snowbound peaks of the Himalayas. A major reason was a change of command in Rawalpindi. The previous October, Nawaz Sharif had forced Jehangir Karamat into early retirement after Karamat proposed the creation of a National

Security Council as an institutional means of providing more formal input from the armed forces into policymaking, especially now that Pakistan was a nuclear power.

It quickly became apparent that the new chief of the army staff, Pervez Musharraf, had even less regard for Sharif and the civilian political leadership than his predecessor Karamat. In particular, Musharraf found the Lahore summit galling. He was one of the millions of Muslims who had been born in what was now India and left during partition. Like so many of his fellow officers and, for that matter, many of his countrymen, he was a revanchist on the issue of Kashmir. He also nurtured an undying bitterness over the dismemberment of Pakistan in 1971, in which India had played a powerful role in support of Bangladeshi secession. He had told Indian classmates at the Royal College of Defence Studies in 1990 that the only way there could be peace between the two countries would be if Pakistan recovered its lost territory and lost honor. He yearned, he said, for the day when he would be in a position to launch a military campaign across the Line of Control.[1]

Musharraf's chance came near the tiny town of Kargil, about five miles on the Indian side of the line. The Pakistani military had been eyeing Kargil as a target of opportunity for some time, in part because it was on the only road between the Kashmiri summer capital Srinagar and the town of Leh in the far northeast of Kashmir near the Chinese border. Since 1997 there had been a pattern of Pakistani incursions in the Kargil area that often triggered bursts of sniper fire and occasional artillery exchanges. The conditions in winter made patrolling the mountain ridges and manning border posts all but impossible. Every year Indian and Pakistani forces pulled back during the harshest months and returned in the spring. By soldierly convention, the two sides had refrained from major attempts to alter the status quo during the ebb and flow of seasonal deployments.

In the early spring 1999, however, Pakistan seized Indian positions above Kargil. Pakistani forces crossed the line and settled in at positions as high as seventeen thousand feet. Most of the infiltrators slept in tents, while a few luckier ones occupied an Indian post that had been abandoned for the winter. They thus acquired a militarily advantageous (though otherwise miserable) perch on the commanding heights over the road connecting Kargil with the valley below. In early May, New Delhi grew alarmed when an Indian reconnaissance unit spotted a column of ten suspicious-looking men in long black coats threading their way along a ridge.

Indian efforts to dislodge the infiltrators prompted Pakistani shelling that hit an ammunition dump in Kargil. Many residents fled, and Pakistan used the ensuing pandemonium to send in reinforcements. By the end of the month, the town had to be evacuated, and the initial skirmishing had grown into a full-fledged border conflict involving infantry assaults, artillery barrages, and aerial operations including attacks on ground positions by helicopter gunships. The Pakistanis shot down two Indian MiGs and moved regular army troops into the Kargil area to construct bunkers on the Indian side of the line.

As casualties mounted, Vajpayee came under withering criticism at home for having let himself be double-crossed by Nawaz Sharif.

Subsequent inquiries, conducted by the Indians but credited by the United States, established that the Pakistani thrust was more than just a serendipitous exploitation of the winter stand-down: it was a preplanned probe mounted by the Pakistani military and intended to create a "new" Line of Control more favorable to Pakistan.[2]

THE AMERICAN GOVERNMENT followed the conflict with growing alarm. The biggest danger was that the Indians would launch an onslaught of their own across the Line of Control. It was conceivable that while mobilizing for all-out war, Pakistan might seek support from China and various Arab states, while India would perhaps turn to its old protector Russia and even to its newer partner Israel. The result could be an international free-for-all in which all the wrong outsiders would be looking for ways to score points against one another rather than concerting their energies to pull the combatants back from the brink of what could easily become a nuclear cataclysm.

Imagining the worst was easy. Doing something to prevent it was not. The Pakistanis were still pretending that the trouble along the disputed frontier had been caused by local freedom fighters provoked by India's depredations in Kashmir, while the Indians professed that they had the matter well in hand and wanted no help from the United States or anyone else.

At the end of May, the two sides were at least beginning to exchange messages that did not explode on impact. That gave the United States an opening to offer its good offices. Rick Inderfurth and Tom Pickering began meeting regularly, and talking bluntly, with the Pakistani and Indian ambassadors in Washington, and Secretary Albright made phone calls to Nawaz Sharif, Jaswant Singh, and the British foreign secretary, Robin Cook. In all these dealings, Madeleine, Tom, and Rick put the blame squarely on Pakistan for instigating the crisis, while urging India not to broaden the conflict.

During the first week in June, just as Milošević was acceding to NATO's demands over Kosovo, Clinton turned his own attention to India and Pakistan. In letters to Nawaz Sharif and Vajpayee, the president went beyond the studied neutrality that both prime ministers were expecting—in Pakistan's case with hope, and in India's with trepidation. Clinton made Pakistan's withdrawal a precondition for a settlement and the price it must pay for the U.S. diplomatic involvement it had long sought. Clinton followed up with phone calls to the two leaders in mid-June emphasizing this point.

I WAS STILL deeply involved in the messy and suspenseful aftermath of the Kosovo war. Russian diplomacy had played a positive role in induc-ing Milošević to pull his forces out of Kosovo, but that contribution almost turned to dust when the Russian military made a mad dash to establish a foothold near the main airport. The Russian forces were act-ing independently—and in defiance—of NATO, which was charged with providing security in the province so that the UN could take over. It took most of June to avert a confrontation and work out an arrangement for Russian troops to serve as part of the NATO-led peacekeeping operation.

In the midst of shuttling between Moscow and allied capitals, I spoke several times with Jaswant by phone about the Kargil crisis. He expressed muted, cautious, but unmistakable relief that this time the United States was tilting in India's direction rather than Pakistan's.

THE EXCHANGES BETWEEN Indian and Pakistani officials sputtered through June while the fighting between military units intensified along a widening front. Indian forces were suffering terrible losses as they tried to fight their way up steep mountainsides against well-dug-in Pakistani positions. Mid-month, the Indians upped the ante by firing on targets on the Pakistani side of the Line of Control.

American experts following the war were more worried than ever that the Indians would attempt an end run, punching through the line at one or more points where they would have the advantage of terrain and supply lines. India's restraint in not exercising this option almost certainly cost it additional casualties around Kargil.

The United States condemned Pakistan's "infiltration of armed intruders" and went public with information that most of the seven hundred men who had crossed the Line of Control were attached to the Pakistani Army's 10th Corps.

In late June Clinton called Nawaz Sharif to stress that the United States saw Pakistan as the aggressor and to reject the fiction that the fighters were separatist guerrillas. He sent Tony Zinni, the Marine general in charge of the U.S. Central Command, to reinforce the message in person to Musharraf and Nawaz Sharif. Tony warned Musharraf that India would cross the Line of Control itself if Pakistan did not pull back. Musharraf professed to be unimpressed. Sharif kept Tony waiting overnight before granting him a meeting, then put on a display of hand-wringing reminiscent of the experience Tony and I had had in May 1998 when we went to Islamabad in a forlorn attempt to dissuade him from testing.

Back in Washington, the administration let it be known that if Sharif did not order a pullback, we would hold up a $100 million International Monetary Fund loan that Pakistan sorely needed. Sharif went to Beijing, hoping for comfort from Pakistan's staunchest friend, but got none. The U.S. embassy in Islamabad reported that he came home desperate.

We did not know whether Sharif had personally ordered the infiltration above Kargil (doubtful), reluctantly acquiesced in it (more likely), or not even known about it until after it happened (possible). But there was no question that he now realized it had been a colossal blunder. Pakistan was almost universally seen to have precipitated the crisis, ruining the promising peace process that had begun in Lahore and inviting an Indian counteroffensive.

Through our ambassador in Islamabad, Bill Milam, who had replaced Tom Simons, Sharif begged Clinton to come to his rescue with a plan that would stop the fighting and set the stage for a U.S.-brokered solution to Kashmir. Clinton, who was finally breathing easier about the transition from war to peace in Kosovo, had plunged back into the task of trying to untangle a new complication in the Northern Ireland peace process.*

On Friday, July 2, Sharif phoned Clinton and pleaded for his personal intervention in South Asia. Clinton replied that he would consider it only if it was understood up-front that Pakistani withdrawal would have to be immediate and unconditional. He then telephoned Vajpayee to report on Sharif's request and his own reply. For someone we thought of as a man of few words, Vajpayee was voluble in his anxiety that Sharif would deceive or co-opt Clinton.

I called Jaswant to reinforce Clinton's assurance that under no circumstances would the United States associate itself with any outcome that rewarded Pakistan for its violation of the line, and Sandy Berger did the same thing with Brajesh Mishra.

As I headed home at the end of the day, I ran into Bruce Riedel, who had come over from the White House to the State Department to consult with Rick Inderfurth.

"Well," I said, "I guess another weekend bites the dust."

"Yep," he said. "Let's just hope the only fireworks are in this country."

THE NEXT DAY Sharif called Clinton to say that he was packing his bags and getting ready to fly immediately to Washington—never mind that he had not been invited. Clinton decided on the spot that he could not say no without losing whatever chance there was of helping to defuse the crisis. He warned Sharif not to come unless he was prepared to announce unconditional withdrawal; otherwise, his trip would make a bad situation worse.

The Pakistani leader did not accept Clinton's condition for the meeting—he just said he was on his way.

"This guy's coming literally on a wing and a prayer," said the president.

"That's right," said Bruce, "and he's praying that we don't make him do the one thing he's got to do to end this thing."

Clinton again called Vajpayee, who was more worried than ever that Sharif's prayer would come true.

Presidential protocol made hurried preparations to put Sharif and his entourage in Blair House, the official guest quarters across Pennsylvania

---

*The Unionist leader, David Trimble, was refusing to endorse the inclusion of Sinn Fein in the government until the Irish Republican Army committed itself to disarm.

Avenue from the White House. The Secret Service felt it necessary to close the area to the tens of thousands of tourists flocking into the capital for the Fourth of July celebrations.

During that hectic day, we got word that Sharif did not have time—or perhaps did not have enough support from the Pakistani military—to arrange for an aircraft to bring him to Washington. He boarded a Pakistan International flight that normally flew from Karachi to New York but would make a special stop at Dulles Airport to drop off Sharif and his retinue. In addition to his advisers he was bringing his wife and children with him. That news caused us to wonder whether he was coming to seek an end to the crisis or political asylum.

IT WAS NOT hard to anticipate what Sharif would ask for. His opening proposal would be a cease-fire to be followed by negotiations under American auspices. His fallback would make Pakistani withdrawal conditional on Indian agreement to direct negotiations sponsored and probably mediated by the United States. Either way, he would be able to claim that the incursion had forced India, under American pressure, to accept Pakistani terms.

After several long meetings in Sandy Berger's office, we decided to recommend that Clinton confront Sharif with a stark choice that included neither of his preferred options. We would put before him two press statements and let Sharif decide which would be released at the end of the Blair House talks. The first would hail him as a peacemaker for retreating—or, as we would put it euphemistically, "restoring and respecting the sanctity of the Line of Control." The second would blame him for starting the crisis and for the escalation sure to follow his failed mission to Washington.

ON THE EVE of Sharif's arrival, we learned that Pakistan might be preparing its nuclear forces for deployment. There was, among those of us preparing for the meeting, a sense of vast and nearly unprecedented peril. We had all lived much of our lives with the danger that the cold war could turn into a global thermonuclear holocaust, and we remembered those thirteen days during the Cuban missile crisis in the fall of 1962. But by and large, the U.S.-Soviet relationship had been stable, in significant measure because an existential threat translated into existential deterrence. As we had argued assiduously in our dialogue with the Indians, there was no reason for confidence that anything similar would keep something like the Kargil crisis from touching off nuclear war between India and Pakistan. Quite the contrary, everything we had seen in years past between those two countries, and everything that had happened in the past several weeks, made that possibility real.

SANDY AND BRUCE arranged for Bandar bin Sultan, a member of the Saudi royal family and the kingdom's ambassador in Washington, to pick Sharif up at the airport. Bandar, the dean of the diplomatic corps, was a wily, well-connected power broker throughout the Greater Middle East and the Islamic world. He would use the car ride into town to soften up Sharif for the president's message. After dropping Sharif at Blair House, Bandar told us that we should be prepared to deal with a man who was not just distraught about the crisis but terrified of the reaction from Musharraf and the military if he gave in to American pressure.

When Clinton assembled his advisers in the Oval Office for a last-minute huddle, Sandy told him that overnight we had gotten more disturbing reports of steps Pakistan was taking with its nuclear arsenal.* Clinton said he would like to use this information "to scare the hell out of Sharif." I telephoned John Gordon, the deputy director of central intelligence (the first colleague I had called on May 11, 1998, after learning about the Indian nuclear test), and asked him if we could refer to the latest reports in broad-brush terms that would not compromise our sources and methods of intelligence-gathering. John said it was completely up to the president.

Sandy told the president that he was heading into what would probably be the single most important meeting with a foreign leader of his entire presidency. It would also be one of the most delicate. The overriding objective was to induce Pakistani withdrawal. But another, probably incompatible, goal was to increase the chances of Sharif's political survival. "If he arrives as a prime minister but stays as an exile," said Sandy, "he's not going to be able to make stick whatever deal you get out of him." We had to find a way to provide Sharif just enough cover to go home and give the necessary orders to Musharraf and the military.

*Madeleine Albright was in Europe over the Fourth of July holiday.

I agreed with the objective as Sandy had framed it, but I added a caution. Even though Clinton would be meeting the prime minister of Pakistan in the most intense, high-stakes circumstances imaginable, he must keep his Indian audience in mind. We were finally making headway with the Indians—not in getting them to address our concern over the future of their nuclear weapons programs, but in allaying their doubts, accumulated over fifty years, about whether we would take their security interests properly into account, especially when push came to shove with Pakistan.

The Kargil crisis had probably shattered Vajpayee's willingness to deal with Sharif. But it might also have created an opportunity for us Americans to show that we could conduct our own dealings with the Pakistanis in a way that protected, and even advanced, India's interests. Therefore, whatever the president was able to accomplish with Sharif, it was crucial that he avoid confirming the Indians' suspicions about our motives. They would be scrutinizing every word that came out of Blair House for evidence that we had fallen into a trap the Pakistanis had set for us—or, worse, that we were colluding with the Pakistanis to force India into negotiating on Kashmir under duress. Providing Sharif with political cover was fine, as long as what we were covering was Pakistan's retreat from the mountaintops.

The Indians would be deeply suspicious of anything that happened at Blair House, so it was essential that the president give Vajpayee personal updates on the talks as they unfolded.

Rick Inderfurth and I had two other pieces of advice for the president, based on our own experience with the Pakistanis. First, the more Foreign Minister Sartaj Aziz and Foreign Secretary Shamshad Ahmad participated in the meeting, the less productive it would be. We had seen on several occasions, most dramatically in early February, how this tag team kept tackling Sharif, preventing him from making concessions or pulling him back from ones he had already made. Second, under no circumstances should Clinton let Sharif insist on a true one-on-one, without at least one other American present. Unless there was a presidential aide taking notes, Sartaj and Shamshad would subsequently put their own spin on what transpired between the two leaders, attributing to Clinton commitments he had not made while denying ones that Sharif had made. We felt the most productive format was two-on-one—Clinton plus

Bruce Riedel, in his capacity as the White House's senior regional expert. If the Pakistanis objected, too bad: Clinton was the host, so it was his call.

Bruce added that if Clinton chose to tell Sharif that we knew his military was already taking steps toward deployment of nuclear weaponry, it was particularly important that Shamshad not be within earshot, since he was known to have close ties to the Pakistani military and the intelligence services.[3]

ONCE WE ARRIVED at Blair House and ushered the weary and visibly tense guests into the sitting room on the first floor, Clinton pulled out an editorial cartoon by Jeff MacNelly from that day's *Chicago Tribune*. It showed Indian and Pakistani soldiers waging a ferocious artillery battle at close quarters from atop two giant nuclear bombs.

I had the impression that Sharif was paying little attention, since he already knew what he was going to say—and we had all heard it before: if Clinton would just devote one percent of the time and energy he had put into the Middle East, there would be no crisis. (It was another sign of his desperation that in earlier appeals he had said ten percent.) He added that India was to blame for the crisis since it had carried out an incursion of its own fifteen years before.*

"I'm a moderate and forward-looking person," said Sharif, in a tone more pleading than boasting. "I have an historic mandate and want to take bold decisions to rid the region of this curse. I'm flexible—India is not." He needed Clinton's help in getting India to move from its uncompromising position. Otherwise, he would be pushed aside and Islamic hard-liners—comparable, he said, to the Hindu militants who were now in charge in India—would come to power in Pakistan.

Clinton refuted Sharif's depiction of the Indians, especially Vajpayee, as instigators of the crisis and intransigents in the ongoing standoff. The Indian prime minister had been more than flexible in going to Lahore—

---

*In April 1984, the Indian army sent its army and air force (using special helicopters that operate in extremely thin air) to the Siachen Glacier in Kashmir. The India-Pakistan border along the glacier had not been demarcated, nor, until then, occupied by military forces. Pakistan soon sent troops of its own into the glacier region, but India already had the high ground. Troops from both countries have remained there ever since, deployed as high as 21,000 feet. Over two thousand Indians have died, mostly from the extreme cold. When the Pakistanis made their move above Kargil, they were hoping to take a page from the Indian book.

he had taken a "risk for peace" (a phrase that Clinton often used in extolling Yitzhak Rabin of Israel, and in exhorting Rabin's Arab neighbors and his successors as Israeli prime minister).

"If you want me to be able to do anything with the Indians, I've got to have some leverage. Only withdrawal will bring this crisis to an end." A Pakistani military pullback across the line had to be unlinked to American diplomatic intervention in the Kashmir dispute: "I can't publicly or privately pretend you're withdrawing in return for my agreeing to be an intermediary. The result will be a war. Plus, I'll have sanctioned your having crossed the Line of Control. I can't let it appear that you held a gun to our head by moving across the line."

Clinton was playing back to Sharif virtually the same words that Vajpayee had used with him in their phone conversation an hour or so earlier.

Instead of relenting, Sharif made the matter worse: "I'm prepared to help resolve the current crisis in Kargil, but India must commit to resolve the larger issue in a specific time frame"—that is, negotiate a settlement on Kashmir under the pressure of a Pakistani-imposed, U.S.-sanctioned deadline.

Clinton came as close as I had ever seen to blowing up in a meeting with a foreign leader: "If I were the Indian prime minister, I'd never do that. I'd be crazy to do it. It would be nuclear blackmail. If you proceed with this line, I'll have no leverage with them. If I tell you what you think you want me to say, I'll be stripped of all influence with the Indians. I'm not—and the Indians are not—going to let you get away with blackmail, and I'll not permit any characterization of this meeting that suggests I'm giving in to blackmail."

Since Sharif had run through the Pakistani version of half a century of conflict in South Asia, Clinton decided to respond with a history lesson of his own. He drew from John Keegan's *The First World War*, which he was reading. European generals and politicians stumbled into World War One when "military plans went onto auto pilot and the diplomats couldn't do anything to stop it. We can't get into a position in which India feels that because of what you've done, it has to cross the Line of Control itself. That would be very dangerous. I genuinely believe you could get into a nuclear war by accident."[4]

Suddenly, Clinton switched from chastising Sharif for the reckless stupidity of Kargil to complimenting him on his earlier contribution to a moment of diplomatic promise. "You had the Lahore process under way. That was great. But if I'm going to do any good for you, I've got to have a restoration of the integrity of your position"—that is, a return of Pakistani forces to their side of the line, and a return of Sharif to the Lahore process.

Then Clinton edged toward giving Sharif one thing he knew he wanted: a signal of American willingness, under the right circumstances and with Indian acceptance, to help in that process.

"I've been fighting with the Irish for the past week," he said. "I haven't had any sleep because of the time difference and I'm on the phone with those guys constantly. I've only got a year and a half left [in office]. I'm committed to working on this, on going to India and Pakistan. But it can't appear that I've agreed to do anything just to get you to withdraw. If you announce you're withdrawing in response to my agreeing to mediate, India will escalate before you even get home, and we'd be a step closer to nuclear war. If you hold out for a date certain [for a resolution of the Kashmir dispute], you would have made a terrible mistake in coming here. . . . What I am prepared to support, however, is a resumption and intensification of the Lahore process and a commitment on the part of the U.S. to work hard on this."

Sharif, just as we had expected, asked for a one-on-one. Sandy and I got up to leave and escorted Shamshad Ahmad and Sartaj Aziz out with us. To the visible consternation of all three Pakistanis, Bruce stayed behind. Sharif repeated, tartly, that he had asked to talk to the president privately. Clinton said he wanted a record of their talks so there would be no misunderstandings afterward. Avoiding the sharp looks of his two advisers, Sharif grudgingly assented.

Once the rest of us were out of the room, Sharif reviewed what he portrayed as his unstinting effort over the past month to work out a deal with Vajpayee that would feature the trade-off between Pakistani withdrawal and a timetable for resolution of Kashmir. His version of events was neither coherent nor, insofar as we could reconstruct and check it afterward, consistent with what we understood to be the facts. The point, however, was clear enough: he had to have something to show for his trip to Washington beyond unconditional surrender over Kargil. Without some sort of face-saver, the army, egged on by fundamentalists back home, would overthrow him.

THE CONVERSATION HAD already convinced Clinton of what he feared: the world was closer even than during the Cuban missile crisis to a nuclear war. Unlike Kennedy and Khrushchev in 1962, Vajpayee and Sharif did not realize how close they were to the brink, so there was an even greater risk that they would blindly stumble across it.[5]

Adding to the danger was evidence that Sharif neither knew everything his military high command was doing nor had complete control over it. When Clinton asked him if he understood how far along his military was in preparing nuclear-armed missiles for possible use in a war against India, Sharif acted as though he was genuinely surprised. He could believe that the Indians were taking such steps, he said, but he neither acknowledged nor seemed aware of anything like that on his own side.

Clinton decided to invoke the Cuban missile crisis, noting that it had been a formative experience for him (he was sixteen at the time). Now India and Pakistan were similarly on the edge of a precipice. If even one bomb were used . . .

Sharif finished the sentence: ". . . it would be a catastrophe."

He then tried again to expel Bruce from the room, but Clinton waved the request aside and returned to the offensive. He could see they were getting nowhere. Fearing that might be the result, he had a statement ready to release to the press in time for the evening news shows that would lay all the blame for the crisis on Pakistan.

Sharif went ashen.

Clinton bore down harder. Having listened to Sharif's complaints against the United States, he had a list of his own, and it started with terrorism. Pakistan was the principal sponsor of the Taliban, which in turn allowed Osama bin Laden to run his worldwide network out of Afghanistan. Clinton had asked Sharif repeatedly to cooperate in bringing Osama to justice. Sharif had promised to do so but failed to deliver. The statement the United States would make to the press would mention Pakistan's role in supporting terrorism in Afghanistan—and, through its backing of Kashmiri militants, in India as well. Was that what Sharif wanted?

Clinton had worked himself back into real anger—his face flushed, eyes narrowed, lips pursed, cheek muscles pulsing, fists clenched. He said it was crazy enough for Sharif to have let his military violate the Line of Control, start a border war with India, and now prepare nuclear forces for action. On top of that, he had put Clinton in the middle of the mess and set him up for a diplomatic failure.

Sharif seemed beaten, physically and emotionally. He denied he had given any orders with regard to nuclear weaponry and said he was worried for his life.

WHEN THE TWO leaders had been at it for an hour and a half, Clinton suggested a break so that both could consult with their teams.

The president and Bruce briefed Sandy, Rick, and me on what had happened. Now that he had made maximum use of the "bad statement" we had prepared in advance, Clinton said, it was time to deploy the good one. He put in a call to Vajpayee. This time Vajpayee was at his most uncommunicative. "What do you want me to say?" he asked after listening silently to Clinton's detailed report. Nothing, Clinton replied; he just wanted Vajpayee to know he was holding firm.

Clinton took a cat nap on a sofa in a small study off the main entryway while Bruce, Sandy, Rick, and I cobbled together a new version of the "good statement," incorporating some of the Pakistani language from the paper that Sharif had claimed was in play between him and Vajpayee. But the key sentence in the new document was ours, not his, and it would nail the one thing we had to get out of the talks: "The prime minister has agreed to take concrete and immediate steps for the restoration of the Line of Control." The paper called for a cease-fire but only after the Pakistanis were back on their side of the line. It reaffirmed Clinton's long-standing plan to visit South Asia.

Clinton gave the statement to Sharif, who read it over carefully several times, asked to review it with his team, and finally accepted it with the request for one addition: a promise that Clinton would take a personal interest in encouraging an expeditious resumption and intensification of the bilateral efforts (that is, the Lahore process) once the sanctity of the Line of Control had been fully restored. This was no problem, since the president already had such an interest, encouragement was not mediation, there was no invidious linkage, and the sequence was right—withdrawal across the line before resumption of Lahore.

The meeting came quickly to a happy and friendly end, at least on Clinton's part. He heaped praise on Sharif for passing the test to which they had subjected their personal relationship.

As the president and his advisers were leaving Blair House, Shamshad Ahmad scurried after Sandy with alterations he wanted in the text. Sandy kept walking and said briskly over his shoulder, "Your boss says it's okay as is."

Before Bruce and Rick briefed the press on the statement, Clinton called Vajpayee to preview the statement. Once again, it was nearly a one-way conversation.

"That guy's from Missouri big-time," said Clinton afterward. "He wants to see those boys get off that mountain before he's going to believe any of this."*

I PUT IN a call to Jaswant, who phoned me back that evening. The State Department operations center tracked me down while Brooke, our sons, and I were on the roof of the Canadian embassy watching the Independence Day fireworks display over the Washington Monument. I took the call on a wall phone in the embassy kitchen, surrounded by waiters who were noisily replenishing trays of hors d'oeuvres. Jaswant spoke more slowly and formally than usual—partly, I'm sure, because of the bad line and the clattering of dishes in the background, but also because he was exhausted—it was the predawn hours of Monday morning in New Delhi. Like Vajpayee, Jaswant was doubtful about whether Nawaz Sharif would follow through on the promise that Clinton had elicited. He was, however, already prepared to acknowledge Clinton had kept his own promise to Vajpayee.

"Something terrible has happened these past several months between us and our neighbors," said Jaswant. "But something quite new and good has happened this weekend between our own countries, yours and mine—something related to the matter of trust. My prime minister and I thank your president for that."

---

*Missourians are known for their skepticism, and Missouri is often called the Show-Me State.

NINE

SISYPHUS AT INDIA HOUSE

Kargil gave President Clinton a jarring look at the danger in South Asia, and Blair House gave him a taste of the new opportunity for American diplomacy in the region. At least half a dozen times in the summer and fall of 1999, when I was in the Oval Office or traveling with the president on other business, he would pull me aside and ask how things were going and instruct me to keep in mind his endgame as I played out my own. In late July he held me back after a meeting on Russia in the Cabinet Room, put his arm around my shoulder, and said that while he wished me luck on the talks I was conducting with "that Jaswant guy," I shouldn't forget that he was determined to "go to India, look those people in the eye, and tell 'em it's a new world out there and we've got to work together."

Kargil made Vajpayee more trusting of Clinton, whom he thanked for being a "facilitator," not a mediator—but it also made him even more wary than before of any diplomatic venture that had anything to do with India's security.

In late July, during an ASEAN Regional Forum meeting in Singapore, Jaswant told Secretary Albright that the aftermath of the crisis and the requirements of domestic politics made it necessary for him to "tread especially carefully" in the next round of meetings with me, since it was due to take place in New York on the margins of the United Nations General Assembly in late September and that would be on the eve of the Indian national elections.

Three weeks later, in mid-August, Brajesh Mishra, Vajpayee's principal secretary, released to the public a draft document containing recommendations for the government's long-awaited nuclear doctrine. It summarized the views of twenty-seven experts who were outside the government but who represented the country's strategic elite. The paper was believed to reflect the preferences of powerful forces in the BJP, and it showed how little inclination there was in New Delhi to give an inch.

The plan was, from the American administration's vantage point, the worst possible answer to the question of how India intended to define "minimum credible deterrence"—worse, certainly, than Jaswant himself had told me in private talks or hinted in his January interview with *India Today*. It called for the development and deployment of a "triad of aircraft, mobile land-based missiles and sea-based assets"—in other words, a replica of the American strategic deterrent. If implemented, it could give India an arsenal not just equal to but bigger than either Britain's or France's, and it would surely provoke an acceleration of China's nuclear buildup.[1]

MEANWHILE, IT WAS clear that Nawaz Sharif had paid a crippling price for having given in to Clinton at Blair House. On his return to Islamabad, the prime minister put out the story that he had not been briefed on Kargil. What was intended as an alibi sounded more like an admission of weakness.

Sharif dragged his feet on a promise he had made at Blair House to name a special envoy to begin working immediately with us to translate into action Clinton's "personal interest" in getting talks started again between Pakistan and India, including on Kashmir. For weeks afterward, when we pressed him for a name, he said it was hard for him to find someone who had his personal trust. Then, in mid-September, he sent his brother Shahbaz Sharif, his closest confidant and the chief minister of Punjab province, to Washington for "exploratory discussions." That choice told us all we needed to know about how isolated the prime minister was within his own government.

Brooke and I gave the First Brother, as we called him, the kitchen table treatment, inviting him for a home-cooked meal on September 15.[2] The next day he met for several hours with Rick Inderfurth and Bruce Riedel at his suite in the Willard Hotel and agreed to let us float with

Jaswant Singh a formula, developed by Rick and Bruce, that might lead to a resumption of the Lahore process without preconditions. Under the plan, Nawaz Sharif would promise to keep Pakistani forces from "straying" across the Line of Control and stop shelling along the Kashmir divide; in addition, the Sharif brothers would open a direct channel to Vajpayee in order to bypass the obstructionists in the Pakistani foreign ministry, military, and intelligence services.

Shahbaz said that since even these modest measures carried a huge political risk, he wanted to wrap them in a "conceptual framework" that ruled out in advance "legitimization of the status quo"—which we took to mean acceptance of the Line of Control as an international border—in whatever agreement ultimately emerged. It sounded like a gimmick designed to guarantee that the negotiations with India went nowhere. Certainly Vajpayee would see it that way.

Rick, Bruce, and I concluded that Shahbaz Sharif's real purpose in coming to Washington was to get U.S. help not so much in engaging India as in protecting Nawaz Sharif and strengthening his grip on political power in Pakistan. Shahbaz would not quite confirm, even in response to direct questions, that a military coup was brewing. But his combination of knowing, mirthless smiles, long silences, and abrupt changes of subject when we asked about the situation at home left us in no doubt that something was afoot.

FIVE DAYS LATER, on September 20, during a private dinner with Jaswant in New York, I registered a strong objection to the draft nuclear doctrine Mishra had presented in August. Jaswant replied that since the paper had no imprimatur from the government, it should not be taken too seriously. It was not really even a doctrine—it was just a set of recommendations that Vajpayee would almost certainly not accept. The United States should not "dignify" it by overreacting. India could not possibly afford a strategic triad. Its nuclear arsenal would "reside in a passive deployment"—presumably meaning not on permanent alert. He had already assigned some of his own experts to examine the "discrepancies" between the advisory board's report and statements that Vajpayee and his ministers (Jaswant himself included) had made about India's commitment to minimum deterrence.

I pointed out that Jaswant was disavowing in private something that Mishra had unveiled in public, which suggested that the more-is-better philosophy of deterrence had significant backing from powerful forces in the government, the BJP, the parliament, the defense and foreign policy establishment, and public opinion.

Not necessarily, Jaswant replied. Everything had to be understood against the backdrop of a hard-fought election campaign. "As our democratic process moves into the home stretch," he said, "it's getting a bit raucous and rough, as I suspect yours may do in due course."

For just that reason, he continued, we should hold off any further meetings at a delegation-to-delegation level until after the BJP victory that he confidently expected in early October 1999. We should also postpone the next scheduled meeting of our technical experts, led by Bob Einhorn and Rakesh Sood—in order "not to let Indo-U.S. relations be affected in any way by our domestic politics."

Meanwhile, he would be keeping his own head down: "Remember, I'm often called a traitor in my own country because of my association with this exceedingly valuable and promising enterprise. I don't mind. In fact, I regard it as a badge of honor as long as I enjoy the confidence of my prime minister, which seems to be the case."

WHEN I TOLD Jaswant about Shahbaz Sharif's visit to Washington, he expressed the deepest doubts about whether there was, or ever would be, anyone on the Pakistani side whom Americans or Indians could trust. He was not in the least impressed either by the substance of the Sharif brothers' latest position ("We've seen it a hundred times"). He seemed worried that we Americans might be betting on the Sharifs and deluding ourselves into thinking that sanctions relief would help them cling to power. "All you're doing is giving the Pakistanis more rope," he said. "We're resigned to your effort" to keep Pakistan afloat economically. "We realize that you've invested so much in that relationship that you don't know how to disinvest. But you would be making a big mistake to try to save Nawaz Sharif's skin. You won't succeed, and even if you do, you'll wish you hadn't. We tried to give him a helping hand ourselves, and look what happened. We held out the hand of friendship, and we got a fist in the face. Even if our view of him—and of his brother—however heartfelt and however rooted in recent experience, is somehow exaggerated or even unjust, I must tell you: I don't think they can deliver. I don't think they're really in control."

The United States's wisest posture toward Pakistan, he said, would be to do what the Indian leadership was doing: sit back, stay cool, avoid any rash moves that might implicate any outsiders in the inevitable—which was a coup d'état that would, yet again, bring a military dictator to power.

I could understand why Vajpayee and Jaswant were angry and mistrustful toward Nawaz Sharif but not why they should resign themselves to Sharif's being replaced by Musharraf, who had been the moving force behind the Pakistani incursion and who would be even more intractable on Kashmir and everything else if he emerged as Pakistan's new leader.

While agreeing that Musharraf was worse than Sharif, Jawant was fatalistic about a coup. There was nothing either India—or, for that matter, the United States—could do to stop it; all we could do was not provoke it. That was why Vajpayee was not beating the war drums in the parliamentary campaign. "We could have exploited the crisis," he said. "We could have held a khaki election, the way Margaret Thatcher did over the Malvinas" (the Spanish name for the Falkland Islands, which were contested by Britain and Argentina in the war they fought in 1982). As a sign of its forbearance, he said, the Indian government had even allowed the Lahore bus service to continue and gone ahead with the purchase of sugar from a factory owned by the Sharif family.

In any event, Jaswant concluded, speculation about what was going to happen in Pakistan was beside the point. In the final analysis, the nature and future of that country did not depend on whether a feckless civilian or a vengeful general was in power there, and the United States should stop thinking otherwise: "You're playing yesterday's chess match—the one you got in the habit of playing during the cold war. The game now is for energy from a region that is falling increasingly into the hands of the forces of radical Islam and the forces of fundamental destabilization and disintegration. No one has had as much experience with Islam as India. You must work with us more in waging our common struggle against those forces," which were, as he saw it, running amok in Pakistan. That country "is falling apart because faith cannot keep it together. It's already a failed state. Things are moving so fast now. Yet India stays together. Your right choice, strategically, is to help the Indian experiment succeed."

I found myself frustrated not just with his side of this now-familiar argument, but with my own as well.

There was, at the core of Jaswant's feelings toward Pakistan, a proposition that I could not fully refute. He was right that partition had been a huge and tragic mistake. He was right that in the fifty intervening years, Pakistan had, more often than not, tended to confirm the apprehension that it was a state based on a flawed—perhaps fatally flawed—idea: a homeland for South Asian Muslims, yet one sharing the subcontinent with a much larger, secular neighbor that was home to even more Muslims. And he was certainly not imagining things when he saw Pakistan as being in danger of becoming a failed state.

Yet while all that was analytically correct, or at least defensible, it was prescriptively wrong. It was true that neither India nor the United States could control Pakistan's evolution; but both could, for better or for worse, *affect* that evolution. If an indictment of Pakistan's origins, a presumption of guilt about its every move, and utter pessimism about its future continued to dominate official attitudes in New Delhi, then India would lose whatever chance it might have of ever exercising a positive influence. The same could be said of assumptions underlying American policy.

On this issue Jaswant and I seemed as much at odds as we had been when we first met in June 1998. Yet this time there was something new and welcome in the exchange. Dismissive as Jaswant was of Shahbaz Sharif's motives in coming to Washington, he betrayed none of the reflexive Indian suspicion of U.S. motives in receiving the First Brother.

Just to be sure of what I was not hearing, I asked him whether he was "comfortable" with the role the United States was playing by exploring the possibility, however remote, of using the Shahbaz Sharif contact to good effect.

"If I felt you had crossed some sort of foul line," he said, "I'd blow a whistle. I didn't bring one with me tonight, and I don't miss it. Your points are worth listening to. They're taken in the spirit intended. There is more good will toward the United States of America in India today than I've ever known in my life." President Clinton's handling of the Kargil crisis had "greatly diminished" Indian mistrust of the United States's strategic orientation in South Asia and therefore "somewhat increased" a tacit Indian willingness to let the United States play a "good-offices" role in the affairs of the subcontinent. For that reason, he was prepared to have "our very best and most trusted associates put their heads together and think through, in a discreet and constructive way, what lessons we should take away from this awful experience [of Kargil] and how we might apply them in the future."

Returning to this idea later, also in private, Jaswant suggested that our governments engage in a joint case study of the crisis. This would be helpful, he said, as "its own kind of confidence-building measure" in that it would transform the Kargil affair from a cautionary tale of Pakistani perfidy into a more positive one about U.S.-Indian mutual trust. After consulting with my team and laying out a few ground rules, I agreed. The resulting consultations, conducted with virtually no publicity, continued into the Bush administration.*

ON OCTOBER 13 Nawaz Sharif committed his final blunder as prime minister of Pakistan: he provided a pretext for the military coup that he so feared—and that Jaswant so confidently predicted. Musharraf was on a trip to Sri Lanka, and Sharif tried to force him into exile by preventing the plane that was bringing him home—a commercial flight with more than one hundred passengers aboard—from landing in Pakistan. While the plane circled, running low on fuel, the army rebelled, forced the airport to open, and arrested Sharif. He was charged with attempted murder (on the grounds that the plane could have crashed) and sentenced to death. Clinton instructed the National Security Council staff to marshal whatever influence the U.S. government had to persuade Musharraf to commute the sentence.

---

*More than a year was spent laying out a framework of questions in which each side was interested. Walter Andersen, then division chief of the Office of Analysis for South Asia in the State Department's Bureau of Intelligence and Research and an important member of our India-Pakistan team, led a delegation made up of State and Defense Department officials. Arun Singh, a minister of state for defense in the late 1980s under Rajiv Gandhi and a close friend of Jaswant's, led the Indian side, which was composed of officials from the External Affairs and Defense Ministries. In the summer of 2001, the two teams met twice, once at the Cooperative Monitoring Center at Sandia National Laboratory in California and once in Washington. For the Indians, a key lesson was that the United States, in exerting its influence to bring the Indo-Pakistani confrontation over Kargil to a close, took account of Indian security concerns. Hence, U.S. involvement in South Asian security issues need not undermine Indian security objectives. The talks also helped on some technical issues, such as increasing the effectiveness of Indian monitoring of military deployments and activities along the Line of Control.

In Washington, there was a sense of bleak anticlimax. We felt as though we were watching a remake of a bad movie with an unhappy ending. Twenty-one years earlier, General Muhammad Zia ul-Haq had overthrown Prime Minister Zulfikar Ali Bhutto and had him hanged on a charge of murder, despite an outpouring of appeals for clemency from around the world, including from President Jimmy Carter.

THE COUP BROUGHT the dialogue with Pakistan to a halt, at least on the issue of nonproliferation. There was a single attempt, at the instigation of various Americans and Pakistanis who were worried about the breakdown in communications, to put me in touch with Sahabzada Yaqub Khan, a military-officer-turned-statesman who had served as foreign minister and ambassador to Paris, Washington, and Moscow. I had known him in the 1970s and 1980s and shared the widespread opinion of him as an able and eloquent diplomat, a broad-gauge thinker, and a political figure of rare integrity. Presumably because of those qualities, he was being brought out of retirement in his eighties, but for what was truly an impossible assignment and with no latitude for negotiations on any issue of substance.

This was the second time Yaqub Khan had been thrown into the fray after 1998. The first time had been that July, when the Pakistanis were suffering from a condition that Rick Inderfurth diagnosed as "Jaswant-envy." On that earlier occasion, Yaqub Khan had come to call on me in Washington but had little to say. He had not been particularly close to Nawaz Sharif then, and there was no reason to think he was any closer to Musharraf now. When he appeared in my office a few weeks after the coup, he did the best he could with what amounted to an empty brief. There was plenty of style—indeed, elegance—but nothing of diplomatic utility.

"You must hear the unheard symphony, the unspoken poem," he mused. "You must see the aura of the fact as opposed to the fact itself." I couldn't tell whether he was talking about Pakistan's new military regime, its nuclear weaponry, or the music of the spheres.

I felt some sympathy for him, and not just because he was someone I had admired in years past. Unlike Jaswant, who was a policymaker in a government that had self-confidence, coherent objectives, and a strategy for achieving them, Yaqub Khan was blowing smoke on behalf of a newly installed regime of dubious legitimacy, a government that was in upheaval, and a state that was deeply insecure.

For the duration of the Clinton administration, we did business with Pakistan through regular diplomatic channels, relying primarily on Ambassadors Bill Milam in Islamabad and Riaz Khokhar in Washington. We focused on two objectives: persuading Musharraf to use Pakistani influence on the Taliban to crack down on al Qaeda, and getting him to restore the democratic process in Pakistan.

We made little progress on either goal. Musharraf acknowledged that the Taliban was a problem and said he intended to go to Kandahar, the stronghold of the Taliban in Afghanistan, and speak to their leader, Mullah Omar. He never did so. On democracy, he assured us he had every intention of holding elections but would not commit himself to a timetable.

Sharif's fate remained in doubt for fourteen months. After strenuous behind-the-scenes intervention by the United States, led by Bruce Riedel, with considerable help from the Saudis, who threatened to cut off Pakistan's access to cheap oil, Musharraf lifted the death sentence and allowed the two Sharif brothers and their families to go into exile in Saudi Arabia in December 2000.

THE SAME WEEK in October that the military overthrew the civilian government in Pakistan, the Indians completed their latest national elections. Over a period of five weeks, 650 million voters had chosen 545 members of parliament, and the result left Vajpayee and the BJP solidly in control.

Commentators drew the obvious conclusion about the contrasting state of democracy in these two major nations of South Asia. But there was also reason to ponder the complexity of Indian democracy and the dilemma it posed for the United States. The BJP had come to power on a platform that included inducting nuclear weapons. In carrying out that campaign promise, the new government upset most of the rest of the world while earning praise and support from vast numbers of its own constituents. For seventeen months, the United States had worked, primarily through Jaswant Singh, to mitigate the damage that the BJP had done to the global nonproliferation regime and to bring India into the fold of the CTBT. But the Indian leaders feared that signing the treaty would cost the BJP crucial support in parliament and with the electorate. Thus, in this respect too, Indian democracy, for all its virtues in American eyes, was a complicating factor in accomplishing an important U.S. goal.

Now that Vajpayee was safely returned to the prime ministership, the Clinton administration held out some hope that he would have the political running room—and the political courage—to sign the CTBT, thereby making good on the statement of intent he had made to the UN.

BUT AT JUST that moment, the vicissitudes of America's own politics kicked in, with consequences for the cause of nonproliferation potentially as disastrous as the Indian test a year and a half earlier. On October 13— the day Vajpayee's government took office with a renewed mandate and the day after the Pakistani coup—the United States Senate rejected the CTBT.

The treaty had been languishing in the Senate Foreign Relations Committee for three years. The Republican leader of the Senate, Trent Lott, seemed bent on letting it die a slow death there. The treaty's proponents, mostly Democrats, demanded action. Knowing there were enough opponents to defeat the treaty, Lott scheduled a vote by the full Senate. Moderate Republicans, fearing the harm that rejection would do to the global nonproliferation regime, urged Lott to call off the showdown, but he was not about to pass up the opportunity to draw blood from the administration and drive a stake through the heart of the CTBT.

As a technical matter, the treaty was not necessarily dead. Clinton could resubmit it the following year, in 2000. But that was a presidential election year, and to try again for ratification then would be to invite, if not guarantee, another rejection. The only hope for the treaty was for Clinton's successor to bring it back to the Senate.

I was traveling in Europe at the time, dealing with another issue of nuclear diplomacy that was not going well—our attempt to persuade our allies and the Russians to accept changes in the Anti-Ballistic Missile Treaty that would permit limited defenses to deal with the emerging threat posed by North Korea's effort to develop rockets that might someday be able to hit the United States.[3] I had just finished yet another round of what turned out to be a fruitless set of negotiations with Yuri Mamedov on this subject in Helsinki and was heading back to my hotel, exhausted and discouraged about how little progress I was making with the Russians, when I heard a radio report of what the Senate had done.

The rejection of the CTBT was not just a political debacle—it was a severe setback to our diplomacy as well, or so it seemed to me and most of my colleagues. After all, the steady erosion of congressional support for sanctions had already deprived us of our principal means of applying pressure in New Delhi and Islamabad to get those governments to sign the CTBT. Now we had lost the credibility of our own signature on the treaty. As the White House press secretary, Joe Lockhart, conceded, the United States was "out of the nonproliferation business until 2001."[4]

Yet when I got back to Washington, I found Clinton, while livid at the Senate, more convinced than ever that he should go to India and Pakistan—and more optimistic about his ability to make the trip worthwhile. As he saw it, we now had nearly as much of a quarrel with our own Senate as with the Indian government over the testing of nuclear weaponry. If we continued to hang tough on the benchmarks as a condition for his trip to the region, we would be the ones bullying from weakness. He was determined to make the journey for the good he felt he could do by going rather than as a reward for progress on the nonproliferation agenda.

Paradoxically, the massive and humiliating defeat he had suffered in the Senate seemed to Clinton, in its consequences for his own long-standing desire to plunge into South Asia diplomacy, almost liberating. Except in the first flush of anger he had felt over the Pokhran II test nearly a year and a half before, he had never been entirely comfortable with sanctions. In general, he did not feel that sanctions did much good, and he found it downright distasteful and counterproductive to use them against countries with which he was trying, despite serious differences, to improve relations.[5]

Clinton was a gut fighter when necessary, a conciliator when possible. He battled hard for the presidency and waged the political equivalent of a mortal combat with Newt Gingrich and other Republican opponents over impeachment. He twice took the nation and the Western alliance to war against Slobodan Milošević. But he preferred managing differences with foreign leaders whom he regarded as essentially decent, conscientious, and deserving of a better relationship with the United States. Vajpayee fit the bill. That, I believe, was why Clinton seemed almost relieved that circumstance had altered the dynamic of U.S.-Indian relations, depriving him of sticks he had never been enthusiastic about wielding. The way was now open for him to do what came most naturally to him—

meet with Vajpayee, and a great many other Indians, face-to-face and, as he often put it, "talk these things through."

Clinton phoned Vajpayee on October 15 and told him that it was his strong desire to make the trip. In reporting publicly on the call, Lockhart said, "The President recognized the restraint India has shown to date in this situation [the coup in Pakistan], and discussed the need for an early restoration of civilian government." On the CTBT, Lockhart said, "The United States will continue to abide by our obligations under the treaty that the President signed. And it's our hope that other countries will move forward in a positive way on nonproliferation and on testing and that other countries will not misread the very misguided decision that the Republican majority in the Senate made."

In a letter to Vajpayee following the phone call, Clinton wrote, "As leaders of the world's two largest democracies you and I have a special responsibility to demonstrate that democracy provides the best foundation not only for domestic prosperity and stability but for cooperation and harmony among democratic nations, [and] I look forward to working with you in this endeavor."

BRUCE RIEDEL AND MATT DALEY flew to New Delhi to begin preparations for the trip. Brajesh Mishra did not disguise his pleasure that the Senate had knocked the administration's legs out from under it on the CTBT. Pressing his advantage both with Bruce and Matt in New Delhi and during a trip of his own to Washington the following week, Mishra tried to talk the administration into ruling out a stop in Pakistan on the grounds that shaking hands with Musharraf would lend legitimacy to a "criminal regime."

Clinton, however, was almost as determined to go to Pakistan as to India. He wanted to use the incentive of a presidential visit as leverage on Musharraf to move against al Qaeda and Osama bin Laden, and also to nudge Musharraf toward restoration of democracy. Therefore the administration would keep the option of a stop in Islamabad open until the last minute.[6]

At the end of October, Clinton waived a significant number of the remaining sanctions against India while easing only a few on Pakistan. It was another attempt—by definition imperfect—to use the meat cleaver of sanctions as though it were a scalpel. We wanted to show that the administration was ready to accelerate the improvement of relations with a democratic though nuclear-armed India, while proceeding more slowly with a Pakistan that was now back under military rule.*

JASWANT AND I held our next formal round of the dialogue, delayed almost ten months because of the Indian governance deadlock and the elections required to end it, on November 16–17, 1999. We met at India House in London, and our host was Lalit Mansingh, the Indian High Commissioner (the Commonwealth equivalent of ambassador). A seasoned diplomat with a gentleness of manner that disguised considerable toughness, Mansingh had just been named to replace Raghunath as foreign secretary. In that new capacity, and in his subsequent posting as ambassador to Washington, he would play an active and constructive role in managing the U.S.-Indian relationship through its ups and downs.

The plenary sessions in London covered much of the ground that Jaswant and I had been over privately in New York in September. He let his team members do most of the talking, and they concentrated their fire on the United States for its refusal to write off Pakistan as a rogue state: the Pakistani leadership, whether civilian or military, was "hopelessly corrupt," "a criminal-terrorist mafia gang"; the whole country was "Taliban East."

Listening impassively, Jaswant spoke up only once to suggest that it was useful for the American delegation to hear a "polite echo of the sentiment back home." The White House's refusal to rule out a presidential stop in Pakistan had not helped. The perception in India that the United States was still in some sense coddling Pakistan had diminished the feeling of gratitude in New Delhi for the role Clinton had played at Blair House. However, Jaswant added, it might reverse the erosion of Indian good will toward the United States if the American government, in addition to taking the Pakistanis to task for their support of the Taliban and

---

*The sanctions relief, formally approved by Clinton on October 27, meant that India was now eligible for loans and other assistance from the Overseas Private Investment Corporation, the Export-Import Bank, and the Trade and Development Agency as well as loans from private American banks to the Indian government. India could also participate in the International Military Education and Training program—a step toward more military cooperation. For Pakistan, the sanctions relief was limited to some agriculture credits and bank loans to the government.

al Qaeda, would also hammer them for backing terrorism in Kashmir. In other words: *Don't have anything to do with the Pakistanis, but if you insist on dealing with them, at least get them to stop the covert war they are waging against us.*

In fact, we were already using our contacts with the Pakistanis to deliver precisely that message.

I HAD COME to London fully expecting Jaswant to tell us to forget about Indian signature on the CTBT, especially after what Bruce Riedel and Matt Daley had heard from Mishra. If that had been Jaswant's message, I would not have had much grounds for protest. Since we could not even keep our own Senate from rejecting the treaty, we could hardly insist that Jaswant get his parliament to accept it.

To my surprise, he told me that Vajpayee was still prepared to try to put India "on par" with the United States—that is, to sign the treaty before Clinton came in March. Ratification, of course, would have to wait until the Indians saw whether Clinton or his successor was able to resuscitate the treaty in the Senate.

Jaswant had set aside the two months before our own next meeting, to be held back in London the third week in January 2000, to build the necessary domestic support. He had a detailed strategy for doing so. It involved lobbying key parliamentary committees, giving interviews and press conferences, and meeting with foreign policy and national security institutes. The plan also called for him to make a public statement, perhaps in parliament, that would distance the government from the draft nuclear doctrine and disavowing the need, under foreseeable circumstances, for a strategic triad.

Over dinner with Brooke and me in an Italian restaurant in Mayfair at the end of a long day, Jaswant explained why he felt we should not give up on the CTBT. He and his prime minister realized how important the treaty was to Clinton personally. They wanted to accommodate him as much as possible, especially after Kargil and Blair House, and now that Clinton had agreed to make the trip to New Delhi "for its own sake, not as part of a pressure campaign. It is easier to do this thing you've asked us to do if it's not under duress. Also, there is, in my country among the political elite, the glimmering of a consensus, albeit wary and inchoate, that there's something new under the Indo-American sun. We've seen it in our many months of dialogue. Your man Zeno might, for once, be wrong. We might actually get where we want to go."

I took Jaswant's willingness to keep pushing for the CTBT within his own government as further indication that he was, and had always been, serious about doing everything he could to have the dialogue produce Indian signature on the treaty. While that was a lot less than we were asking for—in fact, it was partial accommodation on only one quarter of what we were asking for, and not the most important benchmark at that—we would settle for it with relief and gratitude. For India to sign the CTBT—and to do so at our behest—would help counter the worldwide impression that the treaty was dead and that the United States Senate had administered the coup de grâce.

THE NEXT DAY, however, there was a sign that Jaswant was pushing a large boulder up a steep hill within his government. At the end of our final session, he and I went off into a corner and put our heads together for a few minutes on the exact wording of the terse statement that we would, as usual, give to the press. Meanwhile, his key lieutenants, Alok Prasad and Rakesh Sood, handed Rick Inderfurth and Bob Einhorn a document summarizing concessions they wanted from the United States in exchange for CTBT signature. The list included an end to all remaining sanctions by the international financial institutions before India signed up to the CTBT. Alok and Rakesh also dusted off an old demand that India be given various rights and privileges available to signatories of the Nuclear Non-Proliferation Treaty even though India would remain a nonsignatory.

Emboldened by our discomfiture over what the Senate had done, some on the Indian side were making another push to be freed forever from the opprobrium, discrimination, and, of course, sanctions that had come down on their heads after Pokhran II—*and* to be granted the rights and privileges enjoyed by the five nuclear weapons states whose status was enshrined in the NPT.

I had not had many occasions to let my temper show with Jaswant, but I did so on this one. I was going to tear up the Prasad-Sood paper, I said, and strongly urged he do the same. He seemed genuinely embarrassed, not so much by the substance of this last-minute ploy—which I assumed he had approved—as by the appearance that he and his team were trying to pull a fast one on us. He said on the spot I should regard the paper as a "dead letter" and promised to discipline his "otherwise excellent pandits."

Whether Jaswant did that or, more likely, told his aides, "Nice try!" the objectionable document disappeared and a better one took its place. At a subsequent meeting at the expert level in Washington, on December 23, Alok Prasad gave Rick Inderfurth a handwritten note that represented a considerable improvement on the paper we had rejected in London. If the administration would lift all the remaining sanctions and establish a case-by-case review of procedures for licensing India's purchase of high-tech equipment similar to the one that had existed before the Pokhran II test, it would be easier for the Indian government to sign the CTBT, since it could do so without appearing to be under duress.

Jaswant even dropped a public hint that CTBT signature was still a possibility, although he did so in a fashion that was (deliberately, no doubt) so subtle, Delphic, and convoluted that only pandits would understand what he said. "There is no denying that this negative vote by the U.S. Senate does have a bearing on the future of this treaty," he told Raja Mohan, a knowledgeable and respected writer who was the strategic affairs editor of the *Hindu*, in an interview at the end of November. "I would, therefore, consider it natural for India to also disaggregate its decision." Disaggregating, in this context, could be taken to mean signing soon and ratifying later—which was as much as we could hope for.[7]

THEN, ON DECEMBER 24, 1999, bad news intervened again, this time in an especially ugly and, for Jaswant, devastating form. A band of five Pakistan-based Islamic radicals hijacked an Indian Airlines Airbus, en route from Katmandu to New Delhi, with one hundred seventy-eight passengers and eleven crew members aboard.

The crisis arose just as Jaswant was preparing to leave his office and join his family in celebrating the birth of a granddaughter. Because of the extreme sensitivity of the information initially available to the government, Jaswant was, for several hours, not allowed to explain to his wife why he was detained when he phoned her from the office. It pained him to be unable to answer her repeated questions about what could be more important than the birth of a grandchild. Over the next several days, he returned home late and slept fitfully on a chair in his living room in order to be near the secure telephone that awakened him with updates.

The hijackers demanded $200 million and the release of thirty-six Kashmiri guerrillas, many of them notorious in India as terrorists and a Pakistani cleric who was the brother of one of the hijackers. The Indian press, especially television, heightened the dilemma facing the government by playing up the suffering and peril of the hostages and the danger that the imprisoned guerrillas would pose if they were freed as part of a deal. To show they were serious, the hijackers slit the throat of a newly wed passenger who was returning home with his bride from a honeymoon in Nepal.

The plane made brief refueling stops in India, Pakistan, and the United Arab Emirates—where some passengers (mostly women and children) were freed, leaving one hundred fifty-five hostages aboard. After being turned away by several other airports, the plane ended up in Kandahar.

Vajpayee, who had said the Indian government would not negotiate with terrorists, changed his mind after more executions were threatened. He gave Jaswant the thankless task of flying to Kandahar with three of the prisoners whose release the hijackers were demanding. On December 31, after several hours of hard bargaining with a group that included Taliban, Kashmiri secessionists, and al Qaeda operatives—and with Pakistani operatives hovering in the background—Jaswant secured the exchange of the passengers for the three guerrillas.

When word reached me, I put in a call to congratulate Jaswant. I found him at home, sipping champagne and surrounded by friends and family. He was exhausted but satisfied, convinced that he had made the right decision given, as he put it, the "calculus of human life involved." Indian intelligence believed, on the basis of intercepted communications, that unless the standoff had been resolved that day, the hijackers would have forced the plane to take off on New Year's Day and blown it up in the air with all passengers on board—a deliberately timed terrorist fireworks display to mark the new millennium.

The initial relief that swept India quickly gave way to criticism of Jaswant for the price he had paid. On January 2, two days after the end of the hostage crisis, heavy shelling resumed across the Line of Control, killing six people on the Indian side. The next day a bomb ripped through a busy vegetable market in Srinagar, killing eighteen people. The fresh outbursts of violence made the release of the three militants even more controversial in India. The hijacking was now seen by many as a personal victory for Musharraf, who was widely believed to have masterminded the incident as payback for the humiliation he had suffered as a result of Nawaz Sharif's capitulation to Clinton at Blair House.

I KEPT IN touch with Jaswant during this ordeal, primarily to let him know that he had the good wishes of the U.S. government and to ask if there was anything we could do to help, although other than discreetly sharing information, there was not much we could do. The last thing he wanted was any appearance that the United States was, yet again, insinuating itself in India's troubles with its enemies. I would get up early to put in a call to him during what I knew to be the working day in India, and he would call me back many hours later, by then the early hours of the morning on his end. He told me that, while "still at peace with myself," he had found dealing with terrorists exceedingly distasteful, and the flak he was taking on his home front was discouraging and hurtful.

We had some concern in Washington that the Indian government might feel it had to retaliate in some fashion against Pakistan. Once the worst of the crisis was past, I tracked Jaswant down in Rajasthan, where he had gone to get a bit of rest and to see his ailing mother. India, I told him over a bad phone line, had the high ground; everyone in Washington understood the political pressures the government was under, but we hoped Prime Minister Vajpayee would reflect carefully and not embark on a course that would dramatically complicate the situation.

For the first and last time in my dealings with Jaswant, he grew truly angry—not so much exploding as doing a slow burn. It was also the only time he succeeded in making me feel truly guilty.

Why was the United States raising its concern just with India? he asked sharply. There was no doubt about Pakistani complicity in both the hijacking and the massacre in Kashmir. While spending those hazardous hours on the ground in Kandahar, he had seen, with his own eyes, evidence that Pakistanis, Kashmiris, Afghans, and Arabs were tied up in the same diabolical plot. He had been lucky to get out of there alive. India's handling of the situation had nothing whatsoever to do with giving in to domestic political pressure; he and the government were exercising extraordinary restraint, and he found it "strange" that his "American friends" would suggest otherwise.

I backed off fast.

IN THE WAKE of the hijacking, the Indians chose not to take military action against Pakistan. That decision, too, was controversial. Critics in the Congress Party as well as on the right wing of the BJP accused the government of being weak on security issues. Jaswant was already a target on that score because of the perception that the dialogue with the United States would result in India's giving in to American efforts to limit its defenses. Now he had to bear the additional stigma of having met the hijackers' demands.

When we met again at India House in London in mid-January, I could tell that Jaswant's burden had become heavier and the hill steeper. He soldiered through talking points that suggested, more than in the past, close oversight from New Delhi.

A short time later, Rick Inderfurth and Bruce Riedel urged that we attempt what they called a Hail-Mary pass. I should send a message to Jaswant saying that if the Indian government would sign the CTBT before the presidential visit, Clinton would use his waiver authority to announce the lifting of sanctions on the eve of his trip. If we did not make that offer fast, said Rick and Bruce, there was a very real chance that Congress would lift sanctions on its own. Bob Einhorn and his fellow nonproliferationists were against any further concessions, and I agreed with them. Besides, I concluded, the last-ditch effort Rick and Bruce were proposing would have done no good, since the Indians could see for themselves that sanctions were a wasting asset for the administration. Just as they had long hoped, they were getting a presidential visit without having to pay any price.

I had some concern that now it was my own president who was at some political risk. For Clinton to drop all the earlier conditions he had set for going to New Delhi would open him to the charge of having let himself be stared down and thus having devalued American power. I alluded to this danger in private with Clinton only once, and rather diffidently and obliquely at that. It was during a chance opportunity to talk alone with him on the margins of a meeting about Russia. He understood exactly what I was saying and blew it off.

"Listen," he said, "we can't be too hung up about any suggestion that someone else is pushing us around. We're dealing with people here—hell, we're dealing with people *everywhere*—who think we're the ones who have been pushing *them* around. They think we're always laying down the law and telling them what they have to do. Sometimes being big and powerful means recognizing that you can afford to roll with a punch. We can take the occasional bump in the road as long as we're moving along the right road. It's easier for us than just about anybody since we're so strong and everyone knows it. What matters is getting the job done and working with what we've got to do that. Let's face it: we're out of Schlitz on sanctions, and we're in lousy shape on the test ban. So we just have to keep on truckin' with what we've got."

There had been compelling reasons in the past for deferring the trip, and there were new reasons now. However, they did not outweigh Clinton's confidence that the visit would be, as he put it, "a transformational event." Clinton believed that by becoming the principal agent of engagement and by making his trip a dramatic demonstration of improved relations, he could increase the influence that he—and his successors— would have over their South Asian counterparts on all issues, including nonproliferation.

TEN

A GUEST IN THE PARLIAMENT

IN JANUARY 2000, when I returned to London for another round of talks with Jaswant, we were largely marking time. More important than the rather sterile discussions in India House was the trip that Rick Inderfurth made when he peeled off and flew to Islamabad, leading the first high-level American government delegation to Pakistan since the coup. Over the previous year and a half, all such teams had included a senior nonproliferation specialist, usually Bob Einhorn or someone from his shop. This time, Rick took with him instead Michael Sheehan, a State Department official responsible for counterterrorism, which had replaced nonproliferation as Topic A on the agenda with Pakistan. The shift had occurred in part because the administration was getting nowhere in its effort to curb the Pakistani nuclear and missile programs, but also because the bombing of the U.S. embassies in East Africa in August 1998 had been followed by further threats and foiled plots and a crescendo of warnings that al Qaeda and other organizations would usher in the new millennium with a rash of attacks against American targets around New Year's Day 2000.

Rick and his colleagues asked Musharraf for his help in capturing Abu Zubaida, one of Osama bin Laden's key lieutenants believed to be living in Peshawar, the Pakistani city at the foot of the Khyber Pass, and in getting the Taliban to turn over bin Laden himself. They also tried to persuade Musharraf to stop Pakistani sponsorship of terrorism in Kashmir. In reply, Musharraf half-conceded and half-denied that his intelligence services were aiding the militants in Kashmir, then attached conditions to his agreement that they would stop. Pakistan, he said, would use its "influence" in Kashmir to calm the situation there if India reduced its own buildup of troops along the border.

He fended off American exhortations that he quickly restore democracy by saying that he "would not stay in power any longer than required." When told that it would be difficult for Clinton to visit Pakistan with so little progress on any of the issues that mattered to the United States, Musharraf warned that a presidential snub would "strengthen the hand of the extremists"—essentially the same argument that Nawaz Sharif had repeatedly used with me in seeking American leniency before and after the Pakistani nuclear test.

ON MARCH 2, a little more than two weeks before Clinton was due to leave for South Asia, Sandy Berger convened a small group of advisers in the Map Room of the White House residence to present the president with the pros and cons of a trip to Pakistan. The cons had become even more formidable: the Secret Service had reliable indications that al Qaeda was planning to assassinate Clinton if he came to Pakistan.

Sandy told us in advance that Clinton was exhausted and irritable from his battles in Congress—with the Republicans on gun legislation and with many Democrats on trade with China—so we had better talk fast and give the president clear choices and crisp arguments. Sandy's deputy, Jim Steinberg, and I advocated a brief stop in Islamabad on the grounds that it would allow us to retain some leverage over Musharraf. Sandy agreed with us but felt he should hold his own opinion in reserve so that he would be better able to help the president sort through the considerations on both sides.

Someone had to make the case against going to Pakistan, so Sandy assigned the task to Bruce Riedel, who made three points: first, Musharraf and his government were doing nothing to help us rein in the Taliban or al Qaeda; second, the United States should not be the first country to give a coup-plotter and military dictator the political boost of a high-level visit; and third, the president would lose some of the ground he had gained with India if he went to Pakistan on the same trip.

Clinton furrowed his brow at the first two points and blew his top at the third, taking out on Bruce his annoyance at the Indians for acting as though they had a veto over where else he went in the neighborhood. He had done enough to show good faith with the Indians for them to give him a break: "Those guys owe me *something*, and they've got to cut me a little slack. I'm not going to Pakistan for my health, for God's sake! I'm going to try to keep us in the play there—both for what happens inside that country and for getting them to cut out the bad stuff they're doing in the region, and that means Kashmir as well as Afghanistan. Can't you see that, Bruce?"

Sandy intervened, assuring Clinton that of course Bruce could see it, but there were high stakes in the decision, and the president needed to know the risks—including to his own life. Clinton looked a little sheepish and winked at Bruce: "You do a pretty good imitation of a hard-ass." He dismissed the security concerns with a joke: he would invite Newt Gingrich to join him on the plane to Islamabad and let him deplane first—wearing a Clinton mask.

Not long afterward the Secret Service made a direct appeal to Clinton not to go to Pakistan because of the danger of assassination. Pressed by Clinton for his own advice, Sandy said the risk was worth taking, given the need to keep channels open to Musharraf and not to appear to be writing off Pakistan. Clinton thought for a moment, then said he would go, although he wanted his daughter, Chelsea, who would be accompanying him to India, to skip the stop in Pakistan.

"But you, Berger," he added with a grin, "are *definitely* coming with me."

ON MARCH 18, the night before the presidential party was to leave for South Asia, the Secret Service picked up a warning that al Qaeda intended to shoot down Air Force One when it came in for a landing at the airport outside Dhaka, the capital of Bangladesh. The security specialists strongly recommended pulling the plug on that portion of the trip, but Clinton decided to go anyway. If terrorists could keep him from visiting a country simply by threatening him, then they would have won.

The presidential party flew first to New Delhi but just to spend the night before flying to Dhaka for a stripped-down program. I stayed behind to get ready for Clinton's program in India. Because of the danger in Bangladesh, the president left Chelsea and her grandmother, Dorothy Rodham, behind (Hillary was in New York state, campaigning for the Senate).

Jaswant invited Chelsea, Mrs. Rodham, and me to accompany him on a day trip to his home in Rajasthan. We flew on an Indian air force VIP plane to Jodhpur, where I met briefly with Jaswant's wife, Sheetal Kumari, known as Kala, whom I had seen several times on past trips. As before (and since), she chided me for tormenting her husband and dragging him all over the world. Listening to this mock scolding, Jaswant smiled wanly and told Kala, "Strobe is not the worst of my tormentors."

While Jaswant went off to rest and be with his family, Chelsea, Dorothy, and I stayed at the palace of the local maharaja, where I was joined by my friend Nayan Chanda, who had flown out from Hong Kong to cover the Clinton visit for the *Far Eastern Economic Review*. The festival of Holi was in full swing. As part of this Hindu celebration of spring, revelers smear each other with red, green, and yellow powder and spray it with colored water. Nayan and I got into the spirit of the occasion, but Chelsea, who did not want newspapers around the world to carry photographs of her with a multicolored face, watched from a distance.

Flying back to New Delhi that evening, Jaswant and I had a few minutes alone. He seemed pensive, even apprehensive. He had high hopes that the trip would go well, he said, but we would have to cross our fingers and see. Now it was up to the two leaders.

CLINTON'S VISIT TO INDIA—the first by an American president in twenty-two years—was, by any standard and in almost every respect, one of the most successful such trips ever, not just because of the rhapsodic reception he received, but because it marked a pivotal moment in an important and vexed relationship. That was the nearly universal verdict of Indian commentators at the time—and would remain so for years afterward.[1]

The trip began on a grim note. On Monday, March 20, the day Clinton returned to New Delhi from Bangladesh, a group of militants dressed in Indian army uniforms entered a Sikh village about forty miles south of Srinagar. They called for all the male residents to come out from their mud and brick homes and submit to an identity card check, then mowed down thirty-five of them. The Indian government said the killers belonged to two militant groups, Lashkar-e-Taiba and Hizbul Mujahedeen, that were supported by the government of Pakistan.

From the moment he got off the plane, Clinton spoke about "sharing the outrage" of the Indian people and expressing the "heartbreak" he and others around the world felt about the latest atrocity. He did not endorse the accusation that Pakistan was behind the violence since the United States had no independent confirmation, but he used every occasion to express sorrow for the victims of the attacks and their families.

Clinton and Vajpayee signed a five-page "Vision for the 21st Century," filled with what the wordsmiths of the administration called lift-of-a-driving-dream rhetoric that affirmed the leaders' resolve to "create a closer and qualitatively new relationship." The statement reviewed the two sides' differences over nonproliferation and committed the governments to institutionalize the dialogue.[2]

During a session with his advisers to prepare for his first meeting with Vajpayee, Clinton said, "We've got to combine love-in with tough love," both on India's relations with Pakistan and on its nuclear weapons program.

When Clinton and Vajpayee sat down together at Hyderabad House, the president let his host do most of the talking at the outset. Vajpayee treated the nonproliferation benchmarks as though they had already passed into history, rendered moot by the events of the past two years, starting with the Indian test and continuing through the U.S. Senate's rejection of the CTBT. He seemed to regard the dialogue between Jaswant and me as a safety valve that had kept pressure from building up against him to do more, and do it faster, than he wanted. Now that Clinton had made his long-awaited trip, Vajpayee clearly hoped that India had successfully pivoted from being on the defensive over its tests to being able to press for full acceptance as a nuclear weapons state. Looking ahead to the bright future described in the vision statement, when the United States and India would work together on dealing with the world's problems, Vajpayee appealed for Clinton's support in making India a permanent member of the United Nations Security Council.

Clinton replied that there were other major regional powers with similar aspirations, such as Brazil—which, he added, had done the right thing in *not* going nuclear.

Meeting with the press afterward, Vajpayee said as little about nonproliferation as he felt he could get away with. He asserted his "firm commitment not to conduct further nuclear tests"—essentially repeating what he had said on that subject in his first statement announcing the Pokhran II test in May 1998—and referred to the dialogue as being "in progress," which was quite different from "making progress."

In response, Clinton made sure that anyone paying attention understood there were still important differences between the United States and India, but he put a forward spin on the diplomacy that was intended to narrow the gap:

> I felt today that there was a possibility we could reach more common ground on the issues of testing, on the production of fissile material, on export controls and on restraint generally. With regard to the Comprehensive Test Ban Treaty, you heard the prime minister's statement about his position on testing. I would hope that the democratic process would produce a signing and ultimately ratification of the Comprehensive Test Ban in India, just like I hope that the democratic process would ultimately produce a ratification of the test ban treaty in America that I signed. These are contentious issues, but I am actually quite optimistic about our ability to make progress on them. I thank the prime minister for sanctioning what I think has been a very honest and thorough-going dialogue. We have been working on this for some time and we will continue to do it and I believe we will wind up in a common position.

It was a standard diplomatic technique of Clinton's to profess more optimism than was justified and assert more agreement than existed in hopes that by doing so he could prod his negotiating partner in the desired direction. This exchange between the two leaders—the tight-lipped Vajpayee and the ebullient Clinton—captured much of what had gone on over the past twenty-two months between our governments: once again, the United States pushed for specificity and movement, while India hunkered down and hoped that form would substitute for substance, process for progress, and atmosphere for agreement.

TWICE THAT DAY, both at a lunch in Clinton's honor and at a state banquet that evening at the Presidential Palace, Jaswant arranged—with a touch of amusement, I suspect—for me to sit next to A. P. J. Abdul Kalam, the legendary figure of the Indian nuclear weapons and ballistic missile programs who had presided at Pokhran II. He was diminutive, animated, and charming, with a high-pitched voice that buzzed with enthusiasm, no matter what the topic, and long white hair that bounced when he talked. His idiosyncratic but precise, imaginative, and expressive syntax, combined with his rapid-fire delivery and distinctive accent, made his English sound as though it had been translated into words by a computer from some higher form of mathematics. Our conversation ranged over various subjects in which he was expert, but principally Tamil poetry and physics (he made a heroic though not entirely successful effort to help me understand string theory).

Abdul Kalam congratulated me on the wonderful relationship I had developed with Jaswant—as distinct, I sensed, from approving of the work we had done to keep open the possibility of India's signing the CTBT. Jaswant and I, he said, had established the diplomatic equivalent of "impedance matching," which I took to mean something like being on the same wave length. (When I looked up the term it seemed all the more fitting, since it refers to "the opposition in a circuit to the flow of alternating current, consisting of resistance and reactance.") Jaswant and I should write a book together about our experience, he added. As for himself, he was looking forward to retirement and devoting the rest of his life to the cause of disarmament.

ABDUL KALAM AND I had to suspend our conversation when K. R. Narayanan, the president of India, rose to give a lengthy toast. Narayanan, who was by birth a Dalit (a member of a category previously known as untouchables), had served as Indian ambassador in Washington in the early 1980s. His remarks that evening were memorable for two reasons. First, he referred repeatedly and reverently to Gandhi and Nehru, whose names were notably absent in what one heard from BJP spokesmen. Second, he took Clinton to task for having suggested a month earlier that South Asia was the most dangerous place on earth, a line that *The Economist* used on its cover in advance of Clinton's trip.

> It has been suggested [said Narayanan] that the Indian subcontinent is the most dangerous place in the world today and Kashmir is a nuclear flash point. These alarmist descriptions will only encourage those who want to break the peace and indulge in terrorism and violence. The danger is not from us who have declared solemnly

that we will not be the first to use nuclear weapons [a doctrine Vaj-payee had proclaimed to the parliament in August 1998], but rather it is from those who refuse to make any such commitment.

The prime minister's office and the Ministry of External Affairs were mortified that their president would chastise the guest of honor, and Clinton was none too pleased himself. Still, Narayanan's speech was, for me at least, an instructive glimpse into the chasm that divided the traditional Nehruvians, with their dedication to disarmament, from the "realist" BJP. It also provided a useful preview of what would be a standard Indian counterattack for years to come whenever Americans (or anyone else) suggested that there was a real danger of nuclear war between India and Pakistan: *Don't say that! You'll only encourage those crazy people!*

THE NEXT DAY, March 22, Clinton met briefly with Sonia Gandhi at his suite in the Maurya Sheraton. Bruce Riedel and I suggested that he try to succeed where Dick Celeste and I had failed in getting her to make it easier for the government to budge on the benchmarks, particularly the CTBT. Clinton got nowhere. "For someone who smiles a lot and has the gentlest of manners," he remarked after saying good-bye to his visitor, "that's one tough lady. She never said 'no' but she made mighty clear she wasn't saying 'yes' to anything that will get in the way of playing hardball with Vajpayee."

Clinton was, as often, running late for his next appointment—in this case, the most important of the trip, an address to a joint session of the parliament. His staff was in a near-panic to get him to the motorcade waiting in the basement garage of the hotel and from there over to the Central Hall of the Supreme Legislature. Any thought of quiet time to focus his mind was out the window. It did not matter, since he was operating on adrenaline and seemed to derive energy from the anxiety of everyone around him.

On this occasion, as on many others, the prepared text seemed almost incidental to the speech he ended up giving. He would often wait until the last minute to turn his attention to a draft written by his staff, then slash away at it with a felt-tipped pen. Witnessing this process could be hair-raising for his aides, and so it was for me as I rode with him to the parliament, crammed into a jump seat in the back of his limousine. Both in the car and in the holding room before he went to the dais, he was muttering and cursing as he scribbled tag lines for new ideas in the margins.

The speech worked spectacularly. The initially cool, normally jaded politicians interrupted him with rapturous applause. Early on, he expressed compassion for the victims of the latest killings in Kashmir and mentioned that he had met with the widow of the young man murdered by the hijackers in January. He also sought to build up the Indians' self-confidence about their economic potential:

> You liberated your markets and now have one of the ten fastest growing economies in the world. At the rate of growth within your grasp, India's standard of living could rise by 500 percent in just 20 years. You embraced information technology and now, when Americans and other big software companies call for consumer and customer support, they're just as likely to find themselves talking to an expert in Bangalore as in Seattle.*

Only after this audience-friendly opening did he introduce the nuclear issue, and he did so by acknowledging the responsibility that the United States bore for setting an example in nonproliferation and disarmament: "I'm aware that I speak to you on behalf of a nation that has possessed nuclear weapons for fifty-five years and more." He then moved to the main message: if India wanted to join the United States as an equal and be treated as a responsible power, it should look not to the past but to the future: "We are producing no more fissile material, developing no new land- or submarine-based missiles, engaging in no new nuclear testing." India should also look to the rest of the world: "From South America to South Africa, nations are forswearing these weapons, realizing that a nuclear future is not a more secure future. Most of the world is moving toward the elimination of nuclear weapons. That goal is not advanced if any country, in any region, moves in the other direction."

He was inching toward the hard message, but he set it up with an affirmation of Indian sovereignty, which drew another round of applause:

---

*The issue of the outsourcing—or "off-shoring"—of American jobs to India aroused nowhere near as much political controversy in the United States in 2000 than during the presidential campaign of 2004.

Only India can know if it truly is safer today than before the tests. Only India can determine if it will benefit from expanding its nuclear and missile capabilities, if its neighbors respond by doing the same thing. Only India knows if it can afford a sustained increase in both conventional and nuclear forces while meeting its goals for human development. These are questions others may ask, but only you can answer. . . .

India is a leader, a great nation, which by virtue of its size, its achievements and its example, has the ability to shape the character of our time. . . . Great nations with broad horizons must consider whether actions advance or hinder what Nehru called the larger cause of humanity. So India's nuclear policies, inevitably, have consequences beyond your borders, eroding the barriers against the spread of nuclear weapons, discouraging nations that have chosen to forswear these weapons, encouraging others to keep their options open. But if India's nuclear test shook the world, India's leadership for nonproliferation can certainly move the world.

There was a bit of code here that Clinton knew Vajpayee, who was sitting beside him, would understand: India might someday get American support for permanent membership on the Security Council if it found a way of advancing another more immediate, more specific, and much larger cause, which was nonproliferation.

I had attended plenty of Clinton speeches, but the experience this time was especially revealing, perhaps because I had been living with the issues for so long—perhaps, too, because instead of sitting with the traveling White House staff, I found a seat about twenty rows back, surrounded by members of parliament, in order to get a better sense of how the speech worked with that audience. Clinton read the mood of the approximately seven hundred men and women in front of him and recrafted parts of the speech as he talked. He felt particularly comfortable improvising on his signature themes: the tension between the upside and downside of globalization, the struggle between hope and fear, the way in which both optimism and pessimism can be self-fulfilling, the extent to which interdependence was replacing independence as the natural condition of states, the obligation of leaders to imagine a different and better future, the need for nations to define strength and greatness in terms of the twenty-first century rather than those of the nineteenth and twentieth:

> Time and again in my time as president, America has found that it is the weakness of great nations, not their strength, that threatens their vision for tomorrow. So we want India to be strong, to be secure, to be united, to be a force for a safer, more prosperous, more democratic world. Whatever we ask of you, we ask in that spirit alone.

This last point was one he had used, nearly two years earlier, to chastise the Indians after their test.[3] Now that he was in New Delhi and addressing them directly, he recast the same point as an exhortation of what they could do rather than castigation for what they had done.

The setting and the audience that morning were nearly perfect for him. Parliaments are to democratic politics what churches are to religion, and Clinton had a lot of the southern preacher in him. The bully pulpit of his office was a platform from which he did everything but bully, especially when he was abroad. He cajoled, flattered, encouraged, persuaded, evangelized, and, above all, engaged. If there was tough love to administer, he dosed it with empathy. He laid on thick his appreciation of what was most admirable in the past and what was most promising about the future of the nation whose representatives he was addressing. Without seeming either patronizing or Pollyanna-like, he was able to convey the impression that he was even more confident in, and more optimistic about, their country than they were themselves.

Vajpayee's speech in reply finally gave American visitors who had been dealing with him for the last several years, myself included, a chance to see what a powerful orator he was. His peroration brought many of the MPs in the chamber to their feet:

> Mr. President, your visit marks the beginning of a new voyage in the new century by two countries which have all the potential to become natural allies. In this context, we can do no better than to recall to ourselves the stirring words of the great American poet, Walt Whitman. Noting that a "Passage to India" is always a "Passage to more than India," Whitman, in his long and admiring poem on India, called upon our two peoples to:

Sail forth—steer for the deep waters only,
Reckless O soul, exploring, I with thee, and thou with me,
For we are bound where mariner has not yet dared to go.

AFTER ALL THIS soaring rhetoric from the two leaders, Madeleine Albright had the unenviable task of meeting with Jaswant to make sure he understood that there was still plenty of tough, nitty-gritty work to be done. The chemistry had never been good between them, and on this occasion he provoked her by offering a bromide about how there was, on nonproliferation, "no difference in principle between us, just a difficulty in the management of the politics of it."

"Look, Jaswant," said Madeleine, "despite the pleasantries, there are some things that won't go away and that can't go away."

Another thing that would not go away was Indian apprehension about Clinton's forthcoming stop in Islamabad. Jaswant felt he had to repeat a familiar warning: Musharraf would exploit any American attention as supportive of his position and contrary to India's. Pakistan deserved a cold shoulder and nothing else.

"As irritated and disappointed as we are with Pakistan," Madeleine replied, "we can't turn them into a pariah."

"Oh, absolutely!" said Jaswant. Of course India and the United States must do everything they could to keep Pakistan from being isolated and therefore all the more radicalized, and to keep alive the possibility of a settlement. "But someone playing the role of umpire will reduce the possibilities of it working."

Madeleine grew exasperated. "Don't blame the umpire," she said. "Look to yourselves as players. Do something about the nature of the game."

Jaswant was not to be deterred, nor was he going to let her have the final word on this subject. The problem with Pakistan was its ongoing "Talibanization"; the struggle was not so much between Pakistan and any other state as within that country: "Pakistan is much more at war with itself than outside itself."

RELIEVED TO HAVE the meeting over with, Madeleine went off to a reception at Roosevelt House while I accompanied Jaswant back to South Block. He obviously felt he had held his own and dispensed all the warnings and rebuttals that were required for the diplomatic record. When we got to his office he was, by his standards, in a mellow mood. While a stereo system played a Mozart piano concerto softly in the background, he savored what he regarded, all in all, as a good day.

He was effusive in his praise for Clinton's speech in the parliament. He had been attending political and diplomatic spectacles in that chamber for some thirty years, but he had never witnessed anything quite as compelling. Clinton had taken a giant step toward dispelling the mistrust that had accumulated over half a century. The speech, while hortatory, had avoided any impression of arm-twisting. As a result, said Jaswant, what had been impossible before the visit was now merely very, very difficult—namely, progress on the nonproliferation agenda. He knew that people in Washington suspected him and his prime minister of stringing us along—either that, or of not having a firm grip on their own political system. He could understand how it might appear that way, but he wanted me to appreciate the extent to which circumstances had conspired against us both. The four big setbacks over the last year— the parliamentary crisis followed by the long electoral campaign, Kargil, the coup in Islamabad, and the hijacking—had taken a considerable toll on him politically. The last three in particular, since they were Pakistan-instigated and therefore security-related, strengthened opponents of the CTBT within the BJP and further disinclined the Congress Party to help.

Despite all that, Jaswant said, maybe in the wake of the presidential visit, there was still some chance of getting the CTBT done. He was willing to make one more stab at developing the consensus he had been talking about for the last two years; he would put the issue before the appropriate parliamentary committee in May, then take it to the floor.

I listened in astonishment. Maybe he really believed there was such a chance, but I did not. If anything, the CTBT faced more opposition in India than ever. There was, I knew, a technical debate under way in which Jaswant was likely to be in the minority. Influential figures in the scientific and strategic elite—including, perhaps, my exuberant lunch and dinner partner of the day before—believed that while the Pokhran II series of tests had been sufficient for establishing confidence in a basic fission device (that is, an atomic bomb), more tests were necessary to perfect a thermonuclear one (a hydrogen bomb).

I told Jaswant that despite his own good intentions and admirable persistence—and despite my own president's pep talk about the progress

India and the United States could still make on the nuclear issues—I feared time was running out. Jaswant had been candid with me many times about his domestic politics and how they obtruded on our diplomacy, and I now owed him a bit of reciprocity. It would be comforting to think that the visit that Vajpayee would make to Washington in September might be an "action-forcing event," a deadline for Jaswant to use within his own government in getting signature on the CTBT. But the visit would also come at the height of the American presidential election campaign. Al Gore was committed to trying to resurrect the treaty, while the Republican candidate—most likely George W. Bush—would probably stick with his party's decision to kill it.

What I did not say, and didn't need to, was that under those circumstances, Vajpayee would probably choose to wait to see who won the presidency before making any definitive moves on the CTBT.

Jaswant lapsed into a silence of his own for a moment, then acknowledged that I might be right. "Perhaps, much like President Clinton's long trip in coming to New Delhi," he said, "our own venture has been more directional than destinational."

His willingness to give the CTBT one last try, he said, was rooted in a sense of personal obligation to deliver on past promises. But then, after another pause, he added, "An obligation to deliver does not mean an ability to deliver—it means determination to try."

AT THE CONCLUSION of Clinton's program in New Delhi, he set off for Jaipur, Hyderabad, and Mumbai. Since my work was done, I hitched a ride on Secretary Albright's plane to Geneva, where she was scheduled to address the UN Commission on Human Rights. Shortly after takeoff, she and I compared notes briefly; then she had the good sense to get some sleep in the airborne stateroom.

I went back to my seat in the senior-staff section ("business class," we called it), cranked up my laptop, and wrote up my impressions, for her and Sandy, of where we stood with our principal interlocutor. "Jaswant," I wrote, "is feeling once bitten, twice shy—not bitten by us, but by circumstance and by his countrymen." The last several months seemed to have taken a considerable toll on him—politically, physically, and psychically. "Now, more even than when we started in June '98, we must recognize that Jaswant isn't Vajpayee; he isn't the BJP; he isn't the [parliament]; and he isn't India.

"But he is the Minister of External Affairs, and he's committed to testing the questions that I posed very candidly to him: now that the president has delivered the much vaunted, long-awaited opening of [a] new era, can Vajpayee deliver a relatively modest, highly reasonable set of steps that will demonstrate India's determination to make itself part of the solution to the global problem of non-proliferation? His answer, which I endorse: *maybe; let's try.*"

I concluded that we should see if we could get CTBT signature in early summer, followed by major progress on the other three benchmarks when Vajpayee came to the United States in the fall. I couldn't quite dissociate myself from Jaswant's refusal to give up, even though I could see clearly enough how formidable the obstacles to progress were. The president's trip had been, by the standard of achievable results, a stunning success. But the boulder we had been counting on Jaswant to budge was still at the bottom of the hill. He might go through the motion of giving it one more shove, and we must do whatever we could to help him. But the fact was, we had exhausted our leverage on Indian decisionmaking.

WHEN I FINISHED the memo, I should have followed Madeleine's example, put on my sleep mask and unplugged from the world. Instead, I let myself be talked into joining some of her team in watching nearly all thirteen episodes of the first season of *The Sopranos* on the plane's video system. The marathon screening lasted the rest of the flight. Fortunately, the only damage done was to my biorhythms and not to the national interest, since I had no diplomatic duties awaiting me on the ground in Geneva.

From there I flew home, while Madeleine returned to South Asia to join Clinton for a visit to Pakistan that was memorable in its own right and a telling contrast to the one he had just completed to India. Because of the Secret Service's concerns about the threat from al Qaeda, Air Force One leapfrogged ahead to Muscat, Oman.* Clinton traveled into Islamabad aboard an unmarked Gulfstream executive jet with another one, painted with Air Force One's colors and the words "United States of

---

*As a result of this complex arrangement, Oman got its first visit from a U.S. president, although it lasted only an hour—just long enough for Clinton to meet with the country's ruler, Sultan Qaboos, at the airport.

America," leading the way. If terrorists armed with surface-to-air missiles managed to get off a shot, they would likely aim at the first plane.[4]

In addition to meeting with Musharraf, Clinton gave a fifteen-minute speech that was televised live and in full so that Musharraf would not be able to pick and choose which passages were aired.

The president adapted his favorite theme for the Pakistani people: "With the right vision rooted in tomorrow's promise, not yesterday's pain—rooted in dialogue, not destruction, Pakistan can fulfill its destiny as a beacon of democracy in the Muslim world. . . . If you choose that future, the United States will walk with you."

With his audience to the south much in mind, Clinton also said, "We cannot and will not mediate or resolve the dispute in Kashmir. Only you and India can do that, through dialogue."

In an hour-and-a-half meeting with Musharraf, Clinton asked for assurances that Pakistan would return to democracy, show restraint in Kashmir, exert pressure on terrorist groups, and help in apprehending bin Laden. Musharraf, who had, in the previous days, postponed elections and referred publicly to Kashmir militants as freedom fighters, offered only bland statements in reply.

Clinton departed having spent five hours on the ground in Pakistan after five days in India.[5]

ELEVEN

UNFINISHED BUSINESS

JASWANT AND I next saw each other, in July 2000, in Bangkok, where we attended that year's session of the ASEAN Regional Forum. Fortunately, I was spared having to be part of a skit at the closing dinner, since Secretary Albright was there and did another star turn with a song-and-dance routine on the theme of "Thanks for the Memories." Wearing a bowler and a tuxedo jacket, she sang, "I'm so glad Jaswant is here. If he's looking to please me . . . he'll sign CTBT."

Jaswant was in no joking mood on that subject. "I've heard your song," he commented, rather starchily, during an exchange with Madeleine during one of the plenary sessions.

Jaswant and I sat next to each other during a long bus ride to a seaside resort for an audience with King Bhumibol Adulyadej. He then joined me aboard a small plane that the U.S. embassy provided to take us to Bangkok airport for our flights home. During both these journeys, Jaswant spent a lot of time taking in the scenery. His long silences were more awkward than pensive. In the airport departure lounge, we went to a Japanese restaurant for what we had promised each other would be another in our series of working meals. But our work was done and we both knew it. Jaswant said nothing about trying to push the CTBT. I assumed he had given up but did not feel he could tell me since Vajpayee was coming to Washington for an official visit two months later and Jaswant did not want to strike any sour notes before the trip.

Vajpayee's visit in mid-September came off without a hitch. He was invited to address the joint houses of Congress in reciprocity for the chance he had given Clinton to speak to the Indian parliament.

On Sunday evening, September 17, the Clintons threw a lavish banquet under a massive tent on the South Lawn of the White House. Jaswant and I were seated next to each other at the long head table. We didn't get much opportunity to speak, since each of us had to make small talk with the dignitary on the other side—in his case an American official, in mine an Indian. Brooke was at one of the seventy circular tables for the nearly seven hundred guests, the majority of whom were Indian Americans from around the country. It was the largest state dinner of the administration.

While several notches below us in protocol, Brooke had more fun, not least because her dinner partner was the comic actor Chevy Chase. He had known Clinton for years but was reluctant to approach him at the head table in the midst of what might, for all he knew, be a moment of high statesmanship. Brooke said he shouldn't worry, took him by the arm and led him to Clinton at the center of the dais. The president, who was not having much success chatting up Vajpayee, was delighted when Chase appeared before him. In his exuberance, Clinton reached out to shake Chase's hand and knocked over Vajpayee's untouched glass of red wine, causing its contents to gush all over the prime minister's jacket. Clinton's face turned beet-red while waiters and security types rushed over and patted Vajpayee down with wet napkins. Chase, having inadvertently introduced slapstick into the occasion, could not think of anything to do but play out his part in the extended sight gag. He theatrically turned on his heel and, with an I'm-outta-here expression, retreated to his assigned place, pretending to whistle nonchalantly as though nothing had happened. Once he was in his seat, Chase sneaked a look at what was going on at the head table. He and Clinton caught each other's eye and exchanged the faintest and briefest of smiles, suggesting that they were both as amused as they were mortified. Vajpayee remained impassive throughout the incident.

Brooke by then had made her way to where Jaswant and I were sitting, well below the salt. "Are you boys behaving yourselves?" she asked.

Jaswant gave her one of his tired but patient looks, with a hint of amusement. "As much as usual," he said.

Brooke leaned over and gave him a kiss on the cheek. "Thanks for coming to our village, Jaswant." Nodding in the direction of the prime minister, who was suddenly the focus of so much bustling attention, she added, "And thanks for bringing your friend."

"Thank you for coming to mine," Jaswant replied, "and for bringing yours."

TWO DAYS LATER I saw Jaswant for the last time before I left government. We were making our annual pilgrimages to New York for the United Nations General Assembly. He asked to meet me alone at the Waldorf-Astoria so that he could officially notify me—and it came as no surprise—that India was not going to sign the CTBT. He apologized for having, as he put it, "let you down." I told him I knew he had tried but that the confluence of circumstances—like an inauspicious alignment of the stars in Rakesh Sood's astrological charts—had conspired against us.

Those circumstances included an American political environment in which the Republican majority in Congress gave the administration a hard time across the board, including on almost every aspect of foreign policy. It was difficult enough to conduct diplomacy with any semblance of bipartisanship in 1998 and 1999. In 2000, with the presidential campaign in high gear, it was nearly impossible. Clinton was on his way out, and Al Gore was running behind George W. Bush in the polls. It was understandable that the Indians would put their diplomacy with us on hold while we sorted out our political leadership.

Many Indians who followed the American race closely thought they had reason to root for Bush, since his campaign struck a number of themes that were music to their ears. The Texas governor made clear from the beginning that he had little use for traditional nonproliferation measures enshrined in negotiated agreements like the CTBT. For him, the best way to deal with proliferation was technologically and militarily rather than diplomatically, unilaterally rather than multilaterally, and through measures targeted on specific dangerous countries rather than applicable to otherwise friendly states like India. In his first major foreign policy speech as a candidate, on November 19, 1999, at the Ronald Reagan Presidential Library in Simi Valley, California, Bush said: "Our nation must diminish the evil attraction of [nuclear] weapons for rogue states by rendering them useless with missile defense. The Comprehensive

Test Ban Treaty does nothing to gain these goals. It does not stop proliferation, especially to renegade regimes."

Since India was not in that category, its government believed it was
less likely to hear as much about its nuclear and missile programs from a
Bush administration as it had from the Clinton administration—or as it
would hear from a Gore administration.

Bush's repeated criticism of Clinton for failing to recognize that China
was "a competitor, not a strategic partner" was also well received in India.
In an article in *Foreign Affairs* in early 2000, Condoleezza Rice, who
would, a year later, succeed Sandy Berger as national security adviser, put
the candidate's anti-China sentiment in a pro-Indian context:

> China's success in controlling the balance of power depends in large
> part on America's reaction to the challenge. The United States . . .
> should pay closer attention to India's role in the regional balance.
> There is a strong tendency conceptually to connect India with Pak-
> istan and to think only of Kashmir or the nuclear competition
> between the two states. But India is an element in China's calcula-
> tion, and it should be in America's, too. India is not a great power
> yet, but it has the potential to emerge as one.[1]

I had heard something close to this argument from Jaswant and other
Indians in almost every round of the dialogue.

IN JULY 2000 Paul Wolfowitz, the intellectually formidable neoconserv-
ative who would become deputy secretary of defense in the Bush administration, lamented that India had been a "black hole" in American
foreign policymaking and that past administrations had too often substi-
tuted sanctions for policy. While Wolfowitz's comment was widely covered and much applauded in the Indian press, it went largely unnoticed
in the United States.[2] South Asia barely figured as an issue in the campaign. Bush's foreign policy speeches contained brief, carefully crafted
mentions of the region and called for engagement with India balanced
against preservation of America's solid relationship with Pakistan.[3] A version of that mantra appeared in the Republican party platform. The
Democrats included a nearly identical plank in their own platform. Bush
made few targeted appeals to Indian Americans, and on election day that

community, like the country as a whole, split its votes just about evenly between the two candidates.

Once the outcome of the election was settled, the incoming administration at first adopted a posture toward India that was not, in its essence, much different from its predecessor's. When Colin Powell went before the Senate Foreign Relations Committee for hearings on his confirmation as Bush's secretary of state, he repeated the promise to "engage more broadly with India." Then he added, "We have to do what we can to constrain their nuclear program at this time"—a combination of good and bad news for the Indians, close to what they would probably have heard from a Gore nominee for the same post. Pressed by Senator Brownback to commit to a timetable for lifting the remaining sanctions against India, Powell said he needed to study the matter further.

A number of Indian officials and journalists I knew remarked, a bit ruefully, that it looked as though there had been a smooth handoff from one administration to the next—at least with regard to U.S. policy toward their country.

As the Bush presidency got under way, some of those same Indians shifted from disappointment to alarm. They were beginning to have a sense of déjà vu—not from the second Clinton administration but from the first: it looked as though India might be relegated, yet again, to secondary importance by a new administration whose priorities had nothing to do with South Asia. In Bush's case, those were building a national missile defense system, toppling Saddam Hussein, and squaring off against China. Virtually all the Indians I talked to disapproved of the missile defense plan since it meant pulling out of a treaty with Russia that prohibited such a system; the plan was therefore seen as an ominous and provocative manifestation of the American penchant for acting alone. For much the same reason they were aghast at the undisguised determination of the new administration to bring down Saddam, with whom the Indian government had generally smooth relations. While they were glad to see a tougher American stance toward China, they wanted India to be taken seriously as a major power in its own right, not just as a large piece on the Asian chess board.

JASWANT CAME TO Washington in early April 2001 at a moment of heightened tension between the United States and China. Six days before he arrived, a Chinese interceptor collided with an American reconnaissance plane, forcing it to make a crash landing on a Chinese island and touching off an eleven-day altercation over the release of the crew.

When Jaswant called on Condoleezza Rice in the West Wing, Bush did a "drop-by" on their meeting—a carefully choreographed gesture of respect—then invited Jaswant back to the Oval Office for a forty-minute conversation. White House aides put out the story that the special treatment was intended to underscore the potential for U.S.-Indian cooperation against China.

The previous month, George Fernandes had stepped down as defense minister because of a bribery scandal, and Jaswant had replaced Fernandes on an interim basis while retaining his own portfolio as minister of external affairs. He got red-carpet treatment at the Pentagon, where Secretary of Defense Donald Rumsfeld told him that the new administration was prepared to initiate a series of high-level military exchanges.

To reciprocate this good news and solidify ties to the administration, Jaswant told Rumsfeld that he supported the Bush plan for national missile defenses—a position that raised some eyebrows back in New Delhi.

The following day, a Saturday, Jaswant came to Brooke's and my house for lunch. For most of the conversation we steered clear of politics and diplomacy, although he commented wryly that the United States had come a long way since the summer of 1998, when the Clinton administration tried to play the China card against India. He was particularly pleased with the meeting he had held with his new American counterpart. Secretary Powell, said Jaswant, "seems quite prepared to pick up where you and I left off in our journey together."

Powell came close to saying the same thing publicly. "A lot has been done in recent years," he told the press in a joint appearance with Jaswant. "We look forward to building on all that has been accomplished."

In reply, Jaswant said, "Secretary Powell and I have decided that the architecture of the dialogue that had been put in place earlier will be fully implemented."

THE EXCHANGE WAS another indication of Powell's strong—and, as it turned out, stubborn—belief that a certain degree of continuity with the previous administration was not altogether a bad thing. This feature of Powell's approach to his job enhanced his popularity and effectiveness with moderate Republicans, with most Democrats, and with almost all his foreign partners. But it also made him the odd man out in an administration that seemed reflexively inclined to stop, repudiate and, if possible, reverse any policy or project associated with Clinton.

Powell's desire to preserve some of the main strands of U.S. diplomacy extended to the issue of nuclear weaponry in South Asia. His closest colleague in the State Department was my successor as deputy secretary, Richard Armitage, who said during a press conference in Australia, on August 17, 2001, "India is a nuclear power. There are a lot of reasons we ought to engage with India, and we're going to." While robust in tone, this statement could just as well have served as a motto for the Clinton policy—with one addition: having declared and demonstrated itself to be a nuclear power, India had disqualified itself from receiving certain kinds of assistance available to non-nuclear-weapons states. Armitage left that point unstated in public, but for the next two and a half years, the Bush administration maintained the restrictions on various forms of aid and trade imposed on India and Pakistan because of their refusal to abide by the NPT.

In dealing with their Indian counterparts, Powell, Armitage, John Bolton (the under secretary of state for arms control and nonproliferation), and Christina Rocca (a member of Senator Brownback's staff who took Rick Inderfurth's place as assistant secretary for South Asia) pressed for what were essentially the Clinton administration's four nonproliferation benchmarks: no more nuclear testing, a halt in the production of fissile material, strategic restraint, and stricter export controls.

Powell and his colleagues did not advertise the extent to which they were picking up where their predecessors left off, but they did not go out of their way to deny that they were doing so.[4]

When the sanctions were lifted on September 22, 2001, it was because they had long since passed the point of diminishing returns, not because the new administration believed the previous one had been mistaken to impose them in the first place or because it was prepared to give India a pass on the NPT. A "Memorandum of Justification," released by the White House to meet the congressional requirement on lifting sanctions, noted:

> Waiving these sanctions does not reflect a diminution of our concerns over nuclear and missile proliferation in South Asia, or of our

determination to prevent proliferation globally. Rather, it reflects a considered judgment that we are more likely to make progress on our nonproliferation agenda through a cooperative relationship, in which sanctions are no longer an issue.

By then, the post–cold war era of U.S. foreign policy had given way to the post–September 11 era. A Pentagon team was headed toward Pakistan to prepare for the war that would bring down the Taliban regime and drive Osama bin Laden and al Qaeda into the mountains. Virtually every aspect and objective of U.S. foreign policy was subordinated to the war on terrorism.

The ramifications for India were mixed. On the one hand, the government in New Delhi could—and did—reiterate with more force than ever the claim that Jaswant had so often impressed upon me and that Vajpayee had made part of his peroration before the Indian parliament during the Clinton visit in 2000: the United States and India were "natural allies" on a wide range of issues, and they were certainly on the same side in the struggle against radical and violent forces in the Islamic world.

However, the disagreement over how to handle Pakistan was now even more of a complicating factor in U.S.-Indian relations than it had been during the late 1990s. The Indians saw what happened on September 11 as further evidence of what they had been telling the United States for years: Pakistan should be dealt with as a rogue state since it was the principal sponsor and protector of the Taliban.

President Bush's representatives in Washington and New Delhi countered with a version of the Clinton administration's side of that long-running argument: treating Pakistan as an enemy and a lost cause would only drive it further and faster in the direction of behaving like one. Instead, the Bush administration gave Musharraf another chance, but with an explicit warning that it was the last one. Unless he cut off Pakistan's backing for the Taliban and helped crush al Qaeda, his country faced isolation and economic collapse. Washington would maintain sanctions, halt aid, and give Pakistan no help with its massive debt. It was an immediate and precisely targeted application of the new Bush doctrine: you're either with us or against us. But it was also a forceful resort to the channel to Musharraf that Clinton had kept open with his controversial and risky trip to Islamabad in March 2000. If, as the Indians had wanted, Clinton had cast Musharraf into outer darkness after the coup that brought him to power, Bush would probably have had less success in bringing his own influence to bear on the Pakistani leader in late 2001.

American pressure worked. Musharraf allowed the United States to use Pakistani airspace and military bases for attacks on targets in Afghanistan; he banned two Islamist groups in Pakistan that the State Department had designated as sponsors of terrorism; he sacked two top pro-Taliban generals—and he was rewarded with economic aid.

Predictably, some Indian commentators complained about a return to the Nixon-Kissinger "tilt" toward Pakistan.[5] From their vantage point, it looked as though history was repeating itself in a way that was both disadvantageous and unfair to India. Having coddled Pakistan as an ally in the cold war, the United States seemed to be doing so again in the war on terror. Even the geography was the same: Afghanistan had been the last battlefield of the cold war; now it was the first battlefield of the new global struggle.

Nonetheless, the Indians kept in check their official displeasure over America's renewed embrace of Pakistan, in part because the Bush administration made a concerted effort to keep the Indians from feeling neglected even as it blitzed Islamabad with attention. The president met with Vajpayee at the UN, and Powell made three visits to New Delhi in the course of nine months—a record that will probably stand for a long time.

But there was an additional reason why the United States was able to concentrate as much as it did on Pakistan after September 11 without greatly upsetting relations with India: as a result of the buildup in trust between the United States and India during the previous three years, there was a cushion in Washington's bilateral relationship with New Delhi—and additional room for the American leadership to maneuver in the triangular one that included Islamabad.

THAT SALUTARY DYNAMIC was sorely tested by a new crisis between India and Pakistan at the end of 2001. In accommodating the U.S. demands that he crack down on the Taliban, Musharraf overrode the objections of Pakistani Islamists, including many of his fellow army officers as well as militants in the intelligence services. Partly to mollify them and partly out of his own deep-seated antipathy toward India, Musharraf allowed infiltration of Kashmir to continue. On December 13, a five-man suicide squad attacked the Indian parliament building in New Delhi, killing nine people in a forty-minute gun battle. The terrorists were connected with Jaish-e-Mohammad, a Pakistan-based movement led by Maulana Masood Azhar, one of the three hostages Jaswant had traded in Kandahar for the passengers aboard the hijacked Indian Airbus two years earlier.*

George Fernandes—who by then had been reinstated as defense minister—called the outrage "our September 11."[6] India ordered the largest mobilization of its forces ever and proclaimed that it was ready to go to war against Pakistan despite the presence of U.S. troops deployed there as part of the anti-Taliban operation. India reportedly took steps to ensure that its nuclear weapons were ready for use if Pakistan struck first with its own.[7]

After another flare-up in June, the Bush administration sent Rich Armitage on an emergency mission to Islamabad, where he elicited from Musharraf an assurance that infiltration would stop. The episode was—in motivation, execution, and consequence—a replay of the Blair House talks over the Fourth of July weekend in 1999.

The stakes were as high as they had been during the Kargil crisis, and the outcome was as much a cause for relief. This time, however, the urgent business of American "facilitation" could be transacted government-to-government rather than requiring the direct intervention of the American president. The level of deputy secretary of state seemed about right to me.

DURING THIS PERIOD of heightened tension with Pakistan, violence erupted inside India. It started on February 27, 2002, in an incident that remains an object of conflicting interpretations. A scuffle broke out between Hindu activists and Muslim vendors on the outskirts of Ahmedabad, the largest city in Gujarat. A riot ensued, and a Muslim mob set fire to a train carrying Hindu pilgrims, leaving fifty-eight charred corpses. In revenge, Hindus attacked Muslims throughout the state, looting shops, destroying houses, and stabbing, hacking to death, and burning alive as many as two thousand people.

---

*Another of the Pakistani prisoners released in exchange for the hostages was Omar Sheikh, who was centrally involved in the abduction and murder of the *Wall Street Journal* reporter Daniel Pearl in February 2002.

Coming just over two months after the attack on the parliament, the Gujarat massacres brought back to the fore three related issues that had figured in my dialogue with Jaswant: the connection between Indian-Pakistani relations and communal relations within India; the tension between Hindu nationalism and Indian democracy; and the complexity of Indian political culture and of the BJP itself.

Widespread outrage and disgust swept through India, not just at the slaughter but at reports that the state government in Gujarat, led by the BJP, had stood idly by in the early stages of the mayhem and may have been behind some of the violence.[8] Numerous civil society organizations dominated by Hindus took vigorous and courageous steps to stop Hindu-led rampages, bring those responsible to justice, and protect Muslims.

One firebrand, however, who not only escaped accountability but reaped apparent political rewards was the chief minister of Gujarat, Narenda Modi, who went on to lead the BJP to a landslide victory in state elections in Gujarat later in 2002 and made himself into a national figure venerated by many Hindu nationalists. Using posters and video-tapes of the original incident in which Muslims killed Hindus, along with rhetoric that depicted Muslims as terrorists, the BJP did especially well in areas afflicted by communal strife.

The contrast could not have been more stark between Modi and Prime Minister Vajpayee, who denounced the Gujarat bloodbath as a "blot on the face of the country" and the revenge killing of Muslims as "madness."

Vajpayee, however, was on the political defensive. Modi represented forces within the BJP that were then on the rise. At the end of June, in a move widely interpreted as a nod to hard-liners, Vajpayee made Lal Krishna Advani deputy prime minister while keeping him in the power-ful post as home minister.

A week later, Vajpayee shifted Jaswant from the foreign ministry to the finance ministry in a swap with Yashwant Sinha, a BJP stalwart.*

Speculation swirled that Jaswant, the persistent and often beleaguered champion of moderation in Indian foreign and domestic policy, had lost out to Advani, Mishra, and conservatives within the BJP.

There was no doubt a measure of truth in that theory, but Vajpayee's motives in making the change were surely more complicated. He was

*Jaswant Singh and Yashwant Sinha are different transliterations of what is essentially the same name, the first from Rajasthan and the other from Bihar.

hardly exiling his old friend by sending him from the South Block to the North Block, where the finance ministry was located. The need to press ahead with privatization, reform labor laws, and lower budget deficits was of great importance to the prosperity of the country and to the fate of the BJP.

The fact remained, however, that Sinha was neither as forceful as Jaswant in the post of minister of external affairs, nor as encumbered by the baggage that the U.S.-Indian dialogue of 1998–2000 represented in the eyes of nationalists.

Now that Jaswant would be preoccupied with what he called the "dreadful but necessary business of sums," Mishra had even more influence over security policy. When the government finally came forth with its nuclear doctrine early in 2003, it was considerably closer to the draft Mishra had overseen in August 1999 than it was to what Jaswant had told me to expect.[9]

Assessing the cabinet shuffle in the Hindu, Raja Mohan wrote a testimonial to Jaswant for his role as a major force in Indian foreign policy:

> The decision to conduct nuclear tests in May 1998 opened the doors for a creative phase in India's diplomacy, and Mr. Singh rose to the challenge with political aplomb and personal dignity. He brought to office a Realist vision of world affairs, defined India's strategic interests as expansively as Lord Curzon did for British India at the dawn of the 20th century, and pursued them with a boldness that had eluded India for decades. . . . [In the dialogue with the United States] he created the basis for transforming Indo-U.S. relations. The cooperative relationship with Washington, that is taken for granted today, was neither universally desired in New Delhi nor easy to accomplish, given the real hurdles that stood in the way of a greater understanding between India and the U.S. Altering the template of the Indo-U.S. relations during the Clinton era and giving it a strategic content during the Bush administration will go down as the single biggest contribution of Mr. Singh.[10]

Three weeks after the Singh-Sinha switch came a third change in the Indian leadership. A. P. J. Abdul Kalam had to defer his plan, which he had confided to me over dinner in New Delhi during the Clinton visit, to retire and work on disarmament. On July 18, 2002, he was overwhelm-

ingly elected to succeed K. R. Narayanan as president of India. Abdul
Kalam attained that post partly as a demonstration of the pluralism—or
as Jaswant would put it, the civilizational richness—of India's society and
political system. The Vajpayee government, which promoted Abdul
Kalam's candidacy in the electoral college, was especially eager to elevate
a Muslim to the presidency in the wake of the Gujarat bloodbath. But the
government was also rewarding Abdul Kalam for his role in India's acquisition of the bomb and underscoring a determination never to give it up.

IN 2003, THE BUSH ADMINISTRATION—especially Powell, Armitage,
and Rocca—worked quietly behind the scene to nudge India and Pakistan toward a revival of the peace process. Bill Clinton chipped in as well.
Shortly after leaving office, with encouragement from Vajpayee, he had
established a foundation to raise money, largely from Indian Americans,
for reconstructing schools and hospitals in villages devastated by an
earthquake that had struck Gujarat in January 2001. That project took
Clinton to India three months later and kept him in close touch with
events and contacts in South Asia over the next two and a half years.

During a period of heightened tension between India and Pakistan in
early 2003, Clinton received a phone call from Musharraf asking for help
in restarting discussions with Vajpayee. Clinton replied that he would not
be party to any such approach unless he was certain that Musharraf recognized that a demand for India to give up Kashmir could not be part of
the deal. Musharraf said he would be back in touch. Clinton heard nothing more from him for nearly nine months.

In November 2003, Clinton visited New Delhi again, this time in connection with another of his post-presidency ventures, an initiative to
combat HIV/AIDS by making treatment more affordable in developing
countries. In a private meeting, Vajpayee cautiously raised the possibility
of resuming talks with Musharraf. When Clinton told him about the call
he had received from the Pakistani leader earlier in the year, Vajpayee
asked him to get back in touch with Musharraf and convey a simple message: Vajpayee was determined, if possible, to remove once and for all the
"burden" that the India-Pakistan dispute imposed on both countries; he
was prepared to reopen a channel to Islamabad without advance commitments on either side, but only if he was confident he would not be
embarrassed as he had been after Lahore.

In delivering that message to Musharraf, Clinton stressed that Vajpayee's political standing in India and his willingness to venture again down what had already been a treacherous road made him the best hope; Pakistan should seize the opportunity, since it might not have another one for a long time to come.

Two days after Clinton's trip, India and Pakistan announced they had agreed to a cease-fire along the Line of Control. The talks led to a resumption of overflight rights and air links that had been suspended in the wake of the attack on the Indian parliament two years before.

The first week in January 2004, Vajpayee and Musharraf met in Islamabad on the margins of a regional leaders' summit. Vajpayee agreed to talks on all issues, including Kashmir, and Musharraf pledged in writing to end Pakistani support of Kashmiri militants. In mid-February, India and Pakistan agreed on a six-month "roadmap to peace," which would, if pursued, address all outstanding issues, including the nuclear one. The official memorandum that came out of the meetings noted that the two countries would be "undertaking national measures to reduce the risks of accidental or unauthorized use of nuclear weapons under their respective control."

That was not the end of the good news. In the weeks that followed, Musharraf, in part because of prodding from the United States, stopped denying that Pakistan was among the world's most promiscuous black-marketeers in nuclear goods and services. He deflected blame from the Pakistani government and military by focusing on the internationally notorious but until then locally revered and untouchable A. Q. Khan, the mastermind of Pakistan's bomb- and missile-making programs and the principal merchant of its secrets to other countries. Under what amounted to a plea bargain, Khan publicly apologized for his misdeeds, and Musharraf gave him a pardon. American government officials congratulated Musharraf and let him pretend that the Pakistani military establishment had not been complicit in Khan's activities.

IN EARLY FEBRUARY 2004, just as this drama was playing out in Islamabad, Brooke and I visited India as part of a delegation assembled by the Aspen Institute and the Confederation of Indian Industry. Our group held a series of meetings with senior officials—Brajesh Mishra, Yashwant Sinha, and George Fernandes—who all voiced some unease that the

American government was treating Musharraf with kid gloves. But they also expressed general satisfaction with the way things were going between the United States and India. Fernandes, as defense minister, made much of how American-Indian military cooperation was thriving; India, in short, had weathered the storm of American sanctions and was now well on its way to establishing itself as a military partner.[11]

Just as we were saying good-bye to Fernandes, a member of our delegation innocently asked him when he would next be coming to Washington. His demeanor abruptly changed. It was as though he was glad to have an excuse to tell us how he really felt about our country. Ignoring an Ethiopian delegation that was already filing into his office and taking its seats, Fernandes regaled us with the story of how he had been strip-searched by officers of the U.S. Immigration and Naturalization Service at Dulles Airport when he arrived for an official visit in early 2002, and again, in mid-2003, when he was passing through the United States on his way to Brazil. He left us with the impression that he had been forced to take off all his clothes and seemed to enjoy our stupefaction at this tale—which turned out to be something of an exaggeration. Nonetheless, he and other Indians who later referred to the incident clearly regarded it as more than merely a lapse of protocol or just another example of the post-9/11 excesses and indignities that air travelers had to endure for the sake of security. The Indians saw it as a symptom of a deep-rooted, widespread condescension—or worse—on the part of the West toward the East.

The sudden display of rancor and raw nerves was, in its own way, all the more revealing for being completely unscripted.

The tone of our meeting with Jaswant Singh was also in a distinctly minor key. The appointment had been difficult to schedule, since parliament was in its final session before the political parties began all-out campaigning for national elections that the BJP had called for in the spring. Jaswant was busy defending the government's latest budget, which was designed to boost his party's chances at the polls. At the last minute, he found about half an hour to receive us in a conference room off the main lounge area in the parliament building.

After a few opening courtesies, Jaswant delivered what was, by his standards, a head-snapping broadside. He treated us as surrogates for the Bush administration and remonstrated with us accordingly. He gave us a brief but more pointed reprise of what we had already heard from Mishra and Sinha about "the folly of exonerating Pervez Musharraf in the matter of Pakistan's flagrant proliferation activities."

Then came what was clearly the main point: "With much regret and all candor, I must tell you that the Bush administration seems largely to have disengaged from India. . . . The dialogue that we began with the previous American administration and had reason to hope would continue with the current one appears to have gone into hiatus." Yes, Colin Powell had visited several times "when September 11 and events northeast of here were much on your mind," and there had been occasional contacts, especially on Mishra's part, with Condoleezza Rice and her deputy at the NSC, Steve Hadley. "But while we see your senior people from time to time, there is little chance to talk to them in depth and on matters that are of the broad scope befitting our shared interests, and little inclination on their part to probe beyond the issues of the day—and those are confined to ones on their own agenda. When it comes to true, sustained engagement on matters of broad and truly mutual interest, we keep asking ourselves, 'Where are the Americans?'"

All of us arrayed around him understood that it was the one message he wanted our delegation to carry back to Washington. His principal target among the visitors was Brent Scowcroft, a longtime leader of the Aspen Institute's strategic studies program, who had been the first President Bush's national security adviser and therefore had channels to the White House.

Scowcroft listened stone-faced and did not reply, but Sandy Berger, who was also in the group, suggested that India should not feel discriminated against by the episodic nature of U.S. attention. The current administration, he said, was generally less inclined than its predecessors to seek—and to take into account—the views of other governments.

Rather theatrically, Jaswant arched his brow, drew a long face, and replied: "That is regrettable in the leadership of a country—the United States of America—that we otherwise admire and with which we have excellent relations. It is a mistake, in this complex, crowded, and busy world of ours, for those who represent great powers not to venture far and wide in search of the interchange that is the sustenance of wise policy."

Then came an echo of my first conversation with him, in my office at the State Department, nearly six years before: "In the villages I knew as a

boy, people were dependent on a form of animal husbandry that disdained fences and boundaries and did not insist on animals staying on
one piece of property. As my father used to say, 'If the cattle do not roam,
how will they graze?'"

With that, the meeting came to an end. We filed out of the parliament
wondering whether Jaswant had coordinated this mixture of chastise-
ment and exhortation with the prime minister's inner circle, or whether
he was on his own, letting us know what he felt should have been the
view of the government as a whole. That was a question about Jaswant I
had long since grown used to asking myself and not always succeeded in
answering.

A little more than a month later, the entire Indian government had
reason to complain publicly about what it regarded as a flagrant failure on
the part of the Bush administration to consult on a matter of the most
vital importance to India. Secretary Powell made yet another visit to New
Delhi, as usual followed by one to Islamabad. But this time, all the good
he did at the first stop was undone by his announcement at the second
that the United States would designate Pakistan a "Major Non-NATO
Ally" of the United States. The Indians, who had no forewarning of this
development, protested. Lalit Mansingh, who was completing his tour as
ambassador to the United States, gave a farewell speech on April 1, 2004,
at a conference at George Washington University organized by Rick
Inderfurth, who had joined the faculty there after leaving government.
Lalit noted India's "deep disappointment with what has happened. The
disappointment is on account of both substance and style. One of the
biggest achievements, in my mind, of the dialogue we have had with the
United States is the establishment of a level of trust. . . . And I'm afraid
that there was a perception that this was breached."

THERE WAS ONE subject that aroused little discussion and virtually no
debate during the spring 2004 Indian election campaign: who would win.
The conventional wisdom, including on the part of several despondent
friends who were connected with the Congress Party and whom Brooke
and I saw in February during the Aspen trip, overwhelmingly predicted
a solid BJP victory. The American embassy had the same prognosis. The
only person of our acquaintance who categorically and confidently predicted an upset victory by the Congress Party was Mala Singh, Brooke's

friend from the sixties and the editor of *Seminar*, who was a sharp-penned critic of the BJP.

As I finished this book, in late May 2004, India and the world were absorbing the shock of the BJP's defeat. Sonia Gandhi, her Congress Party colleagues, and their coalition partners were forming a new government with Manmohan Singh, the highly regarded former finance minister, as prime minister, and Natwar Singh as minister of external affairs. The BJP leadership changed after the election. Vajpayee stepped down, taking the newly created post of party chairman. Advani became opposition leader in the lower house of parliament, and Jaswant was chosen as leader in the upper house.

EVEN THOUGH ATAL BIHARI VAJPAYEE's prime ministership came to an abrupt end, leaving him with a sense of frustration and disappointment, he left India, South Asia and the world with a considerable though fragile legacy in all that he accomplished with Pervez Musharraf in late 2003 and early 2004. One of the many questions hanging over the region as India's new leaders sorted themselves out and went to work is whether they could build on that legacy, and whether their Pakistani counterparts would make it possible for them to do so. The surprise produced by Indian voters in May 2004 was a reminder of the vigor of their nation's democracy. But it also generated new uncertainties about the future of relations with Pakistan, given how productive and promising the personal relationship between Vajpayee and Musharraf turned out to be in making diplomatic progress. Pakistan's own on-again/off-again experience with democracy has, in the past, produced surprises of its own, including those of the most unpleasant kind.

Nonetheless, as India passed from six years of BJP-led government to a restoration, for however long it lasts, of Congress Party rule, the possibility of nuclear war seemed to have faded as a widely perceived threat to the people of South Asia and, accordingly, as a focal point of American diplomacy. This was just what the Indians had hoped would eventually happen when they conducted the Pokhran II tests.

But while the bomb receded as a preoccupying and contentious issue between Washington and New Delhi, it remained—and, indeed, grew—as a dangerous reality on the subcontinent. How many nuclear weapons India had was a question that officials continued to evade, as did the

Pakistanis about their own program. Public estimates in 2003 put both countries' operational warheads at just above forty.[12] The practical definition of "minimum credible deterrence" was no clearer, and no more reassuring, than it had been in the summer of 1999, when Brajesh Mishra's panel of experts first recommended a strategic triad. Work was under way on an Agni-III missile capable of striking deep into eastern China. Some in the Indian military and strategic communities were still tempted by the idea of developing a submarine-launched missile, even though the technical obstacles and financial costs are considerable.

When the Bush administration, during its first term, appealed to India to make good on its protestations of wanting only a minimal deterrent and having no intention of conducting an arms race with its neighbors, a chorus of voices in the Indian government and media howled in protest. An example occurred in mid-October 2003. In response to a Pakistani missile test, the State Department spokesman, Richard Boucher, read out a carefully worded statement: "We urge Pakistan and other countries in the region to take steps to restrain their nuclear weapons and missile programs, including the operational deployment of nuclear-armed ballistic missiles."

It was a reiteration of what we had called, during the Clinton administration, the third benchmark. Even though Boucher had not even mentioned India by name, his counterpart in the Indian Ministry of External Affairs, Navtej Sarna, objected: Boucher "ought to have confined himself to reacting to the Pakistani missile test rather than cluttering up what he had to say by thinly disguised, unwarranted references to India."

Yet it was precisely the "clutter" of India-Pakistan animosity that remained very much at issue, and that threatened to prove in the future even more perilous than it was when Clinton spoke publicly about the danger on the eve of his March 2000 trip. A Kargil-like incident might someday explode before the combatants can stop it, even with a Blair House–like intervention by an American president.

Therefore the United States must not diminish the attention it pays to the nettlesome issues that brought Jaswant and me together six years ago.

The improvement in U.S.-Indian relations in the late 1990s and the consequent broadening of the agenda on which the two countries are now finding ways to cooperate do not constitute an argument or an excuse for letting disagreement over nuclear weaponry and nonproliferation slip into the past or off to one side. Quite the contrary, the intensification of engagement across the board should give India and the United States an additional reason—and an additional means—to address those vital though difficult questions. More particularly, it should give them a compelling inducement to find a way to define India's relationship to the Nuclear Non-Proliferation Treaty that serves the interests of everyone.

THE NPT HAS SOMETHING in common with other international agreements, arrangements, and institutions—the United Nations, NATO, the World Bank, and the International Monetary Fund—that were put in place just before or during the cold war and that now invite debate over whether they should be retained, reformed, transformed, or retired. Like those other mechanisms, the NPT is based on realities that were once indisputable but that have now either evolved or passed into history. The original bargain underlying the treaty was simple enough: the nuclear haves said to the have-nots, "If you abstain from acquiring nuclear weapons, you will get nuclear energy to generate electricity." That offer has not worked with countries that want the power that comes from the bomb much more than the kind that comes out of an electrical grid. Also, peaceful nuclear energy has—for a mixture of environmental, political, and economic reasons—proved controversial and therefore has not been quite the incentive for abstention from seeking the bomb that Dwight Eisenhower and others hoped would be the case when they proposed "atoms for peace." Furthermore, as the North Korean case most dramatically demonstrates, the NPT suffers from a loophole: it allows countries to put in place, under the guise of peaceful purposes, the building blocks of a nuclear weapons program and then withdraw from the treaty without penalty.

All that is an argument for updating and improving the NPT, not for scrapping it. A non-NPT world would be more dangerous than one in which the treaty undergoes adjustment. Despite its imperfections, until recently the NPT showed itself to be a remarkably sturdy construct. Contrary to what pessimists thought at the time it was signed in 1968, the NPT succeeded for thirty years in holding to five the number of countries that tested weapons. Even when India and Pakistan detonated their devices and proclaimed themselves nuclear weapons states in May 1998, the international reaction overwhelmingly favored keeping the treaty intact rather than carving out exceptions. The United States shared that preference and reflected it in its diplomacy.

Since then, however, nonproliferation has suffered further setbacks, including several caused by the Bush administration. Its idea, put forward during the first term, of developing a new generation of "bunker-busting" nuclear weapons would, if pursued, give those in the United States who want to resume testing a pretext for doing so. That inescapable fact weakens the case for other countries to avoid the temptation to test.

In short, to echo a phrase that American and other officials around the world used with their Indian and Pakistani interlocutors after May 1998, the Bush administration has, through some of its own policies and programs, risked making the United States part of the problem of proliferation. It might have gone some way toward making itself, once again, unambiguously part of the solution had it recommitted itself to a treaty-based global nonproliferation regime—and then found a way of bringing India and Pakistan into that regime, even if not formally into the NPT itself. That would have meant accepting the irreversible reality of India's and Pakistan's nuclear weapons programs while providing them with additional incentives for more responsible custodianship of their bombs.

Shoring up the nuclear peace in South Asia is a worthy goal in itself, and progress in that direction will have global benefits as well. With more stringent controls over the export of nuclear equipment and technology, there will be less danger that Pakistan will continue to trade and sell its nuclear technology around the world. Only if they adhere to the highest international standards of security for their nuclear installations, materials, and weapons can India and Pakistan do their share to prevent militant "nonstate actors" like al Qaeda from being able to carry out acts of nuclear terrorism.

The United States and other countries are going to need all the help they can get from India and Pakistan in dealing with the two principal remaining proliferation threats that have so preoccupied the Bush administration since it toppled Saddam Hussein's regime in Iraq in the spring of 2003: Iran and North Korea. While the NPT remained intact despite what happened at Pokhran and Chagai in May 1998, it might well come unraveled if Iran makes its own desert rise or if North Korea turns one of its mountains white. A demonstrably—as opposed to presumptively—nuclear-armed (and nuclear-exporting) North Korea would generate pressures on South Korea, Japan, and Taiwan to rethink and perhaps rescind their decisions of long ago to remain non-nuclear-weapons states under the NPT. An Iranian bomb could touch off a comparable contagion in its volatile neighborhood.

The chances of keeping Northeast Asia and the Greater Middle East from going nuclear will be marginally better if South Asia can be transformed from a region where the global nonproliferation regime has failed into one where it has been imaginatively—and very, very carefully—modified to deal with the business that remains unfinished at the end of the story told here.

IF THERE IS EVER a truly salutary nuclear deal to be done with India, my guess is that it will be a version of the one offered by the Clinton administration and rejected by the BJP-led government. The four U.S.-proposed nonproliferation benchmarks put forward in 1998—joining the CTBT, making progress on a fissile material treaty, exercising strategic restraint (by that or some other name), and meeting the highest standard of export controls—took account of India's accomplishments and aspirations, its rights and anxieties, its opportunities and obligations, and the dangers that its nuclear test was meant to deter as well as those that the test created or exacerbated. The benchmarks represented a compromise that, if accepted in 1999 or 2000, would have worked to the benefit of India, Pakistan, the United States, and the international community. Indeed, the American proposal might have been accepted, at least in part, had the domestic political environments in both India and the United States been more propitious.

The benchmarks, in substance, even if not so designated, should become, once again, the basis of American policy in the future. That would mean having a U.S. administration that persisted until the four areas of restraint become the basis of Indian policy. There would, no doubt, have to be adjustments to accommodate the realities that unfolded in the late 1990s. Those of us who grappled with those realities occasionally speculated about what the United States might be able to offer the Indian leadership if it were to exceed our hopes and demonstrate a high degree of strategic wisdom, global responsibility, and political courage by committing itself to real strategic restraint rather than resisting the term, the concept, and the policy. Bob Einhorn was thinking ahead in this respect, as in others. On a couple of occasions in 1998 and 1999, during blue-sky brainstorming sessions in my conference room with the core India-Pakistan team, Bob ruminated about a way of giving the Indians more than just sanctions relief if they made significant progress on the benchmarks. We did not, however, spend much time developing the notion within our own government or figuring out how to rebut the many arguments against it, since Indian stonewalling gave us no reason to do so. The Indians wanted—and still want—total acceptance as a nuclear power without having to accept any meaningful restrictions on their programs.

Nonetheless, the attempt to engage India as a constructive force in global nonproliferation efforts should continue. That effort will stand a better chance of success if genuine and sweeping reform of the United Nations ever occurs. In that case, permanent membership on the Security Council might be available as an incentive for India to meet some version of the benchmarks. Being among the first to join an expanded Security Council is a paramount and undisguised imperative of Indian foreign policy.

Having tried to blast their way into the nuclear club in 1998, the Indians set back their chances for joining the Security Council. That was Clinton's tough-love message to Vajpayee in their meeting in New Delhi in 2000. In future conversations with an Indian prime minister, an American president might use the prospect of Security Council membership and other possible sources of leverage to coax India into the nonproliferation mainstream. New Delhi might be asked—once again—to forswear further nuclear testing, stop producing fissile material, accept international safeguards on its nuclear facilities, go much further than it has to date in strengthening its controls over transfers of technologies relating to weapons of mass destruction, redouble efforts to ensure that its nuclear installations and materials are effectively protected against theft or seizure, and limit its nuclear-capable ballistic missile programs, especially the operational deployment of those systems.

As for its end of the bargain, the United States—in addition to considering India for a place on an expanded or reconstituted Security Council—might offer the government in New Delhi several other policy changes. Those might include the international help India seeks in developing its civilian nuclear power and its commercial space-launch

capacities, and a relaxation of whatever procedural hurdles and legal restrictions the Bush administration, during its first term, kept in place with
regard to India's desire for high-technology items from the United States.

Since India would never agree to restrictions on its military programs
unless Pakistan accepted similar ones, Pakistan would have to be offered
the same carrots with regard to nuclear energy, commercial space launch,
and high-technology trade.

UNFORTUNATELY, LATE IN its first term and then again during its
second, the Bush administration gave up much of the leverage it had
earlier retained for itself and its successors in this regard. In early 2004,
just as India and Pakistan together took a giant step forward on the fifth
benchmark, on their own relationship, India and the United States
announced what was billed as a reconciliation of a far less welcome sort,
since it hinted that the administration was abandoning all efforts at
progress on the four nonproliferation benchmarks and preparing to give
India a free pass into the nuclear club.

On January 13, 2004, President Bush and Prime Minister Vajpayee released a matched set of statements (that is, with virtually identical texts)
announcing that they had agreed to "enhance cooperation in peaceful uses
of space technology and . . . create the appropriate environment for successful high technology commerce." When I first read the statement in the
newspapers, it sounded like a victory for the Indian stonewallers and a
defeat for the American nonproliferationists. In the spin they put on the
parallel statements, the Indians did everything they could to make it
sound as though they had gone a long way toward persuading the United
States to grant India all the rights and privileges of an NPT-recognized
nuclear weapons state. They managed to include reference to how "the
expanded cooperation launched today is an important milestone in transforming the relationship between India and the United States of America."
But then I read the statement again and zeroed in on the following passage:

> In order to combat the proliferation of weapons of mass destruc-
> tion, relevant laws, regulations and procedures will be strengthened
> and measures to increase bilateral and international cooperation in
> this area will be employed. These cooperative efforts will be under-
> taken in accordance with our respective national laws and interna-
> tional obligations.

Whenever a joint communiqué contains a paragraph as convoluted and heavily weighted with passive-voice verb constructions as this one, you can be sure that it is the most significant, and the most painfully negotiated, in the document. In this case, while the Indians had successfully avoided being named, they were promising to adopt stringent, world-class, and U.S.-certified controls on the export of nuclear and ballistic-missile technology: the fourth benchmark.

I checked my impression with senior people in the White House and State Department. They took pains to assure me that the prospect of loosening curbs on high-tech commerce was conditional on Indian export controls and that, even in the best case, India would not be entitled to the level of assistance and trade available to NPT-compliant countries.

For months leading up to the January 13, 2004, joint statement, Indian officials had pressed hard to get themselves grandfathered out of the NPT restrictions. That subject had dominated the exchanges that went on in the Mishra-Rice channel, mostly because it was just about the only thing Mishra wanted to talk about. In parallel with those talks, the Indians had sought, and received, some support for grandfathering from the Russians and French, but the Bush administration replied that it would not happen.

"We're not going to unravel the NPT for the Indians," Steve Hadley told me. "We aren't going to let whatever is permitted in [commercial space-launch and peaceful nuclear commerce] bleed over into their military missile or nuclear weapons program. We'll have firewalls to prevent that." The "endstate," he assured me, would be "within the context of the existing NPT and U.S. legal structures."

As another official, who had worked with me in the previous administration and who stayed on under Bush, put it, "Jaswant's village, when we get there, won't be a Nirvana for the Indians."

Yet in the wake of the Congress Party victory over the BJP, the Indians' goal continued to be Nirvana. Nothing I heard from Sonia Gandhi, Natwar Singh, or her other advisers during my visits to New Delhi, and nothing in the Congress Party's campaign statements, suggested there would be any significant change in India's nuclear policy. Nor is any American administration likely to find a Congress-led government more receptive to the American case for negotiated restraints on India's programs than President Clinton and I found Mrs. Gandhi to be during our conversations with her. India's demonstration of its nuclear weapons capability and assertion of its status as a nuclear weapons state were popular from the moment Vajpayee announced the test that Monday in May 1998, and they remained so with the change of government in New Delhi. The bomb was seen as a winner, both politically and geopolitically; it was firmly established as both an indispensable instrument of hard power and a talisman of India's having arrived at a place in the sun that it will never abandon; and it remained a centerpiece of Indian diplomacy to get the United States to abandon its own defense of the NPT insofar as that treaty was an affront to India's sense of its rightful place in the world.[13]

WHEN PRIME MINISTER MANMOHAN SINGH came to Washington to meet with President Bush in the summer of 2005, he significantly advanced precisely that goal. The result of the summit made a mockery of earlier assurances from the Bush administration about its determination to preserve the "red lines" between those countries within the NPT and those outside its bounds. The two leaders released a joint statement on July 18 in which the administration granted India almost all the privileges of an NPT member, especially with regard to helping India develop its civilian nuclear power industry. Bush had agreed to give India virtual membership in the club of recognized nuclear-weapons states. In return, the United States (and the world) received nothing in the form of concrete Indian steps toward nuclear restraint in its military programs. In fact, in one important respect, the Indians received more leniency than the five established nuclear "haves": The United States, Britain, France, Russia, and China say they have halted the production of fissile material, while India (echoing a position it had taken for several years) promised only to join a universal ban that would include Pakistan—if such a thing ever materializes.

The U.S.-Indian nuclear deal bore a dubious trademark of Bush foreign policy. Since Bush came into office, he had made clear in word and deed that he did not share his predecessors' confidence in international treaties and institutions. In addition to putting the kibosh on the International Criminal Court and the Kyoto Protocol on climate change, he pulled the United States out of the Anti-Ballistic Missile Treaty, significantly weakened the strategic arms reduction process, suspended or halted a variety of other arms-control and nonproliferation agreements, and associated himself with the Republican refusal in the Senate to ratify the CTBT. Hints continued to come from the Pentagon and elsewhere that the United States might proceed with a new generation of nuclear weapons that will, some of its advocates say, require a resumption of American testing.

No wonder the NPT—originally an American idea that depended for its efficacy on unstinting American support—was almost universally feared to be in jeopardy, including among some influential Republicans in the U.S. Senate. The world had been watching warily to see how the Bush administration handled India and other outliers of the NPT. The short answer coming out of the July 2005 summit was: selectively and unilaterally, without much regard for rules that apply to everyone. In this respect, there was a lamentable symmetry between Indian and American policy: both countries had, in recent years, shown a penchant for going it alone—India in defying the international community (including the United States) with its tests, the Bush administration in attacking Iraq over the objections of the United Nations and many of its own closest allies. If the Indian and American versions of unilateralism continued to reinforce each other, it would work to the detriment of institutions like the United Nations and risk turning treaties like the NPT from imperfect but useful mechanisms into increasingly ineffectual ones.

The American administration—taking its lead from the president himself—tended to see the world in black-and-white, good-versus-evil terms. That view had translated into a nonproliferation policy that cut extra slack for "good" countries, like India, while cracking down on "bad" ones—rogue states like North Korea and Iran. Yet the world is full of countries—many of them, like India, certifiably "good" ones—but also ones that, unlike India, have, for decades, stuck with the original NPT deal and forgone the nuclear option. Seeing the outcome of Manmohan Singh's visit to Washington, some—perhaps many—of those nuclear have-nots would be more inclined to regard the NPT as an anachronism, reconsider their self-restraint, and be tempted by the precedent that India had successfully established and that now seemed to have an American president's blessing.

It was in that context that what both the Indian and American governments hailed as a breakthrough in relations between the two countries in July 2005 was really a step toward a breakdown in the international nonproliferation regime. That did not negate the importance of the many welcome improvements the Bush administration had made possible in U.S.-Indian relations—in trade, counterterrorism, and other areas. Bush and his Indian counterparts—first Vajpayee, then Manmohan Singh—had indeed advanced the goal of making their countries into "natural allies." But they and their successors would, as a result of the short-sighted nuclear deal, face a more dangerous world.

IT IS CRUCIAL that the next American president be far more steadfast than George W. Bush has been in shoring up the global nonproliferation regime. The result need not be an impasse. A set of agreements is imaginable that would stop short of granting India and Pakistan equal status with the five "nuclear haves" in the eyes of the NPT. Rather than expanding the club to seven, there could be, in effect, a "5+2" arrangement, whereby India and Pakistan would earn a degree of leniency in exchange for their yielding to international arms control measures and nonproliferation safeguards. They would be treated as NPT outliers rather than outlaws.

Like several of the diplomatic exertions recounted in this book, trying to get India to accept the 5+2 deal may be Mission Impossible. If the experience of 1998–2000 is any guide, India will resist any bargain that does not give it exactly the same standing as the NPT nuclear weapons states. The Indians will, under any imaginable government, continue to press for removal of the last, detested, though now mostly symbolic, vestiges of what they see as a discriminatory, U.S.-conceived, and U.S.-enforced nuclear order.

The only way the plan can work in New Delhi is if the Indians see it as demanding of them nothing that is incompatible with their security interests in general and, specifically, their doctrine of minimum credible deterrence.

Even then, the 5+2 concept will not be easy to sell in the U.S. Congress, since it would require changing American law over the objections of nonproliferation hawks. It would also require changing the international rules barring India and Pakistan from nuclear trade and aid, and that would mean overriding the protests from countries that were forced, years ago, to make a choice between nuclear weapons and nuclear commerce.

Moreover, resolving the dilemma that was at the heart of my dialogue with Jaswant—that is, partially reconciling India's status as a de facto nuclear weapons state with the need to maintain the NPT as a de jure system—could, inadvertently, create a new, larger dilemma. However firm the intention to make 5+2 a one-time-only accommodation exclusively available to India and Pakistan, other states with nuclear ambitions might still seize upon it as a precedent for themselves and demand the same deal. Why, they would ask, should 5+2 not become 5+X, with X an ever-growing number?

The best (though less than perfect) answer would have to be that non-nuclear states should welcome any outcome that draws India and Pakistan into the orbit of the NPT and therefore into the gravitational pull of internationally agreed standards of responsible nonproliferation behavior. As Jaswant (or Zeno) might put it, the strategy here would be more directional than destinational.

Making meaningful progress of that kind will be difficult, especially given the formidable opposition that will face anyone in India arguing for movement—virtually regardless of who governs that country.[14]

Still, we have to try—and that means a genuinely international "we," very much including the Indians themselves. We may be in the paradoxical situation where offering India and Pakistan special terms of association with the community of nations that are bound by the NPT is the only way to ensure the treaty's vitality. If India can bring itself to be part of the solution to that problem, not least by setting an example for its neighbor, it will have gone a long way toward securing what it sees as its rightful position of international leadership. Presumably that is something India's leaders and people want every bit as much as they want the bomb. It is certainly something that the rest of us should want for them.

ACKNOWLEDGMENTS

THE EXPERIENCES RECOUNTED here were rewarding largely because of the quality of the people I worked with in the U.S. government. Bob Einhorn, Rick Inderfurth, and Bruce Riedel, my three principal associates on the India-Pakistan team, pored over long portions of the manuscript of this book in multiple iterations. They gave me the benefit of their memory, expertise, and judgment and indulged me in my relentless exploitation of their good will. Sandy Berger, who headed a much larger and longer-serving team—the NSC staff—was characteristically assiduous and wise in the help he gave me. Our ultimate captain, President Clinton, found time, in the midst of a particularly intense phase of work on his own memoir, to subject another of mine to a careful read.

My thanks for assistance and advice from others in official positions during the period covered here: Walter Andersen, Bill Antholis, Matt Daley, Bob Gallucci, Phil Goldberg, John Gordon, Jan Lodal, Polly Nayak, Phyllis Oakley, Tom Pickering, Geoff Pyatt, Joe Ralston, Bill Richardson, Caroline Russell, Gary Samore, Melanne Verveer, Frank Wisner, and Tony Zinni. Richard Holbrooke yet again proved to be as good an editor as he is a friend.

I'm doubly indebted to Jim Steinberg, who read an early draft from the vantage point of both a former colleague and a current one. Jim and I worked closely together, including on South Asia, when he was at State and the NSC, and it is under the aegis of the Brookings department of Foreign Policy Studies, which he directs, that this book is published.

Steve Smith, who is now at Brookings, and Walter Isaacson, who is nearby at the Aspen Institute, had plenty of experience improving my copy years ago when I wrote for them at *Time*. I appreciate their willingness to give me the benefit of their prodigious editing skills as the book assumed its final form.

Steve Cohen, Brookings's distinguished South Asian scholar, shared with me his vast knowledge of the region, its history, and its politics. My gratitude also to other colleagues at Brookings, Sunil Dasgupta, Tanvi Madan, and Mike O'Hanlon, and also to Dennis Kux and Michael Krepon, who provided independent reviews of the manuscript for the Brookings Institution Press. I am grateful for their detailed and expert guidance.

Others who gave me valuable help were M. J. Akbar, Alan Batkin, C. Uday Bhaskar, Marshall Bouton, Sid Drell, Jim Goodby, Selig Harrison, Sunil Khilnani, Rajan Menon, R. K. and Renuka Mishra, Eric Nonacs, Bob Oakley, George Perkovich, Jairam Ramesh, Joshua Ramo, Rakesh Sood, and Shashi Tharoor.

My appreciation, also, to Ambassador Lalit Mansingh and his wife, Indira, for their hospitality and friendship to Brooke and me on three continents, and for the skill and grace with which they represented their country in Washington.

Andreas Xenachis's title as my research assistant doesn't begin to do justice to the role he plays at Brookings, the help he has given me in my own work, or the contribution he made to this and other projects over the past two years. Every page of this book has profited from his conscientiousness, common sense and, crucially, his good cheer and stamina. Andreas joins me in thanking Derek Chollet for his advice at several points along the way.

My account of the various meetings and events that constitute this episode in diplomatic history is based on my personal notes, memorandums of conversation, and contemporaneous reports to colleagues, supplemented by the recollections of other participants. In reconstructing the record, I had the cooperation of the Department of State, which gave Andreas access to official papers. According to long-standing practice, the department, in coordination with other agencies of the government, subjected the manuscript to a review intended to ensure that the contents would not compromise national security. Thanks in particular to Richard Boucher, assistant secretary of state for public affairs and chief spokesman of the department. He has, to put it mildly, several duties other than overseeing the clearance process; yet his accessibility, courtesy, and diligence were unflagging, and his counsel was much appreciated. Tim Carney, Jane Diedrich, Paul Hilburn, and Mark Ramee shepherded the manuscript through the system. Don Camp, Christina Rocca, and Jim Thessin provided assistance at key moments. The department's clearance should not be construed as concurrence with my opinions, interpretations, or recommendations.

I also want to acknowledge the Brookings Institution Press: Bob Faherty, its director, along with Larry Converse, Nicole Pagano, John Sherer, Janet Walker, Susan Woollen—and, most of all, Marty Gottron, who displayed exemplary proficiency with the text and inexhaustible patience with the author.

Thanks, also, to John Carbaugh for his support of the Brookings South Asia Policy Forum, a discussion series that gave me frequent opportunities to meet and compare impressions with experts from and on the region.

A special note of gratitude to O'Neal Page. I am reminded of his skill as a craftsman and his steadfastness as a friend over thirty years every time I settle into my study for a bout of work on projects like this one.

This book is dedicated to Nayan Chanda, his wife, Geetanjali, their sons Amit and Ateesh, and Geeta's parents, Amarjit and Bhagwant Singh. The Singhs' adoption of Brooke as their American daughter in 1968 coincided with my courtship of her and was therefore my personal introduction to their country. Nayan and I married into the Singh family around the same time. Not long afterward, he and I became journalistic colleagues and began a friendship that has enriched my life in many ways. Brooke and I see Amarjit and Bhagwant when we travel to New Delhi; Geeta now teaches literature and culture in the Women's and Gender Studies Program at Yale, and Nayan is the founding editor of YaleGlobal, an on-line magazine at the Yale Center for the Study of Globalization. When he gave the manuscript of this book a thorough and expert scrub, it was just the latest in a long list of debts I owe him.

A concluding word about Brooke, who figures in the story told here. Throughout our thirty-three years of marriage, she has been at my side during various journalistic, diplomatic, and academic adventures. She provided the impulse to begin work on this book. I'd been thinking about writing it since leaving government in January 2001, but several other endeavors intervened. I didn't open a file labeled "India book" in my laptop and start typing until February 2003, when Brooke and I boarded a flight bound for New Delhi. I was returning there for the first time since accompanying President Clinton nearly three years earlier. I would, over the next ten days, see more of the country than ever before, not just because it was the longest trip I've made to India but because of the company I was keeping. Brooke is a member of the board of the International Center for Research on Women, a Washington-based NGO that works in developing countries on projects aimed at improving women's lives. She suggested to Geeta Rao Gupta, the president of ICRW, a board field trip to see the effect that Center-sponsored programs are having on the ground. Our traveling companions were Brooke's fellow directors of ICRW, Joanna Breyer and Matt Mallow, and my fellow spouses, Stephen Breyer and Ellen Chesler, as well as Brooke's mother, Marva Shearer, and our friend Marion Guggenheim. My thanks to all members of that happy and intrepid band, including our guide Ratna Barua, for the movable seminar we conducted as we bounced from New Delhi to Ahmedabad to Mumbai.

Almost exactly a year later, as I was finishing this book, Brooke and I were back in New Delhi, this time thanks to an invitation from the Aspen Institute and the Confederation of Indian Industry to take part in—naturally—a dialogue on U.S.-Indian relations. My appreciation (again) to Walter Isaacson and his fellow Aspenites, Kurt Campbell and Darcy Willow, and to Tarun Das and Kiran Pasricha of CII. We also had a chance, thanks to Mukesh and Nita Ambani, to visit Goa and join in discussions with the Indian Young Presidents Organization—and, significantly, with a sizable delegation from the Pakistani YPO.

Those two journeys to India, bracketing as they did the writing of this story, gave me a chance to reflect on the social, economic, and political context of my dealings with Jaswant Singh. On both trips, shortly after Brooke's and my arrival in New Delhi, Jaswant and his wife, Kala, received us, jet-lagged but appreciative, for visits with them and members of their family. I hope my regard for the way Jaswant advanced his nation's interests and sought, as he put it, to harmonize U.S.-Indian relations speaks for itself in these pages. Indeed, it is a major reason why I wanted to write about what we did, and tried to do, together.

S.T.
Washington, D.C.
June 1, 2004

NOTES

1. "Estrangement" gained currency as a description of the U.S.-Indian relationship largely because it resonated with the title of Dennis Kux's influential and respected study, *India and the United States: Estranged Democracies* (Washington: National Defense University Press, 1992). "Engagement" has become a common part of the vocabulary of both the conduct of and the commentary on U.S.-Indian relations since the late 1990s, to wit: at least one other book shares part of the title with the current one: *Engaging India: U.S.-Strategic Relations with the World's Largest Democracy* (New York: Routledge, 1999). It is a collection of probing essays edited by Gary K. Bertsch, Seema Gahlaut, and Anupam Srivastava, all at the Center for International Trade and Security at the University of Georgia.

2. For a comprehensive study of Pakistanis' sense of their national identity, see Stephen P. Cohen, *The Idea of Pakistan: The Future of a Troubled State* (Brookings, forthcoming). For a clear and knowledgeable history of the Kashmir issue, see Sumantra Bose, *Kashmir: Roots of Conflict, Paths to Peace* (Harvard University Press, 2003).

3. Sally Bedell Smith, *Grace and Power* (Random House, 2004), pp. 260–63.

4. The term *tilt* first became part of the policy debate in late July 1971, when snippets of a discussion in a senior foreign policy meeting chaired by Henry Kissinger leaked to the press. Kissinger, according to the published report, told the group, "The President always said to tilt toward Pakistan, but every proposal I get [from the State Department] is in the opposite direction." See Walter Issacson, *Kissinger* (Simon and Schuster, 1992), p. 373. Kissinger addressed the strategic rationale of the tilt in his memoirs, *The White House Years* (Little, Brown, 1979), pp. 913–15: "The issue burst upon us while Pakistan was our only channel to China; we had no other means of communication with Peking. A major American

initiative of fundamental importance to the global balance of power could not have survived if we colluded with the Soviet Union in the public humiliation of China's friend—and our ally. The naked recourse to force by a partner of the Soviet Union backed by Soviet arms and buttressed by Soviet assurances threatened the very structure of international order just when our whole Middle East Strategy depended on proving the inefficacy of such tactics and when America's weight as a factor in the world was already being undercut by our divisions over Indochina. . . . Had we followed . . . recommendations [to pursue a more evenhanded policy in South Asia], Pakistan, after losing its eastern wing, would have lost Kashmir and possibly Baluchistan and other portions of its western wing—in other words, it would have totally disintegrated. . . . We succeeded in confining the impact of the conflict to the Subcontinent. The Indian power play did not shake the foundations of our foreign policy and wreck our China initiative as it well might have, and as the Soviets undoubtedly hoped it would." Isaacson notes in his book that Nixon "referred to her [Indira Gandhi] as 'the bitch,' except when he was angry; then he called her worse" (Isaacson, *Kissinger*, p. 373).

5. Kissinger, *The White House Years*, p. 848.

6. George Perkovich, *India's Nuclear Bomb* (University of California Press, 1999), p. 185.

7. Ibid. p. 184.

8. Ibid., p. 193. Perkovich uncovered this 1975 State Department memorandum while researching his book.

9. Ibid., p. 243. See also K. Subrahmanyam's "Indian Nuclear Policy— 1964–1988: A Personal Recollection," in Jasjit Singh, ed., *Nuclear India* (New Delhi: Knowledge World, 1998), pp. 37, 44–46. Throughout Subrahmanyam's career—working in the civil service; directing the Institute for Defence Studies and Analyses, a think tank; and writing columns—he had long been, according to Perkovich, India's "most sophisticated proponent of 'going nuclear.'" His expertise was sought by Rajiv Gandhi in 1985, when he was appointed to a secret committee to evaluate India's nuclear needs and options, and in 1990, when he joined another group to draw up contingency plans in case of a preemptive Pakistani nuclear strike. Subrahmanyam would later chair two Indian commissions mentioned in this book—the panel of experts that would draw up the August 1999 "draft nuclear doctrine" and the Indian government's inquiry panel on Kargil.

10. See Federation of American Scientists (FAS), "Hatf-3 / Shaheen-I / M-11," in *WMD around the World* (www.fas.org/nuke/guide/pakistan/missile/hatf-3.htm): "In the early 1980s China is widely reported to have provided Pakistan with the blueprints for a 1966 design of a U-235 nuclear-implosion device, of the type used in the warhead that China flew on a DF-2A missile during its fourth nuclear test on 27 October 1966. This missile warhead was reported to weigh about 1,300 kilograms with a yield of about 12–25 kt [kilotons]." See also the report "Pakistan Nuclear Weapons" by FAS (www.fas.org/nuke/guide/pakistan/nuke/index.html): "China is reported to have provided Pakistan with the design of one of its warheads, as well as sufficient HEU [highly enriched uranium] for a few weapons. The

25-kiloton design was the one used in China's fourth nuclear test, which was an atmospheric test using a ballistic missile launch. This configuration is said to be a fairly sophisticated design, with each warhead weighing considerably less than the unwieldy, first-generation US and Soviet weapons which weighed several thousand kilograms. Pakistan Foreign Minister Yakub Khan was present at the Chinese Lop Nor test site to witness the test of a small nuclear device in May 1983, giving rise to speculation that a Pakistani-assembled device was detonated in this test."

11. See Stephen P. Cohen, *The Idea of Pakistan,* chapter 2. "The bomb," writes Cohen, "was a magic bullet that could resolve any problem."

12. "Knocking at the Nuclear Door; A Key Ally Confirms that His Scientists Can Build the Bomb," *Time,* March 30, 1987, p. 42.

13. The nuclear aspect of the 1990 crisis was aired publicly in an article by Seymour Hersh ("On the Nuclear Edge," *The New Yorker,* March 29, 1993, pp. 56–73). Although later public literature discounted some aspects of Hersh's piece (see Michael Krepon and Mishi Faruqee, eds., "Conflict Prevention and Confidence-Building Measures in South Asia: The 1990 Crisis," Occasional Paper 17, Henry L. Stimson Center, Washington, April 1994), the part of Hersh's story concerning the assembly of at least one nuclear weapon by the Pakistanis coincides with what other experts have written (see Perkovich, *India's Nuclear Bomb,* p. 308–09, p. 551).

14. Such was the Indians' allergy to anything that looked like an admission of their need for American mediation in dealing with Pakistan that officials in both Washington and New Delhi did everything they could to play down the severity of the crisis and play up the discretion and modesty the United States showed in its own role. "We were concerned they were on the brink of war," said Richard Haass afterward, but "not nuclear war" (Perkovich, *India's Nuclear Bomb,* p. 310). For an authoritative—and much delayed Indian perspective—see C. Uday Bhaskar, "The May 1990 'Crisis,'" in *Studies in Conflict & Terrorism,* vol. 20 (October-December 1997), pp. 317–32. Bhaskar, a commodore in the Indian Navy, is deputy director of the Institute for Defence Studies and Analyses in New Delhi. He argued that whatever the anxieties of the American government, the Indians were not aware that the Pakistanis were seriously considering deploying nuclear weapons: "From the Indian perspective . . . it appears that there was little or no awareness of the magnitude or nature of the danger that cast an ominous shadow over the Subcontinent."

CHAPTER TWO

1. Hillary Rodham Clinton, *Living History* (Simon and Schuster, 2003), pp. 268–86.

2. *Public Papers of the President of the United States: John F. Kennedy, 1963* (Government Printing Office, 1964), p. 280.

3. See, among many public sources, Amos Elon, "A Very Special Relationship," *New York Review of Books,* vol. 51 (January 15, 2004), pp. 15–19.

4. For an account of this episode in U.S.-Russian relations, see chapters 4, 6, and 7 of my earlier memoir, *The Russia Hand* (Random House, 2002).

5. Raj Chengappa, "The Missile Man," *India Today*, April 15, 1994, p. 66. See also Perkovich, *India's Nuclear Bomb*, p. 344.

6. Perkovich, *India's Nuclear Bomb,* p. 345.

7. "BJP Embarks on Ambitious Plan," *News-India Times*, June 17, 1994, p. 1.

8. See Robert M. Hathaway, "Unfinished Passage: India, Indian-Americans and the U.S.-Congress," *Washington Quarterly*, vol. 24 (Spring 2001), pp. 21-34.

9. Tim Weiner, "U.S. Suspects India Prepares to Conduct Nuclear Test," *New York Times*, December 15, 1995, p. A9.

10. Perkovich, *India's Nuclear Bomb*, p. 370: "Rao was prepared to risk American dissatisfaction over nuclear tests but felt that it made more strategic sense to wait until the Indian economy was stronger and the missile program was more advanced. Congress party leaders reportedly had concluded that inflation had contributed heavily to party losses in late-1994 and early-1995 state elections. . . . [A]dvisers reportedly told [Rao] that sanctions would raise inflation." Also, see Raja Mohan's *Crossing the Rubicon* (New Delhi: Penguin/Viking, 2003), pp. 6-7.

11. "Opposition flays US for comments on reports of Indian nuke test plan," Agence France-Presse, December 17, 1995.

12. Jaswant Singh made these comments on several occasions. See, for example, Prabhu Chawla and Raj Chengappa, "Jaswant Singh: 'Let's not take the worm's eye view,'" *India Today*, January 11, 1999, p. 34.

13. Perkovich, *India's Nuclear Bomb*, pp. 374-5.

14. For more on this feature of the CTBT, see Michael Krepon, *Cooperative Threat Reduction: Missile Defense, and the Nuclear Future* (Washington: Palgrave Macmillan, 2002), pp. 29-30.

15. The chair of the council task force was Richard Haass, then a vice president at the Brookings Institution in charge of foreign policy studies. Haass would later be director of policy planning in the administration of George W. Bush, and, in 2003, he succeeded Gelb as president of the Council on Foreign Relations. The other members of the task force included Stephen P. Cohen, then at the University of Illinois, later a senior fellow at Brookings; Robert Oakley, a former U.S. ambassador to Pakistan (and the husband of Phyllis Oakley, who broke the news of the Pokhran II test to me on May 11, 1998); and two other friends and colleagues who assisted me in writing this book, George Perkovich, then of the W. Alton Jones Foundation and now at the Carnegie Endowment for International Peace, and Marshall Bouton, then at the Asia Society and now president of the Chicago Council on Foreign Relations.

16. Other think tanks, notably the Carnegie Endowment and the Asia Society, produced similar studies and recommendations around the same time. See Selig Harrison and Geoffrey Kemp, *India and America after the Cold War* (Washington: Carnegie Endowment, 1993) and the Asia Society, *South Asia and the United States after the Cold War: A Study Mission* (New York, 1994). In 1998 Brookings and the

Council on Foreign Relations formed a task force that yielded a report that influenced the attitudes and objectives of the Clinton administration. See Richard Haass and Morton H. Halperin, co-chairs, *After the Tests: U.S. Policy toward India and Pakistan* (New York: Council on Foreign Relations, 1998).

17. On Robin Raphel's statement regarding Kashmir and her subsequent lambasting by the Indians, see Dennis Kux, *The United States and Pakistan 1947–2000: Disenchanted Allies* (Washington: Woodrow Wilson Center Press, 2001), pp. 327–28. On "cap, roll back, eliminate," see Robin Raphel, testimony before the Subcommittee on Near Eastern and South Asian Affairs of the Senate Foreign Relations Committee, March 9, 1995.

18. For an erudite, eloquent, and essentially positive exposition of Indian democracy, see Sunil Khilnani's *The Idea of India* (Farrar, Strauss, Giroux, 1999), pp. 15–60. For a critical and pessimistic treatment of India, especially under the BJP, as an example of "illiberal democracy," see Fareed Zakaria's *The Future of Freedom* (W.W. Norton, 2003), pp. 106–13.

19. McCurry was asked, during the press briefing about the nuclear issue, why he had not included it in the readout and why it had not come up in the call. His answer: "We have previously expressed our views on some of those questions; I know that the United States would look forward to continuing a fruitful exchange of views with the Government of India on those subjects, including the nuclear issue."

20. Raghunath paid a brief courtesy call on me as well, and there was little of substance in our conversation.

21. See Perkovich, *India's Nuclear Bomb*, p. 416: "As in 1974 only a handful of officials knew of the tests beforehand, and even fewer participated in deliberations over whether and when to conduct them. Vajpayee, Mishra, and Jaswant Singh participated in the relevant deliberations with the top scientists. . . . Fernandes was told only two days before the event, while the three military service chiefs and the foreign secretary were informed on May 10." Also pp. 408–09: "[N]o one but Vajpayee, Jaswant Singh, Brajesh Mishra, perhaps L. K. Advani . . . and a handful of other top scientists knew what 'the government' actually was intending to do. Everyone else, including cabinet ministers, was just guessing."

22. The seismic data were collected by the Comprehensive Test Ban Treaty Prototype International Data Center (PIDC) in Arlington, Virginia, as a central repository for treaty monitoring station readings from around the world. The Center's archives are available online (www.pidc.org/pidc [May 12, 2003]).

23. Khilnani, *The Idea of India*, p. ix.

24. The scientist, G. Balachandran, is quoted in an unpublished paper, "The Indian Nuclear Tests: Parsing the U.S. Intelligence Failure," by Polly Nayak, a retired U.S. intelligence officer who was, while at the CIA, an active member of the interagency team working on India and Pakistan and, subsequently, a Federal Executive Fellow at the Brookings Institution.

25. A boosted fission device is a regular fission bomb with just a small amount

of material that can undergo fusion added to "boost" the size of the fission explosion. A fusion device contains much more fusion fuel and operates in two stages: a fission stage triggers the second fusion stage that generates a very large explosion. Scientists at the Lawrence Livermore National Laboratory ascertained that one of the devices tested on May 11 was indeed a true two-stage fusion device, but believed the second stage did not go off as planned. (See Mark Hibbs, "India May Test Again because H-Bomb Failed, U.S. Believes," *Nucleonics Week*, November 26, 1998, www.nyu.edu/globalbeat/nucwatch.html). The U.S. government neither confirmed nor denied the Lawrence Livermore analysis in public, for fear that it would push India into testing again.

CHAPTER THREE

1. Vajpayee's letter was subsequently leaked to the *New York Times*, but his defense minister, George Fernandes, had already gone public with the same argument on China (see John F. Burns, "India's New Defense Chief Sees Chinese Military Threat," *New York Times*, May 5, 1998, p. A6).

2. Kissinger made this comment at the 46th Bilderberg Meeting in Turnberry, Scotland, held May 14–17, 1998.

3. Moynihan made similar statements in public. See Aziz Haniffa, "U.S. Adopts a Carrot-and-Stick Policy toward India," *India Abroad*, June 12, 1998, p. 8.

4. The G-8 statement, issued on May 15, read: "We condemn the nuclear tests which were carried out by India on 11 and 13 May. Such action runs counter to the will expressed by 149 signatories to the CTBT to cease nuclear testing, to efforts to strengthen the global non-proliferation regime and to steps to enhance regional and international peace and security. It has been met by immediate international concern and opposition, from governments and more widely. We underline our full commitment to the Non-Proliferation Treaty and to the Comprehensive Test Ban Treaty as the cornerstones of the global non-proliferation regime and the essential foundations for the pursuit of nuclear disarmament. We express our grave concern about the increased risk of nuclear and missile proliferation in South Asia and elsewhere. We urge India and other states in the region to refrain from further tests and the deployment of nuclear weapons or ballistic missiles. We call upon India to rejoin the mainstream of international opinion, to adhere unconditionally to the NPT and the CTBT and to enter into negotiations on a global treaty to stop the production of fissile material for nuclear weapons. India's relationship with each of us has been affected by these developments. We are making this clear in our own direct exchanges and dealings with the Indian Government and we call upon other states similarly to address their concerns to India. We call upon and encourage Pakistan to exercise maximum restraint in the face of these tests and to adhere to international non-proliferation norms."

5. As an example of the recurring attraction of Primakov's idea, when Yeltsin's successor, Vladimir Putin, visited New Delhi in early December 2002, spokesmen

for both governments put out the story that the agenda included a "strategic triangle" with China, with strong hints that the purpose was to serve as a counterbalance to U.S. hegemony.

6. According to the Federation of American Scientists, "Pakistani claims concerning the number and yields of their underground tests cannot be independently confirmed by seismic means, and it has been suggested by Indian sources that as few as two weapons were actually detonated, each with yields considerably lower than claimed by Pakistan. However, seismic data showed at least two and possibly a third, much smaller, test in the initial round of tests at the Ras Koh range. The single test on 30 May provided a clear seismic signal." ("Pakistan Nuclear Weapons" on FAS *WMD around the World* website, www.fas.org/nuke/guide/pakistan/nuke/index.html.)

CHAPTER FOUR

1. Reddy was quoted in Kenneth J. Cooper, "India's Leaders Speak of Vindication, Urge Calm and Unity," *Washington Post*, May 29, 1998, p. A33, right after the first Pakistani test. Shekhar Gupta's commentary, "Test of Wisdom," appeared in the *Indian Express*, on May 29.

2. Perkovich had been a member of the Council on Foreign Relations task force on U.S. policy toward South Asia in 1997 (see chapter 2).

3. On April 10, 1919, a group of Indians demonstrating in front of a prison in Amritsar that held two nationalist leaders were fired upon. A riot broke out in the old city of Amritsar. Several British banks were burned, several men were killed, and two women, including Marcella Sherwood, a mission doctor, were said to be beaten up, molested, or both. On April 13, 1919, British troops fired on unarmed Indians protesting in a crowded plaza, leaving around 400 dead and 1,200 wounded. On April 19, Brigadier General Reginald Dyer, issued an order requiring all Indians using the street on which Sherwood was attacked to crawl its 200-yard length on their hands and knees. Dyer later explained to a British inspector: "Some Indians crawl face downwards in front of their gods. I wanted them to know that a British woman is as sacred as a Hindu god, and, therefore, they have to crawl in front of her, too."

4. Josef Korbel, *Danger in Kashmir* (Princeton University Press, 1954).

5. India was not the only country that Clinton compared to the sad-sack comedian: he used the same line in reference to Russia.

6. Jaswant Singh was interviewed by Elizabeth Farnsworth on *The NewsHour with Jim Lehrer*, June 11, 1998.

7. Robert H. Reid, "India Defends Nuclear Tests, Saying They Reflect Unique Security Situation," Associated Press Worldstream, June 9, 1998. Raja Mohan, the strategic affairs editor of *The Hindu*, elaborated on the post-cold-war rationale for India's going nuclear in his book *Crossing the Rubicon* (pp. 9, 11): "The end of the cold war removed one of the most important constraints against India's overt

nuclearization: the strength of the Soviet Union, India's de facto military and political ally"; India was now on its own in "the new world order dominated by one superpower." In 1999 and 2000 Mohan played a role in the story told in chapter 9 of this book.

8. Jaswant Singh made this comment in a press conference at the UN on June 9.

9. In Hindi, *Jis gaon nahin jaana, uska raasta mat poocho.*

10. This interview was published on May 19, 2003.

CHAPTER FIVE

1. "Notwithstanding their recent nuclear tests," said the U.S.-Chinese presidential statement on June 27, "India and Pakistan do not have the status of nuclear weapons states in accordance with the NPT." The United States and China should "jointly and individually contribute to the achievement of a peaceful, prosperous, and secure South Asia," and engage in "close coordination . . . in response to nuclear testing by India and Pakistan."

2. The BJP's website (bjp.org/major/fpoll-sm.html) says the following about the party's position on Kashmir: "Since the Jan Sangh days [Jan Sangh was the predecessor of the BJP], it has been seeking Jammu and Kashmir's total integration with India."

3. Stephen I. Schwartz, ed., *Atomic Audit: The Costs and Consequences of U.S. Nuclear Weapons since 1940* (Brookings, 1998).

4. For a concise summary of the different nuclear factions, see Kanti Bajpai, "The Great Indian Nuclear Debate," *The Hindu*, November 12, 1999. Bajpai notes, "Operationally, moderates take the view that a small nuclear force in the two-digit or three-digit range will suffice for deterrence. Moderates estimate that between 60-140 Hiroshima-type weapons will do, that in addition the warheads and delivery vehicles (airplanes, missiles) can be 'de-coupled' (ergo, deployed separately and mated only when it is necessary to retaliate), that command and control can be modest, and that no first use is politically and strategically viable. Maximalists, by contrast, want a much larger force, perhaps as many as 500-1000 weapons, warheads that are 'ready to go' rather than de-coupled, and a much more extensive command and control system. . . . In short, the pro-bomb lobby is divided on a series of vital issues relating to India's nuclear posture. Rejectionists and pragmatists believe in a relaxed deterrent; maximalists want a more classical posture. Pragmatists want India to sign the CTBT and be active in negotiating an FMCT; rejectionists and maximalists see this is as capitulation and fatal to the deterrent, respectively. Finally, rejectionists believe in both the feasibility and desirability of complete nuclear disarmament; pragmatists and maximalists do not."

5. BJP-related political and religious organizations had, in the past, propounded the concept of *Akhand Bharat*, or United India, which would comprise the whole of South Asia. Three years later, in 2001, Advani floated the idea himself in public.

6. Sartaj Aziz made this comment to me during a visit I made to Islamabad in early February 1999, shortly after he became foreign minister.

CHAPTER SIX

1. The United States also struck a suspected chemical weapons facility in Sudan believed to be associated with bin Laden.

2. Karamat told Dennis Kux of Nawaz Sharif's anger, and Kux passed it along to me in his comments on the manuscript of this book.

3. In addition to suspicion of a Pakistani tipoff, there has been public speculation that a decision by the United States to withdraw dependents of government personnel from posts in Pakistan in advance of the raid may have alerted the Taliban and al Qaeda to the likelihood of an attack.

4. For a detailed account of al Qaeda's jihad and the American response, see Daniel Benjamin and Steven Simon, *The Age of Sacred Terror* (Random House, 2002).

5. Huntington's *The Clash of Civilizations and the Remaking of World Order* (Simon & Schuster, 1996) postulated nine contending civilizations in the post-cold-war world: Western, Latin American, African, Islamic, Sinic [that is, Chinese], Hindu, Orthodox, Buddhist, and Japanese.

6. Senators Richard Shelby of Alabama and Tim Hutchinson of Arkansas, who had just been in India, had asserted there that the U.S. Senate would not ratify the treaty anytime soon—or, as they clearly preferred, ever.

7. An account of Indian decisionmaking published two years later confirms the reports we heard at the time. See Raj Chengappa, deputy editor of *India Today*, in his book *Weapons of Peace: The Secret Story of India's Quest to Be a Nuclear Power* (New Delhi: HarperCollins India, 2000).

8. Jaswant's article in *Foreign Affairs* acknowledged that the Pokhran test represented a break with Indian policy of the Nehru period: "The earliest Indian forays into the question of nuclear disarmament were admittedly more moralistic than realistic. The current disharmony, therefore, between India and the rest of the globe is that India has moved from being totally moralistic to being a little more realistic." The indefinite extension of the NPT in 1995, he asserted, "legitimized in perpetuity existing nuclear arsenals and, in effect, an unequal nuclear regime." His country, he said, had now righted that wrong: "India is now a nuclear weapons state, as is Pakistan. That reality can neither be denied nor wished away. This category of 'nuclear weapons state' is not, in actuality, a conferment. Nor is it a status for others to grant. It is, rather, an objective reality. India's strengthened nuclear capability adds to its sense of responsibility—the obligation of power." Jaswant Singh, "Against Nuclear Apartheid," *Foreign Affairs*, vol. 77 (September/October 1998), pp. 41–53.

9. On November 13, the day after my speech, the *Indian Express* editorialized, "Well, now at last we have an idea of what Jaswant Singh and Strobe Talbott have

been telling each other." The Indian "government has not been eager to throw light on the subject, only to provide itself with instant deniability in case of need. Meanwhile, the Americans have seized the initiative to inform the Indian public about the agenda and progress of the talks. On the Indian side, negotiations are treated as a matter of the greatest sensitivity, so much so that the less said publicly the better."

10. Vajpayee's letter cited the U.S. government's publication of a list of two hundred Indian companies that would be barred from doing business with American firms under the terms of those sanctions that remained in place, but it also strongly implied that he was upset over my speech at Brookings. Officials in New Delhi gave background briefings to the Indian press in which they alleged that I had provided "revelations" about the "exact contents" of the negotiations and that I had, in my public remarks, taken a harder line on key questions than in the dialogue itself. See BBC summary of world broadcasts for November 16 and "Vajpayee Conveys His Unhappiness to Clinton" in *India Abroad*, November 20, 1998, p. 14, which reviewed coverage in several Indian newspapers, especially a November 14 report in *The Hindustan Times*: "What particularly worried the government was Talbott's explicit statement on India's nuclear policy, particularly when New Delhi had started believing that Washington was finally beginning to understand its security concerns. . . . India first felt that the U.S. was softening its stand [on development and deployment of nuclear weapons]. . . . Talbott's Brookings speech, however, changed that perception." My colleagues and I later conjectured that some analysts in the Indian government, parsing the small print of every statement coming out of Washington, had incorrectly detected in testimony by Rick Inderfurth before the Senate Foreign Relations Committee on July 14 signs that the United States was dropping the benchmark on strategic restraint. Apparently I disabused them of that mistaken impression when I reiterated the importance of all the benchmarks in my Brookings speech.

CHAPTER SEVEN

1. *Defending India* was published by Macmillan India and by St. Martin's Press in the United States. Singh's other books were *National Security: An Outline of Our Concerns* (1996) and *Shaurya Tejo* ("The Valorous"; in Hindi with S. P. Bhatia, 1997), and he later published *District Diary*, a collection of articles about his district from when he was a parliamentarian (Macmillan, 2001).

2. On Carter's efforts in the Balkans, see Richard C. Holbrooke, *To End a War* (Random House, 1998), pp. 121, 149–50.

3. Letters of this kind were a device I used frequently over the eight years that I worked with Yuri Mamedov, the Russian deputy foreign minister, who repeatedly proved to be indispensable in solving, or at least managing, the many problems that arose between the White House and the Kremlin. Fairly early in my association with Jaswant, a number of my colleagues in the State Department

made cracks about how I had found in him an Indian Mamedov. I had written Jaswant letters of this kind twice before, in mid-July and early August, but the one in December was considerably longer and more substantive. It began by reviewing the rationale for writing him in this vein: "[I am departing] from the forms and tactics of traditional diplomacy. The conventional, and in some ways safer, practice would be for each of us to prepare the strongest possible negotiating position for a face-to-face encounter in which we would play out the hands our governments have dealt us. I believe that would be neither wise nor necessary in this case. In our very first meeting last June, you and I agreed that we were going to tackle our assignment in a spirit fundamentally different from that of time-honored diplomatic stratagems. We agreed that we're not playing poker; rather, we're working together to solve a mutual problem. We started out in June by laying out to each other as clearly as we could the irreducible requirements of our national interests and goals; we identified the fixed points on the landscape as well as potential areas of flexibility. Since then, we have sought, in effect, to reverse-engineer from those fundamentals on which we could agree."

4. This interview ran in *India Today*, January 11, 1999, p. 34.

5. In addition to the regulars—Rick Inderfurth, Bob Einhorn, Matt Daley of State, and Karen Mathiasen of Treasury—we added Bob's NSC counterpart, Gary Samore.

6. It was actually one of our Pakistani interlocutors, Riaz Muhammad Khan, the director of the policy planning office of the Pakistani foreign ministry, who first commented that *both* dialogues reminded him of the paradox identified by Zeno of Elea, the fifth-century-B.C. Greek philosopher who posited that a runner cannot ever reach his goal because, in order to cover a certain distance, he must first cover half of it, then half of the remainder, and so on, ad infinitum.

7. See Joby Warrick, "Nuclear Program in Iran Tied to Pakistan: Complex Network Acquired Technology and Blueprints," *Washington Post*, December 21, 2003; William J. Broad, David Rohde, and David E. Sanger, "Inquiry Suggests Pakistan Sold Nuclear Secrets," *New York Times*, December 22, 2003. A *New York Times* article noted that North Korea likely sold a package similar to what Libya received: $60 million for "nuclear fuel, centrifuges and one or more warhead designs." (See David E. Sanger, "U.S. Sees More Arms Ties between Pakistan and Korea," *New York Times*, March 14, 2004.) On the Iraq relationship, see Gary Milhollin and Kelly Motz, "Nukes 'R' Us," *New York Times*, March 4, 2004.

8. Védrine expanded on his 1999 concept of America as *l'hyperpuissance* on a visit to New Delhi in February 2000: "The current state of the world is not satisfactory. . . . [T]his unipolar system is excessive, questionable and has negative implications"; it was "high time that our two countries, both of which are committed to making their own assessments of world realities and autonomous decision-making with regard to the major issues affecting the planet, take the time for an in-depth dialogue. . . . If a multipolar system is built, I am convinced that India will be, and must be one of its poles."

CHAPTER EIGHT

1. This insight into Musharraf's long-standing determination to send Pakistani forces across the Line of Control comes from Bruce Riedel, who heard it during a government posting to London in 2002 from a retired Indian military officer who had been a classmate and friend of Musharraf's at the Royal College of Defense Studies in 1990.

2. See *From Surprise to Reckoning: The Kargil Review Committee Report* (New Delhi: Sage Publications, December 1999). For a day-by-day timeline, see a website created by *India Today* (www.india-today.com/kargil/index.html).

3. Bruce Riedel has written his own detailed account of the July 4 Blair House meetings, "American Diplomacy and the 1999 Kargil Summit at Blair House," Policy Paper Series 2002, Center for the Advanced Study of India, University of Pennsylvania.

4. Keegan's book had just been published by Knopf.

5. Berger later commented in public that India and Pakistan "don't know much about each other's capabilities, red lines, doctrine. I think the closest we came to a nuclear conflict, other than the 1962 Cuban missile crisis, was in 1999, the last time these two nations clashed over Kargil, and where we saw, in fact, the Pakistanis moving toward deployment of missiles." (Aziz Haniffa, "Pressure Must Also Be Put on India to De-escalate," *India Abroad*, June 14, 2002, p. 16.)

CHAPTER NINE

1. *India Today*, January 11, 1999 (p. 34).

2. I had met Shahbaz Sharif once before, on August 23, 1998, the same day Brooke, Sandy Berger, and I had our private dinner with Jaswant.

3. For a full account of the national missile defense issue and the negotiations with Mamedov, see *The Russia Hand*, chapter 15.

4. See Kevin Galvin, "Senate May Vote on Test Ban Treaty," Associated Press Online, October 12, 1999; Tuesday 15:20 EST.

5. Similarly, with Russia Clinton went to considerable lengths to avoid imposing sanctions over the transfer of dangerous technology to Iran. See *The Russia Hand*, chapter 10.

6. When the announcement that Clinton would travel to India and Bangladesh was finally made on February 1, 2000, the White House added, "No decisions have been made about other stops."

7. The interview was the first in a pair that Jaswant and I gave to Raja Mohan in a coordinated effort to improve the climate for consideration of the CTBT in India. Both of us played up the extent to which we were, in the phrase favored by Jaswant, "harmonizing" our interests, and we played down all implications of compromise or concession. Jaswant took advantage of the opportunity to build the case for CTBT signature and to refute, albeit ever so subtly, the standing of the draft

nuclear doctrine and, in particular, the need for an Indian triad. Jaswant and I called these the "bookend" interviews. His ran in the *Hindu* on November 29, 1999, under a headline saying he was "for a Consensus on CTBT"; mine appeared on January 14, 2000, under a headline that summarized the U.S. position as being "for a Qualitatively Better Relationship with India."

The key passages in Jaswant's public explanation of policy: "The objectives from our side are two fold: in the first place, to reconcile the stated US non-proliferation concerns with India's national security objectives; secondly, and, in a broader context, to develop greater mutual understanding so that both countries are enabled to work together in tapping the real potential of a qualitatively new relationship, essential in this post–Cold War environment. The results of my discussions with Strobe Talbott are encouraging. There is recognition that India shall maintain a minimum nuclear deterrent as determined by us. There is now no longer any talk of 'roll-back.' The US also accepts that India's security concerns are not geographically limited. Foreign policy tasks and challenges are a continuing process[;] therefore, we need to consolidate these understandings across all sections that make up the US foreign policy establishment. . . . Our stand on the CTBT has been clear. In 1996, we decided that we could not accept the CTBT because it was not consistent with India's national security interest. Over decades, successive governments took necessary steps to safeguard India's nuclear option. In 1996, it was clear to all that subscription to the CTBT at that time would have limited India's nuclear potential at an unacceptably low level. After conducting the nuclear tests of May, 1998, to validate and update our technology, we have ensured the credibility of our nuclear deterrent into the foreseeable future; our scientists are now confident of conducting sub-critical tests, also other non-explosive R&D activity necessary for the purpose. That is why we declared a voluntary moratorium. This, in essence, meets the basic obligations of the CTBT. We also announced a willingness to convert this undertaking into a de jure obligation.

"Clearly," he continued, "this could not be done in a political vacuum. A positive environment had to be created. In reaction, a number of countries decided to impose restrictive economic measures on India. We have conveyed our disappointment at these actions. That, however, does not mean that we do not value our bilateral relationships with these countries. Our endeavor has been to generate a better appreciation of India's security concerns. Obviously, this is possible only through a sustained, bilateral dialogue process. An understanding in this regard will restore our relationship to the pre–May 1998 position. I am also optimistic that this process of restoration will result in an acceptance of a secure, self-confident India, thus imparting a new momentum to these ties. At the same time, there is no denying that the manner in which the CTBT was negotiated, particularly during the last stages, left a great deal to be desired. This led to resentment against the proposed treaty. Many in India see it as part of a discriminatory, nuclear non-proliferation regime. The Government's commitment to nuclear non-proliferation remains unchanged. The priority of our meeting the country's national security concerns having been addressed, the government believes that we now need to convey reassurance to the international community and, in this regard, desires to develop a national consensus. The need for a consensus in any democratic society is self-evident. I have explained this in the past to the U.S. administration, and they better understand this approach after their own difficulties on this issue in their Senate."

On the subject of the draft nuclear doctrine, Jaswant said, "There is a perception in the international community that the document prepared by the National Security Advisory Board for the National Security Council is India's official nuclear doctrine. What is the status of this document? Let me correct this misperception. The National Security Advisory Board is a group of non-official strategic experts and analysts. It was tasked by the National Security Council to prepare a number of papers including one on a possible 'Indian Nuclear Doctrine.' This they prepared and submitted to the National Security Advisor, also releasing it publicly for larger debate. That debate is now under way. It is thus not a policy document of the Government of India. The key elements of India's nuclear policy were spelt out by [the] Prime Minister in Parliament last December. To recapitulate briefly: India shall maintain a minimum nuclear deterrent and shall undertake necessary measures to ensure the credibility of it. India has declared a moratorium on undertaking any further underground nuclear test explosions but R&D activity including computer simulation and sub-critical tests will be conducted as necessary. Development work on an extended range Agni missile is under way and a successful flight test was carried out earlier this year. Additional flight testing will be undertaken in a manner that is non-provocative, transparent, and consistent with all established international norms and practices. India has declared a no-first-use doctrine. This has implicit the principle that India shall not use nuclear weapons against non-nuclear-weapons states. In order that our minimum deterrent be credible, we shall adopt and maintain a deployment posture that ensures survivability of assets. Such a posture, obviously, provides for greater safety and security. India will not engage in any arms race. We shall not, therefore, pursue an open-ended program. A civilian command and control system, with necessary safeguards, shall cater for all possible contingencies. . . . Let me address the issue of 'triad', not because it is part of the NSAB paper, but because there may be genuine misperceptions. It is a known fact that today India has nuclear capable aircraft and mobile land based nuclear capable missiles. We have an R&D program for a naval version of Prithvi that has been a part of the IGMDP launched in 1983. It is also a fact that many analysts, particularly in Western countries, consider nuclear missiles on submarines to be the most survivable nuclear asset in the scenarios that they have thought of—first strike, second strike, war fighting and so on. Our approach is different. It is, therefore, premature to talk of an Indian 'triad.' R&D programs will certainly continue, aimed at enhancing survivability and thus, credibility, but decisions on production, deployment and employment etc will be taken on the basis of factors that I have outlined earlier. In short, just as parity is not essential for deterrence, neither is a triad a pre-requisite for credibility. Let me suggest that you look at the Indian nuclear deterrent as a 'triad' based on a different set of three dimensions—a deterrent that is minimum but credible because it is survivable and backed by effective civilian command and control to ensure retaliation."

CHAPTER TEN

1. On May 13, 2003, more than three years after Clinton was in India—and five years to the day after the conclusion of the Pokhran II tests—Brajesh Mishra returned to New Delhi after an official visit to Washington and recalled the presidential trip as the "turning point" in U.S.-Indian relations.

2. A sample of the language from the preamble to the vision statement: "At the dawn of a new century, Prime Minister Vajpayee and President Clinton resolve to create a closer and qualitatively new relationship between the United States and India. . . . There have been times in the past when our relationship drifted without a steady course. As we now look towards the future, we are convinced that it is time to chart a new and purposeful direction in our relationship. . . . In the new century, India and the United States will be partners in peace, with a common interest in, and complementary responsibility for, ensuring regional and international security. We will engage in regular consultations on, and work together for, strategic stability in Asia and beyond. We will bolster joint efforts to counter terrorism and meet other challenges to regional peace. We will strengthen the international security system, including in the United Nations and support the United Nations in its peacekeeping efforts. . . . India and the United States share a commitment to reducing and ultimately eliminating nuclear weapons, but we have not always agreed on how to reach this common goal. The United States believes India should forgo nuclear weapons. India believes that it needs to maintain a credible minimum nuclear deterrent in keeping with its own assessment of its security needs. Nonetheless, India and the U.S. are prepared to work together to prevent the proliferation of nuclear weapons and their means of delivery. To this end, we will persist with and build upon the productive bilateral dialogue already underway. We reaffirm our respective voluntary commitments to forgo further nuclear explosive tests. We will work together and with others for an early commencement of negotiations on a treaty to end the production of fissile materials for nuclear weapons. We have both shown strong commitments to export controls, and will continue to strengthen them. We will work together to prevent the spread of dangerous technologies. We are committed to build confidence and reduce the chances of miscalculation. We will pursue our security needs in a restrained and responsible manner, and will not engage in nuclear and missile arms races. We will seek to narrow our differences and increase mutual understanding on non-proliferation and security issues. This will help us to realize the full potential of Indo-U.S. relations and contribute significantly to regional and global security. . . . Today, we pledge to deepen the Indian-American partnership in tangible ways, always seeking to reconcile our

NOTES TO PAGES 200-09

differences through dialogue and engagement, always seizing opportunity to advance the countless interests we have in common. . . . Henceforth, the President of the United States and the Prime Minister of India should meet regularly to institutionalize our dialogue. We have also agreed on, and separately outlined an architecture of additional high-level consultations, and of joint working groups, across the broad spectrum of areas in which we are determined to institutionalize our enhanced cooperation. And we will encourage even stronger people-to-people ties. . . . For India and the United States, this is a day of new beginnings. We have before us for the first time in fifty years the possibility to realize the full potential of our relationship. We will work to seize that chance, for our benefit and all those with whom we share this increasingly interdependent world."

3. See chapter 3, p. 58, for his first use of the line two days after the Pokhran II test in May 1998, in a long answer to a question at a joint press conference with Helmut Kohl in Potsdam. He used it again, a little more than a week later, on May 21, 1998, in a meeting with a bipartisan group of senators in the Cabinet Room just after the Birmingham Summit, when he accused India of having "adopted a horse-and-buggy definition of national greatness. We've got to get those folks to get with the program that other countries are on if they want to be a leader in the world."

4. For the details of these security measures, see Jane Perlez, "Clinton Entreats Pakistan to Tread Lightly in Kashmir," *New York Times*, March 26, 2000, p. 1. See also Benjamin and Simon, *The Age of Sacred Terror*, pp. 316-7.

5. Dennis Kux noted the contrast between the India and Pakistan stops in his book *The United States and Pakistan 1947-2000: Disenchanted Allies*, p. 357: "[Clinton's] stop in Pakistan was very different. . . . The president himself landed in an unmarked aircraft and then, shielded from the press and television cameras, quickly drove off to the seat of government fifteen miles away. The presidential motorcade sped along an eerily empty highway. The public was kept away and the only Pakistanis the president saw were soldiers, special forces personnel, and police who lined the roadway. Every few hundred yards, however, banners urging U.S. action on Kashmir reminded the president of Pakistan's single-minded focus on this issue."

CHAPTER ELEVEN

1. Condoleezza Rice, "Promoting the National Interest," *Foreign Affairs*, vol. 79 (January-February 2000), pp. 45-63.

2. See Sridhar Krishnaswami, "'N-Proliferation Views Must Be Realistic,'" *The Hindu*, July 13, 2000.

3. This line was established in another passage from Bush's November 1999 speech at the Ronald Reagan Presidential Library: "This coming century will see democratic India's arrival as a force in the world . . . and the United States must pay it more attention. . . . We should establish more trade and investment with

India as it opens to the world. We should work with the Indian government, ensuring it is a force for stability and security in Asia. We should be able to do all this without undermining our long-standing relationship with Pakistan, which remains crucial to the peace of the region."

4. The one prominent exception was Bush's ambassador to New Delhi. Robert Blackwill, a former foreign service officer who had been one of Bush's foreign policy advisers ("the Vulcans") during the 2000 campaign, made it a constant theme of his public statements and background briefings for the press to trumpet the contrast between Bush's engagement of India and the policy of neglect and patronizing that had come before. Typical was a valedictory address he gave to the Confederation of Indian Industry on July 17, 2003, shortly before the end of his ambassadorship. He hailed the transition from "the bad old days" to "President Bush's big idea. . . . No longer does the United States fixate on India's nuclear weapons and missile programs. No more constant American nagging nanny on these subjects, and no longer does the U.S. largely view its relationship with India through a prism that must always include India's next-door neighbor. In short, the Bush Administration perceives India as a strategic opportunity for the United States, not as an irritating recalcitrant." What had transpired during the Clinton administration, he said, was nothing more than "an intermittent dialogue of the deaf."

5. See, for example, Shibi Alex Chandy, "U.S. Tilt toward Pakistan Causes Consternation," News-India Times, September 28, 2001, p. 18. Raja Mohan ("India and U.S.-Pak Ties," The Hindu, September 21, 2001) was not as alarmist, mentioning that both India and the United States had it in their power to keep bilateral ties strong: "It will be tempting to interpret the reported American plans to resume economic assistance to Pakistan—in return for Gen. Pervez Musharraf's support for U.S. military operations against Afghanistan—as a throwback to the bad old days of American endearment to Pakistan. But the past may not always be a reliable guide to the future."

6. Vajpayee had reinstated Fernandes in October despite protests by the parliamentary opposition. Vajpayee defended his decision on the grounds that no charge had been brought specifically against Fernandes in the bribery scandal and that defense was such an important portfolio that it needed a full-time minister, especially in view of a "fast-changing world situation" after September 11.

7. See, for example, Rahul Bedi, "India's Nuclear Struggles," *Jane's Defence Weekly*, February 5, 2003, which notes: "Security officials said a 'basic' nuclear weapons system was temporarily 'in place' during the Kargil crisis last year [2002] when tensions with Pakistan were high. 'India was in a position to retaliate with nuclear weapons if the need arose,' the official said."

8. See the two major Human Rights Watch reports on the violence, which gathered first-hand evidence as well as synthesizing the various Indian government investigations on the issue: Human Rights Watch, "'We Have No Orders To Save You': State Participation and Complicity in Communal Violence in Gujarat," vol.

14, No. 3 (C), April 2002 (www.hrw.org/reports/2002/india/); and "Compounding Injustice: The Government's Failure to Redress Massacres in Gujarat," vol. 15, no. 3 (C), July 2003 (www.hrw.org/reports/2003/india0703/).

9. The Cabinet Committee on Security Reviews announced the "operationalization" of India's nuclear doctrine on January 4, 2003. The word "triad," which had aroused such agitation in the U.S. government in the August 1999 draft, did not appear in the final version, but the document as a whole left that option wide open, along with virtually all others. Comparing the draft and the outcome, Raja Mohan concluded, simply, "Today's announcement confirmed the essence of that draft as official policy." (See "Nuclear Command Authority Comes into Being," *The Hindu,* January 5, 2003, p. 1.)

10. C. Raja Mohan, "Jaswant Moves Out after a Good Inning at South Block," *The Hindu,* July 1, 2002.

11. The increase in military-to-military relations during the Bush administration had been marked, in 2001, by the visit to India of General Hugh Shelton, the first ever by a chairman of the joints chief of staff. His successor, General Richard Myers, made a visit of his own two years later. Other military leaders and Pentagon officials who traveled to India included the commander-in-chief for the Pacific, Admiral Dennis Blair; Under Secretary of Defense for Policy Douglas Feith; and Secretary Donald Rumsfeld himself. In return, the Indian Army Chief, General S. Padmanabhan, and Defense Secretary Ajay Prasad visited the United States. There were also a variety of joint naval and military exercises, including the first ever on American soil (in Alaska), and joint patrols in the Strait of Malacca.

12. See International Institute of Strategic Studies, The Military Balance 2003–2004 (Oxford University Press, 2003), p. 229.

13. See, for example, "The Congress Agenda: Security, Defence and Foreign Policy," in effect the national-security plank on which the Congress Party waged its campaign. By implication, the document stresses a high degree of continuity with the BJP on nuclear weapons policy, promising only to do an even better job of ensuring command and control over the weapons and to maintain flexibility and freedom for future developments and deployments. The party agenda's ten-point program includes the following (numbers 5 and 6): "The Congress will take necessary steps to fine tune the higher command for India's nuclear and missile capabilities," and, "The Congress will safeguard and maintain these capacities at [the] appropriate level in the context of changing security environments, particularly in the Asian region."

The Congress agenda also criticized the BJP government for "lack of transparency" in the conduct of the dialogue that is the subject of this book: "Till this day, the country has never been taken into confidence about the outcome of several rounds of discussions which Shri Jaswant Singh as Minister of External Affairs had with Mr. Strobe Talbott, Deputy Secretary of State of the USA." The next sentence is either a non sequitur or an insinuation that Jaswant made secret concessions to the Clinton administration in the course of the dialogue: "Sadly, a great country like India has been reduced to having a subordinate relationship with the USA where the USA takes India for granted. This is the result of the [BJP government's] willingness to adjust [to] the US priorities and policies without giving due attention to India's own vital foreign policy and national security interests."

In fact, while Jaswant and I had agreed from the outset to keep the details of our exchanges confidential, the broad outlines of what we were talking about—that is, the benchmarks—were made public and discussed with strategic experts and opposition figures: in my Brookings speech, Jaswant's and my "bookend" interviews with Raja Mohan, my sessions with think tanks, and, pertinently, my courtesy calls on Gujral and Mrs. Gandhi. To be sure, the Indian government often showed itself to be extremely skittish about shedding light of its own on what was going on and sometimes complained that I was going too far. But the opposition could not plausibly claim to be completely in the dark, nor, as this book attests, can Jaswant or his prime minister be fairly charged with being excessively accommodating of "US priorities and policies."

14. While most authoritative Indians have either maintained a stony silence on arrangements of the kind proposed here or dismissed the idea out of hand, there have been occasional veiled hints from Pakistan that there might be official interest in something of the sort. See, for example, a chapter by Abdul Sattar, a former foreign minister, "Nuclear Non-Proliferation and Regional Order," in *Nuclear Non-Proliferation Issues in South Asia*, edited by Ishtiaq Ahmad, 1996, a joint publication of the Islamabad Council of World Affairs and the Hanns-Seidel Foundation of Germany. Sattar writes: "Pakistan's existing policy of restraint is likely to continue, and may even be reinforced, if the sponsors of the NPT—which are also permanent members of the Security Council—strengthen assurances of effective action in the event of aggression or coercion with nuclear or conventional forces." This is a restatement of Pakistan's long-standing pursuit of international security guarantees to protect it from India. However, he adds that "custodial arrangements for fissile materials should be improved. It should be possible also to strengthen assurances against transfer of fissile material and explosion technology. A fair treatment by NPT sponsors will strengthen existing impulses for responsible policies."

As for thinking on the American side, in November 2003 the Council on Foreign Relations and the Asia Society issued a task force report on South Asia, cochaired by Frank Wisner and Marshall Bouton. The report, *New Priorities in South Asia: U.S. Policy toward India, Pakistan, and Afghanistan* (New York: Council on Foreign Relations, 2003), gestured in the direction of what I have suggested here. With regard to American carrots, the report recommended easing of restrictions on export licenses for the sale of American defense equipment to India and cooperation with the Indians in the civilian satellite sector. As for bringing the South Asian nuclear-armed states into the fold of the nonproliferation regime, it avoided specifics, urging only that the U.S. government "think much more searchingly about possible ways to fit India (and Pakistan) into the global nonproliferation system. This presents a tough policy challenge, but that is no reason for not trying to explore options and devise steps to avoid the dangers that a likely nuclear arms race between India and Pakistan will pose for regional and global stability. Although any proposal on this issue will be difficult to implement given the restraints posed by current nonproliferation ground rules, the U.S. government and others should be trying harder to come up with constructive ideas."

INDEX

Abdullah, Sheikh, 9

Adulyadej, Bhumibol, 206

Advani, Lal Krishna: after BJP election loss (May *2004*), 223; appointment to deputy prime minister, 216; as BJP president, 27; as home minister, 47; on nuclear weapons, 34; resignation due to scandal, 39; Talbott visit with (*1998*), 101

Afghanistan: al Qaeda protected by, 117; Bush attack on, 214; Clinton attack on al Qaeda camps in, 115; Russian invasion of, 18; Jaswant Singh's views on, 118–19. *See also* Taliban

Ahmad, Shamshad: Kashmir as focus of, 109–10; meeting with Talbott (London, August *1998*), 124–25; meeting with Talbott (Pakistan, July *1998*), 105; meeting with Talbott after Indian nuclear testing, 59–61, 65–66; relations with Raghunath, 153; role during armed conflict between India and Pak-

istan, 163, 164, 169; Talbott view of, 152

Albright, Madeleine: at ARF meeting (July *1998*), 112–14; at ARF meeting (July *1999*), 170; at ARF meeting (July *2000*), 206; on Carter as possible mediator between India and Pakistan, 139; and counterterrorism, 116; Indian view of, 77; on India-Pakistan relations, 75; meeting with Singh (March *2000*), 201; and nuclear weapons policy, 3, 60, 80; on Pakistan's incursions into Kashmir, 158; relations with India, 82, 137; relations with Pakistan, 57, 64, 65; Talbott memo to, after India and Pakistan meetings (January *1999*), 151–52; visit to India, 42

al Qaeda: and attack threats, 190–92, 204; and embassy bombings, 115; hijacking of Indian plane, 186; and nuclear terrorism, 226; Singh's views on, 119, 120; and South Asian policy of U.S., 117; Ameri-

259

B THE BROOKINGS INSTITUTION

The Brookings Institution is a private nonprofit organization devoted to research, education, and publication on important issues of domestic and foreign policy. Its principal purpose is to bring the highest quality independent research and analysis to bear on current and emerging policy problems. The Institution was founded on December 8, 1927, to merge the activities of the Institute for Government Research, founded in 1916, the Institute of Economics, founded in 1922, and the Robert Brookings Graduate School of Economics and Government, founded in 1924. Interpretations or conclusions in Brookings publications should be understood to be solely those of the authors.

Board of Trustees

John L. Thornton
Chair
Strobe Talbott
President
Zoë Baird
Alan R. Batkin
Richard C. Blum
Geoffrey T. Boisi
James W. Cicconi
Arthur B. Culvahouse Jr.
Kenneth W. Dam
Vishakha N. Desai
Thomas E. Donilon
Mario Draghi
Kenneth M. Duberstein

Lawrence K. Fish
Cyrus F. Freidheim Jr.
Bart Friedman
David Friend
Ann M. Fudge
Jeffrey W. Greenberg
Brian L. Greenspun
William A. Haseltine
Teresa Heinz
Samuel Hellman
Glenn Hutchins
Joel Z. Hyatt
Shirley Ann Jackson
Kenneth Jacobs
Suzanne Nora Johnson

Michael H. Jordan
Harold Hongju Koh
William A. Owens
Frank H. Pearl
John Edward Porter
Steven Rattner
Haim Saban
Leonard D. Schaeffer
Lawrence H. Summers
David F. Swensen
Larry D. Thompson
Laura D'Andrea Tyson
Antoine W. van Agtmael
Beatrice W. Welters
Daniel Yergin

Honorary Trustees

Leonard Abramson
Elizabeth E. Bailey
Rex J. Bates
Louis W. Cabot
A. W. Clausen
William T. Coleman Jr.
Alan M. Dachs
D. Ronald Daniel
Robert A. Day
Bruce B. Dayton
Charles W. Duncan Jr.
Walter Y. Elisha
Robert F. Erburu
Henry Louis Gates Jr.
Robert D. Haas
Lee H. Hamilton
F. Warren Hellman

Robert A. Helman
Roy M. Huffington
James A. Johnson
Ann Dibble Jordan
Vernon E. Jordan Jr.
Breene M. Kerr
Marie L. Knowles
James T. Lynn
Jessica Tuchman Mathews
David O. Maxwell
Donald F. McHenry
Robert S. McNamara
Mary Patterson McPherson
Arjay Miller
Mario M. Morino
Maconda Brown O'Connor

Samuel Pisar
J. Woodward Redmond
Charles W. Robinson
James D. Robinson III
Judith Rodin
Warren B. Rudman
B. Francis Saul II
Ralph S. Saul
Henry B. Schacht
Michael P. Schulhof
Joan E. Spero
Vincent J. Trosino
John C. Whitehead
Stephen M. Wolf
James D. Wolfensohn
Ezra K. Zilkha